AF580679

Birds *of the* West

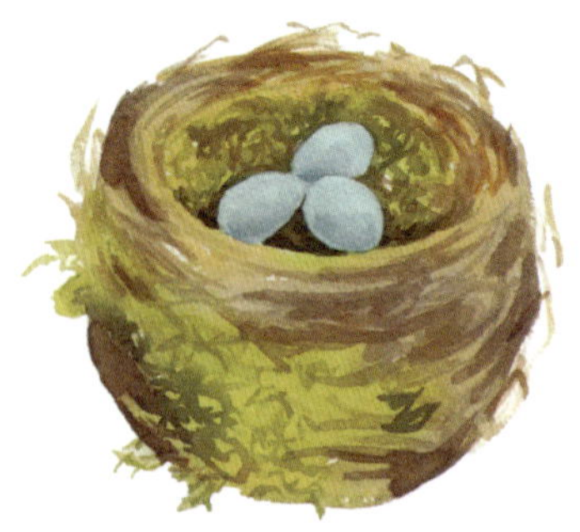

Birds *of the* West

AN ARTIST'S GUIDE

MOLLY HASHIMOTO

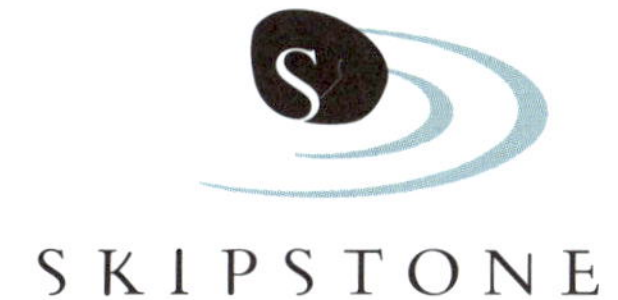

SKIPSTONE

Copyright © 2019 by Molly Hashimoto
All rights reserved. No part of this book may be reproduced or utilized in any form, or by any electronic, mechanical, or other means, without the prior written permission of the publisher.

Published by Skipstone, an imprint of Mountaineers Books—an independent, nonprofit publisher
Skipstone and its colophons are registered trademarks of Mountaineers Books.
Printed in China

28 27 26 25   3 4 5 6 7

"Goldfinches," by Saul Weisberg (from *Headwaters: Poems & Field Notes,* published by Pleasure Boat Studio, 2015) included with permission of the writer.
"Oystercatcher," by Jane Graham George included with permission of the writer.
"To the Scrub Jay on My Office Mate's Desk," by John Daniel (from *Of Earth: New and Selected Poems,* published by Lost Horse Press, 2012) included with permission of the writer.
"Stars," by Ilona Popper included with permission of the writer.
"One for the Dipper," by Tim McNulty (from *In Blue Mountain Dusk: Poems by Tim McNulty,* published by Pleasure Boat Studio, 1992) included with permission of the writer.

Copyeditor: Linda Gunnarson
Design: Kate Basart/Union Pageworks
Page 5: *red-tailed hawk feather*; page 11: *snowy owl feather*; page 123: *golden eagle feather*; page 176: *mallard feather*

Library of Congress Cataloging-in-Publication Data
Names: Hashimoto, Molly, author.
Title: Birds of the West : an artist's guide / by Molly Hashimoto.
Description: Seattle, Washington : Skipstone, 2019. | Includes bibliographical references and index.
Identifiers: LCCN 2018033508 | ISBN 9781680511505
Subjects: LCSH: Birds in art. | Art—Technique. | Birds—West (U.S.) | Hashimoto, Molly—Themes, motives.
Classification: LCC N7665 .H37 2019 | DDC 704.9/4328—dc23
LC record available at https://lccn.loc.gov/2018033508

Printed on FSC®-certified materials

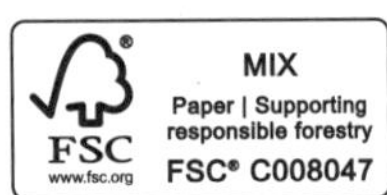

ISBN (hardcover): 978-1-68051-150-5

Skipstone books may be purchased for corporate, educational, or other promotional sales, and our authors are available for a wide range of events. For information on special discounts or booking an author, contact our customer service at 800.553.4453 or mbooks@mountaineersbooks.org.

Skipstone
1001 SW Klickitat Way
Suite 201
Seattle, Washington 98134
206.223.6303
www.skipstonebooks.org
www.mountaineersbooks.org

LIVE LIFE. MAKE RIPPLES.

To David

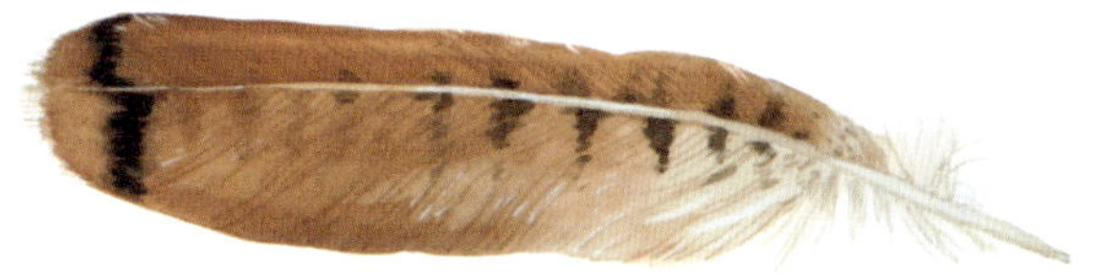

Contents

Introduction: First Birds

Curiosity . . . evokes "concern"; it evokes the care one takes for what exists and could exist; a readiness to find strange and singular what surrounds us; a certain relentlessness to break up our familiarities and to regard otherwise the same things; a fervor to grasp what is happening and what passes . . .

—**Michel Foucault,** "The Masked Philosopher"

When my siblings and I were young, our father bought us a set of Herbert S. Zim's Golden Nature Guides. There was one for almost every subject; my favorites were mammals and birds. I used to study the books endlessly and must confess it was the art that kept me turning pages. In my mind's eye I can still picture the robin pair on the cover of *Birds: A Guide to the Most Familiar American Birds*, their rust-orange breasts posed on a flowering apple bough beneath a pale blue sky.

My other first birds of note were on two bird posters that my parents hung in the basement of our Denver home—one of owls and one of woodpeckers, species beloved by novice and seasoned bird-watchers alike, perhaps because of their size, appearance, and remarkable habits. The birds were illustrations for educators, done in the low-key palette of the late fifties, when commercial printing was unable to capture the brilliant hues we are so used to in the twenty-first century. Now they would look dated and drab, but at the time I thought they were beautiful, and I remember staring at them for hours.

Was that apparently idle gazing at posters and books something like the imprinting that occurs with young birds and their parents? Even though we spent a lot of time outdoors, our home was in the city, with little access to the wildlife of the Rockies. Since then, I've often thought about how many urban children

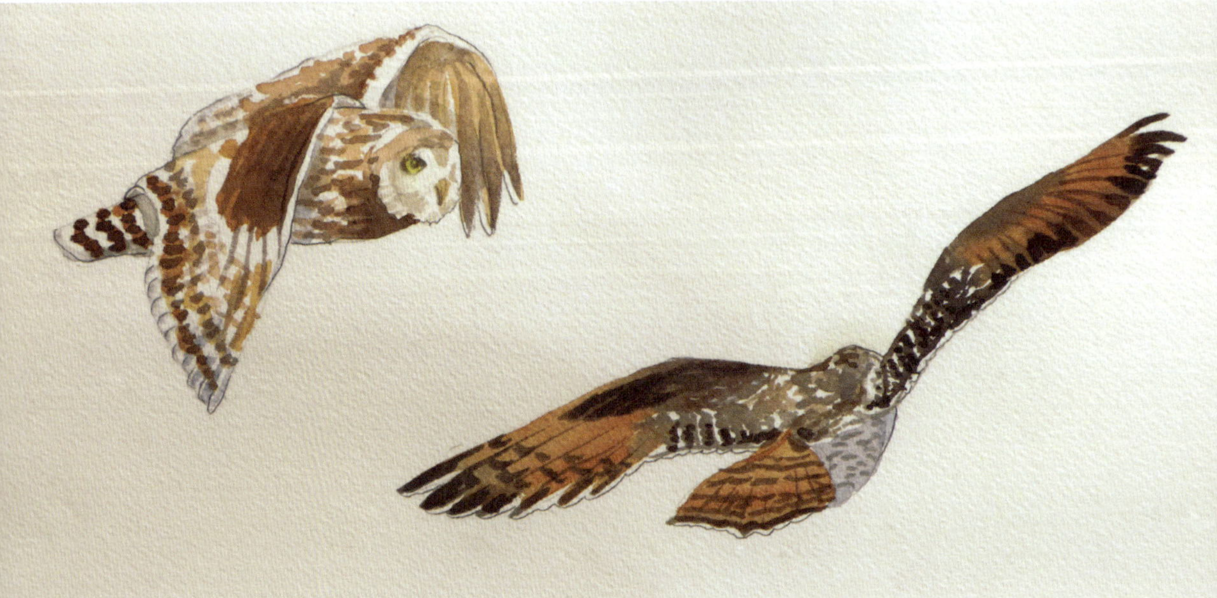

don't have the opportunity to visit parks—a book or poster may be their first introduction to the wild. It was books and art that determined my future as an artist; those images have stayed with me for a lifetime.

Curiosity about the natural world was encouraged in our family even though our parents were busy—there were five children, and our father was in the military and deployed overseas. They couldn't lead us by the hand to nature. But our mother loved sending us outdoors, granting herself a little peace. My sisters and I spent hours with our dogs in the backyard, where one of our favorite pastimes was creating small plastic zoos beneath the hollowed-out lower branches of hedges. When our dad was in the States he took us camping. On one trip we went to Great Smoky Mountains National Park and slept on Army-issued cots, the entire family lined up under a huge tarp pitched in an inverted V shape, wide open on both ends. One night we woke up when a black bear came snuffling through, looking for food.

I didn't attempt to draw birds as a child, although I started making art when I was young, drawing cartoons about my family and friends. Later I refined my human figures by taking life drawing and painting classes. After moving to Seattle, I hiked and skied in the Cascades nearly every weekend, and I wanted to honor those experiences by painting landscapes. When I began to visit national

SHORT-EARED OWLS (*ASIO FLAMMEUS*) WATERCOLOR SKETCH

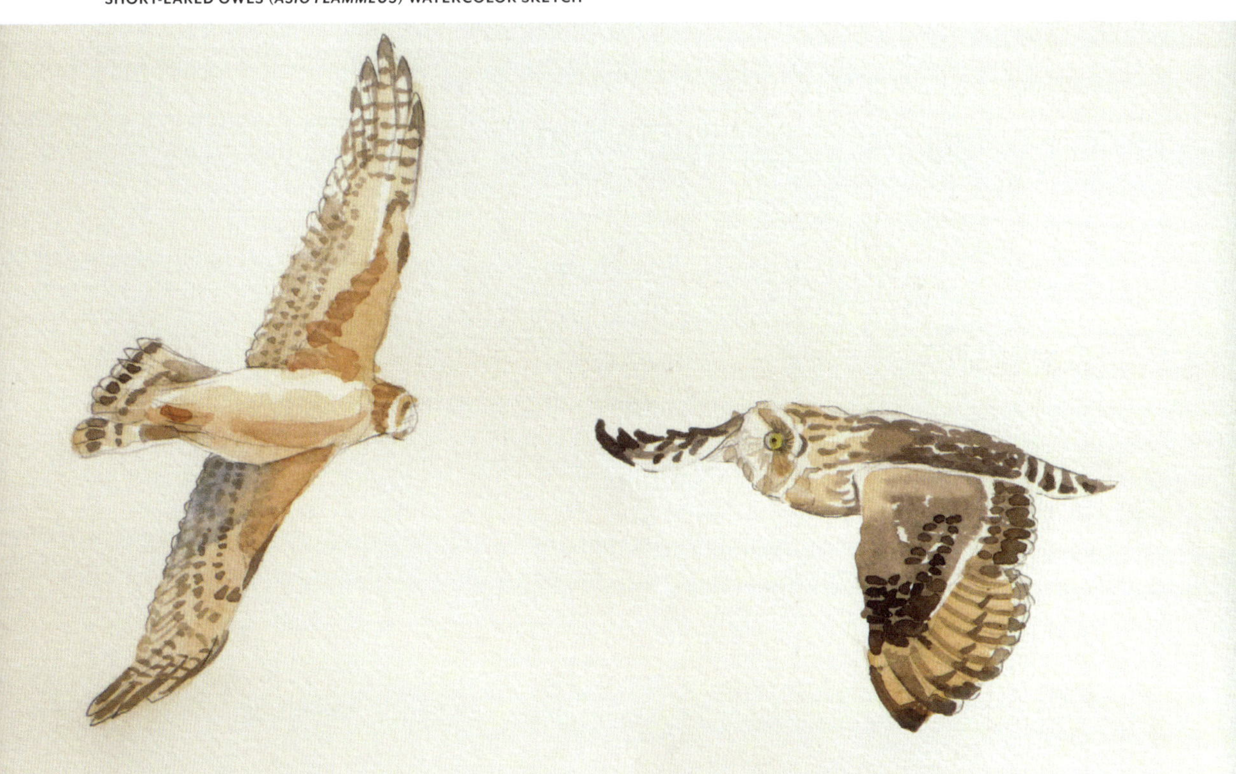

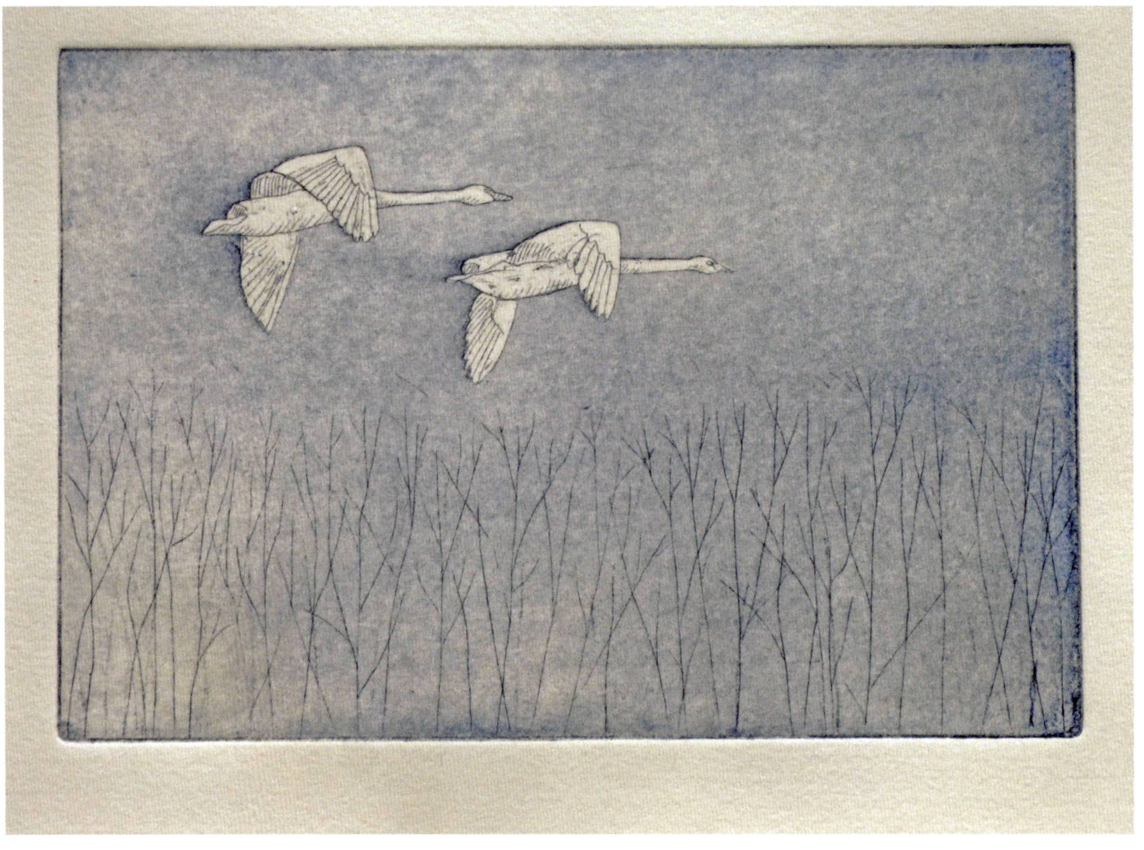

TRUMPETER SWANS (*CYGNUS BUCCINATORS*), SKAGIT VALLEY, ETCHING

parks a little farther afield, I saw bird species I'd never encountered in western Washington: bluebirds, three-toed woodpeckers, and sandhill cranes. I knew I had to try to make art of those experiences. It was difficult at first, and my attempts were very clumsy. I once told someone my birds looked more like dogs! (I was very used to dogs, as I had looked at my pets every day of my life. Not so birds.) But the more I looked at birds, attracted them to my yard with new feeders, photographed them, and sketched them, the better my art became. It wasn't just the rare birds of distant national parks that intrigued me. I began to understand that the birds in my own backyard were equally interesting and worthy of art. Sometimes it takes the rare sighting in a more exotic locale to make you appreciate what's in your own neighborhood—so many of our local species are just as remarkable and colorful as more unfamiliar species.

I was primarily working in watercolor at that time. As my skill increased, I took up a new medium, printmaking, and found that it beautifully expressed the surprise and delight I experienced as a birdwatcher.

The Beauty of Birds

On the whole, birds appear to be the most aesthetic of all animals, excepting of course man, and they have nearly the same taste for the beautiful as we have.

—**Charles Darwin,** *The Descent of Man*

Many mammals—both males and females—are camouflaged in browns, ochres, and earth colors. They need to stay safe from predators since they can't fly away. Female birds, having to incubate and raise broods in a stationary position, require the same protective coloring. But male birds can take flight at any time. What they need is gorgeous ornamentation to attract mates. In his recent book *The Evolution of Beauty,* Richard O. Prum writes, "Birds have been beautiful since the age of the dinosaurs." He says that birds developed their flight feathers not so that they could fly, but as a kind of "canvas" upon which they could evolve complex feather patterns as sexual ornaments for courtship and mating. He believes that flight came later, as a secondary development, and theorizes that birds create art, just as we do. He continues, "the repertoire of aesthetic traits and mating preferences has continued to coevolve and radiate into the many thousands of distinct forms of avian beauty that exist today."

One of the most remarkable examples is the bowerbird, found in New Guinea. Bowerbirds collect ornamental objects and materials and decorate the interior walls of their bowers with blue, green, and black plant material. One species actually lines up stones on a path in order to create the illusion of perspective, flattening the visual space so that when the bird is in the bower, the stones appear to be the same size. Birds themselves are artists—they're the closest living creatures to us in that way. It's no wonder that we love them and make them the subjects of our own art; this is the way we give them the credit they are due as our aesthetic forerunners and equals.

Although I love creating art about many different natural subjects, there's nothing quite as inspiring as a bird in its habitat—the ecosystem and the bird belong together in a coherent and necessary way. Think of a great blue heron wading among chartreuse water lilies, where fish and amphibians hide, or a short-eared owl in search of voles gliding on silent wings above a golden meadow.

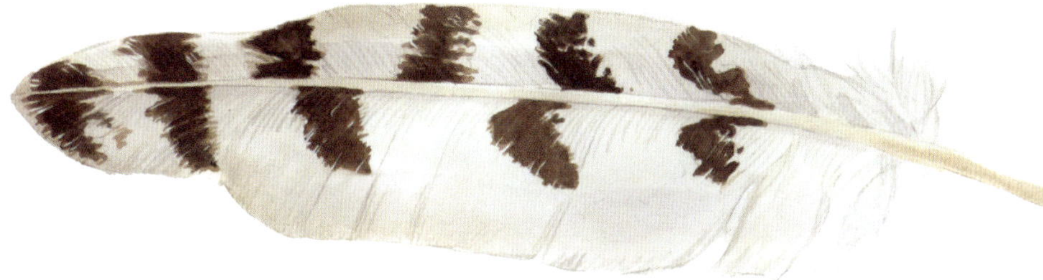

Birds in Art and Illustration

The brush is for saving things from chaos.

—**Shitao,** seventeenth-century Chinese painter, from John Berger's *The Shape of a Pocket*

The beauty of birds has made them the subject of artists throughout history. The earliest cave art at the Chauvet Cave, in France, from as long as 30,000 years ago, includes a powerful engraved image of a long-eared owl, its head turned 180 degrees. In many cave art sites, a hand is stenciled alongside the wild creatures. Art historian and critic John Berger guessed that the cave hands confirm "a magical companionship between prey and hunter" and that painting was "the means of making this companionship explicit . . . and therefore (hopefully) permanent."

In ancient Egypt, falcons were revered in the form of the god Horus, son of Osiris and Isis, and the pharaoh was often depicted as the living embodiment, a man-god, with the head of a peregrine. One ancient tomb, Meidum, from 2500 BCE, contains a surprisingly naturalistic wall frieze depicting geese, graceful creatures of the countryside that were expected to accompany the dead in the afterlife.

There are many examples of birds in the traditional art of Native Americans. Among my favorites is the Raven in Northwest Coast art. Raven was the creator of the world and known as the Transformer. He could turn himself into anything, human or animal, and make things happen through an act of will. Raven transformation masks played an important part in religious ritual; other three-dimensional raven representations appear on totem poles, spoons, and ceremonial rattles.

Birds have always been favored in the art of Asia, along with flowers, insects, mountains, and trees, owing to the Shinto and Buddhist conception of the oneness of nature. In the earliest Asian art, nature depictions were religious in purpose, but beginning around 800 CE, nature became a subject in its own right. Rocks, cliffs, and twisted trees, along with flowing water and birds, were painted on elegant scrolls.

In Europe, bird motifs began to appear as decorative elements in the stone carvings, choir stalls, and capital decorations of Romanesque and Gothic cathedrals. But until the Renaissance, these birds carried only religious meanings, such as the dove symbolizing the Holy Spirit, and the art was included to teach the tenets of faith to a mostly illiterate population. A notable exception is one of Giotto's frescoes in the Basilica of St. Francis in Assisi. In this famous painting, Francis is seen

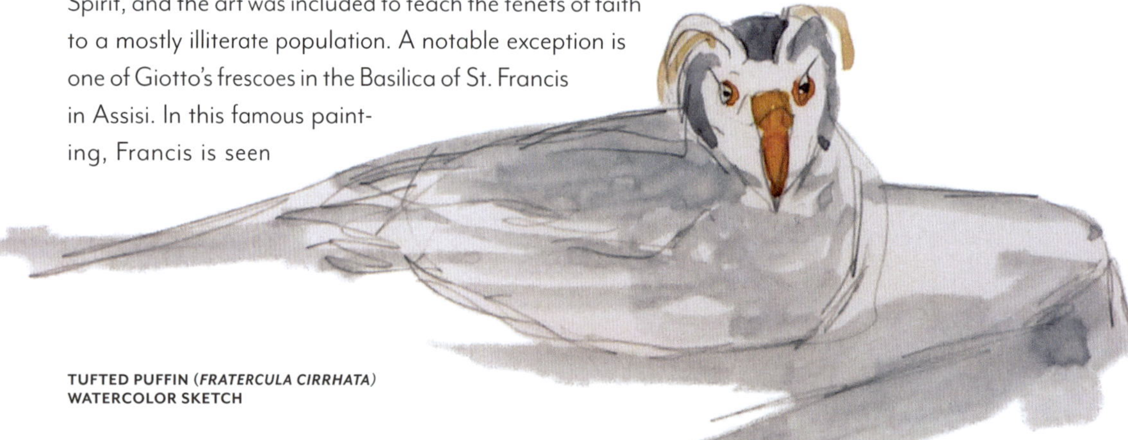

TUFTED PUFFIN (*FRATERCULA CIRRHATA*)
WATERCOLOR SKETCH

preaching his sermon to the birds, upsetting the traditional Christian hierarchy of creation with human beings at the apex and all other creatures subservient. Francis has been called the first environmentalist.

In the fifteenth century, Europeans' perception of nature and birds changed dramatically. Artists such as Leonardo da Vinci began to observe birds more closely. Da Vinci was influenced by the fourteenth-century artist Paolo di Dono, who became known as Paolo Uccello, meaning "of the birds," because of his fondness for painting animals and birds. Da Vinci discovered that the upward and downward wingbeats of birds created the lift they needed to remain airborne, and he used that knowledge to create his designs for flying machines.

Albrecht Dürer, da Vinci's near-contemporary, who was also inspired by Paolo Uccello, was one of the first artists to create full-color watercolors of birds, studies that he used for his larger, more developed oil paintings. These were not stylized depictions, but quite naturalistic. Through his studies and sketches he learned that unrefined nature, without artifice, could be more beautiful than the highest and most technically accomplished art. He wrote, "Nature holds the beautiful, for the artist who has the insight to extract it. Thus, beauty lies even in humble . . . things, and the ideal, which bypasses or improves on nature, may not be truly beautiful in the end."

The Renaissance marked an awakening to the wonders of nature that was crucial to the development of both science and art. The discoveries in the New World prompted a new interest in the natural world as explorers returned with objects never before seen and scientists collected and attempted to categorize them. *Wunderkammern* (German for "cabinets of wonder," or more often translated as "cabinets of curiosity") became popular during this time. These collections of natural and manmade objects always included unusual items such as exotic shells, stones, gems, and feathers from the natural world and were frequently enhanced with gilding, woodwork, and other elaborate craftsmanship for the princes, aristocrats, and merchants who owned them. It was common for these wealthy individuals to have a serious interest in natural history and philosophy, which they either indulged as amateurs or supported as patrons, giving financial help to new branches of science, including the nascent fields of

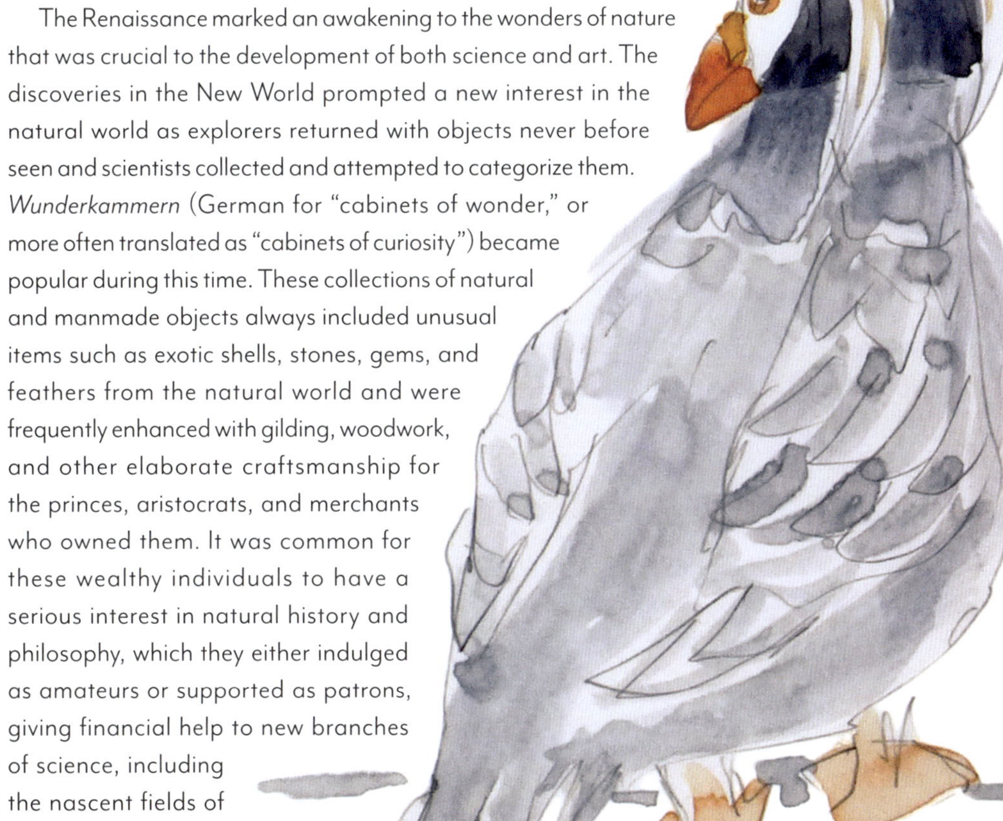

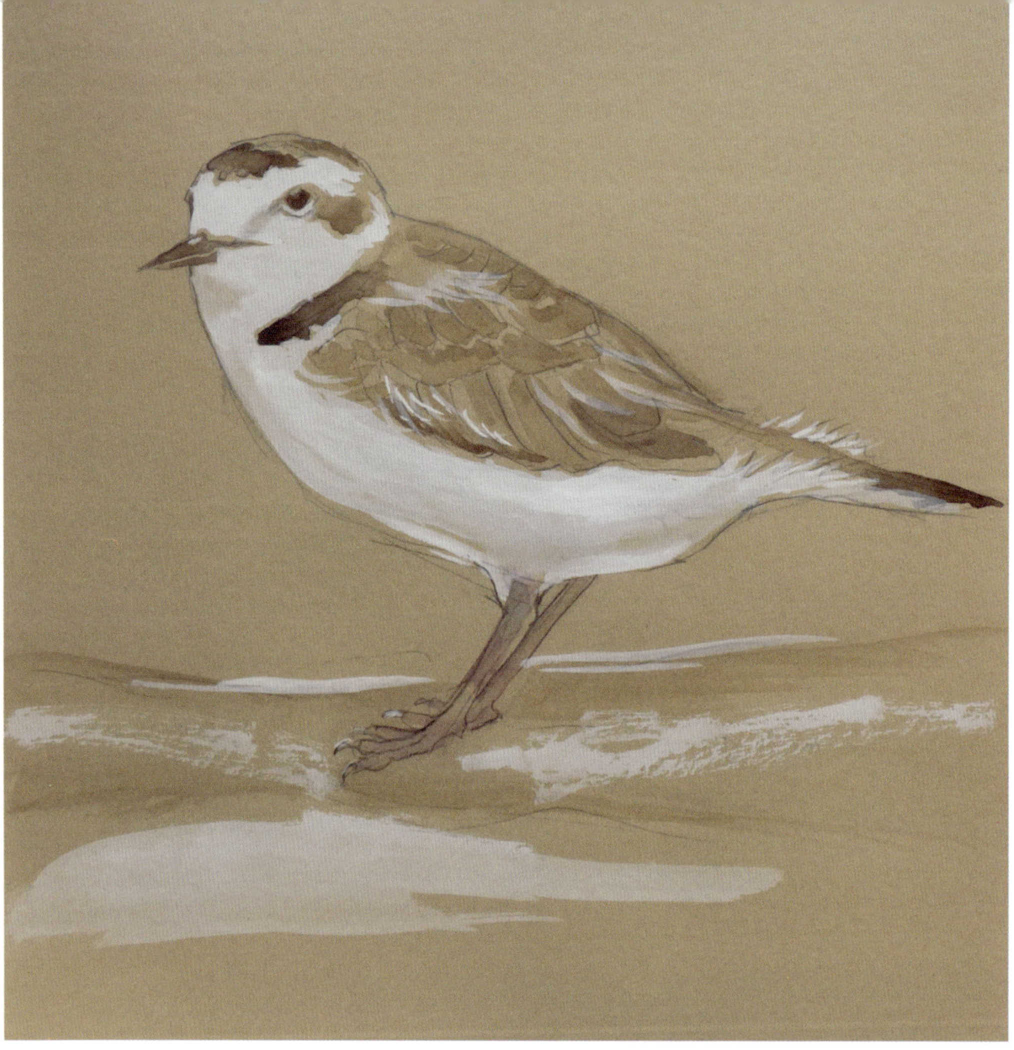

SNOWY PLOVER (*CHARADRIUS ALEXANDRINUS*) WATERCOLOR AND GOUACHE ON TONED PAPER

botany and biology. The cabinet collections were displayed in cupboards and sometimes encompassed huge galleries in the homes of wealthier collectors, and became great spectacles. Everyone who viewed them relished the sense of astonishment—probably in much the same way we do when we see a movie that employs new and dazzling special effects.

Visiting the cabinets, as well as creating them, was a popular pastime among the rich and educated classes and became an addiction for many. Artists also began creating versions of the cabinets on paper, substituting illustrations of subjects such as flowers, seeds, insects, and birds for the natural specimens that would wither or degenerate over time. In the sixteenth century, Flemish painter Joris Hoefnagel developed brilliant trompe l'oeil (French for "deceive the eye") techniques that so realistically depicted three-dimensional natural objects that he was hired by the Holy Roman Emperor Rudolf II to illuminate a manuscript. The way in which this art of illustration developed to preserve a record of rare and newly discovered creatures, both ideal types and sui generis oddities, laid the groundwork for later nature guidebooks and encyclopedias, and even taxonomies, all this in spite of the fact that the *Wunderkammern* may have been a blind alley and inaccurate in the way they categorized species. It was the extreme interest and excitement generated by the collections that was so significant and the way it tied into the highest art and craft being practiced at that time. Stephen Jay Gould wrote, "Nature is full of facts, but any 'album' for their arrangement must record human decision about order and cause. Thus, taxonomies represent the height of human creativity . . . "

The art of illustration continued to develop throughout the Enlightenment as new species were discovered in the Americas. The Royal Society of the United Kingdom, founded in 1660, and the oldest national scientific institution in the world, helped to fund many expeditions on which early botanists and natural scientists often served as their own illustrators. Mark Catesby was one such scientist. Catesby created numerous engravings depicting the birds of Florida, the Carolinas, and the Bahamas and learned how to etch on copper so that he could create his own engravings.

One of the first guidebooks written in a form we would recognize today was the enormously popular *A History of British Birds* (published in two volumes and a supplement from 1797 to 1804), which author Thomas Bewick illustrated with 233 wood engravings. Bewick invented a new form of woodcut that used the end grain of boxwood and employed metal-engraving tools. These proved to last much longer than traditional woodcuts, allowing for large editions with beautiful illustrations. A pacifist, Bewick objected to the then-widespread cruelty he observed in the treatment of horses, dogs, and species employed as circus performers, showing that empathy is inevitable when studying and making art about animals. When John James Audubon came to England seeking a printer for his own bird guide, *Birds of America*, he met Bewick, who gave a copy of one of his books on animals for Audubon's children.

Audubon, born in the Caribbean and of Creole heritage, was in love with nature and birds from his childhood in France onward. His father's efforts to prepare him for seafaring and other serious business pursuits didn't bear fruit. But Audubon learned to hunt and shoot as a child and used those tracking and outdoors skills to collect bird specimens. He moved to the United States in the early 1800s and finally embarked in the 1820s on his life's work, *Birds of America*. He traveled the

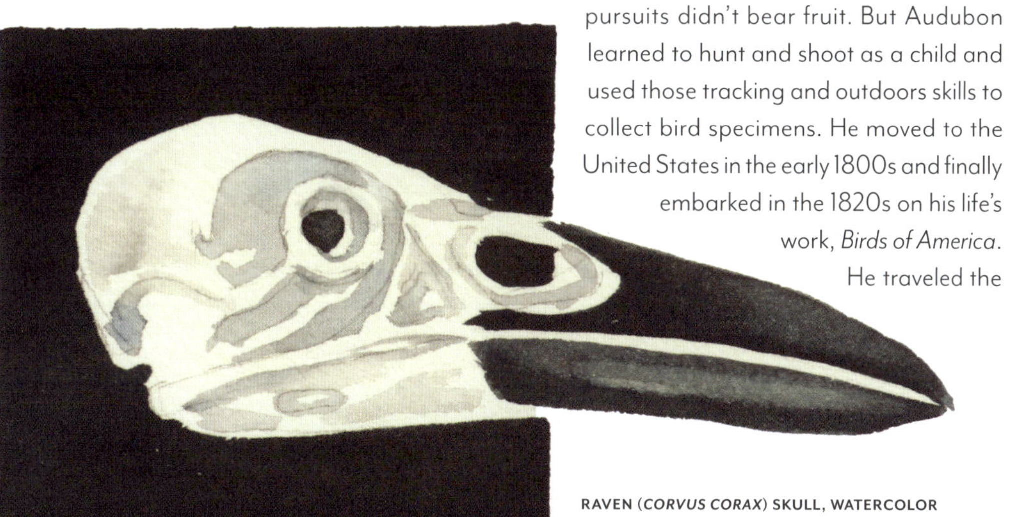

RAVEN (*CORVUS CORAX*) SKULL, WATERCOLOR

North American continent to gather and illustrate all the bird specimens that he could find, often in unexplored areas. After shooting the birds, he would arrange them in lifelike poses, many with wings extended, and by pinning and wiring he was able to achieve a relative likeness to their living behavior. Lamentable as this seems to us today, there were few options to the practice of studying dead specimens before the invention of photography. Audubon quickly sketched and painted the birds while their colors remained vibrant, using watercolor as his primary medium. He made an effort to place the birds in their natural habitats, complete with the fruits and other food they would seek. Later, Robert Havell Jr., one of the leading engravers in Great Britain, began printing faithful reproductions of Audubon's watercolors. Adapting the 435 plates to book form, supervising the engraving and hand coloring, arranging the financing for the project (which cost $100,000), and working tirelessly to promote the necessary subscriptions was an enormous undertaking. Audubon wrote, "I am persuaded that alone in the woods, or at my work, I can make better use of the whole of myself than in any other situation . . . " The fact that he found the birds, painted them, supervised the reproductions, and secured the financing and subscribers was unprecedented—all this aside from the great beauty of his work! No other figure so deserved having a conservation organization named after him, considering that his art brought a wider knowledge of birds to the public and helped establish the dedicated community that continues to advocate for birds, enlarging the scope from art to political action.

Deeply inspired by Audubon's *Birds of America*, Genevieve Estelle Jones, scarcely known today or in her lifetime, conceived of a book project, *Illustrations of the Nests and Eggs of Birds of Ohio*, which she imagined would be issued in approximately twenty-three parts and sold by subscription. Her very close family (mother, father, and brother) and dear friend Eliza Schulze supported her in the effort, with her brother doing much of the collecting and Eliza helping with the art. Genevieve Jones's untimely death at the age of thirty-two from typhoid in 1879 didn't put a stop to the project; though grief-stricken, her family resolved to complete her book. Her mother, Virginia Jones, undertook to finish the engravings and tinting of the plates, her brother completed the egg art, her father put up the money, and work proceeded. Ornithological publications reviewed the book, originally published in 1886, quite favorably, and copies even made their way into the hands of former President Rutherford B. Hayes and

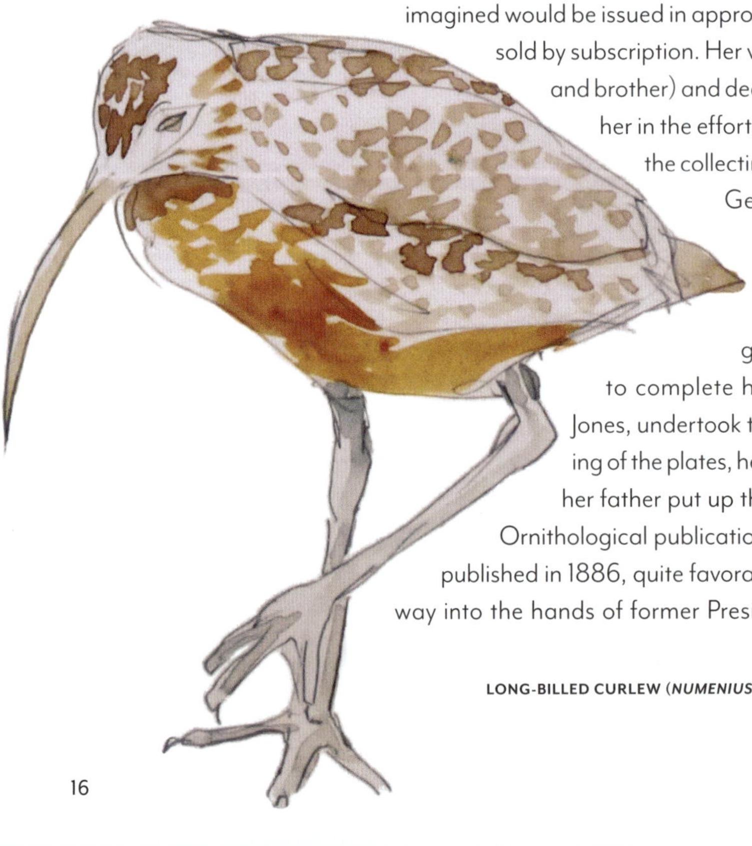

LONG-BILLED CURLEW (*NUMENIUS AMERICANUS*) PENCIL AND WATERCOLOR

Harvard College student Theodore Roosevelt. In 1917, members of the American Ornithologists' Union met to celebrate several members' seventieth birthdays. Seven individuals were honored who had not lived to see their seventieth but had still "left their names indelibly impressed on the records of ornithology." Gennie Jones, as she was affectionately known by her family, was among those honored.

Another follower of Audubon, Louis Agassiz Fuertes, created more than seventy paintings for *Audubon* magazine's predecessor, *Bird-Lore*, between 1904 and 1927, many of them species he observed on an Alaskan expedition, as well as birds from other scientific explorations. Fuertes also painted illustrations for many ornithological works and for *The Auk*, the official publication of the American Ornithologists' Union. He met his own successor, the young Roger Tory Peterson, when Peterson was only seventeen years old. Fuertes gave Peterson a sable brush, which he kept as a memento and never used. Though Fuertes invited him to send him some of his sketches, Peterson felt they weren't good enough at the time. Tragically, Fuertes died in a train crossing accident when he was only fifty-three years old, so he never got to see Peterson's work.

After graduating high school, Peterson decided to study art rather than biology, and had some regrets about that, but he once said, "My primary contribution—field recognition—could not have been made had I followed the traditional path as a biologist. Because of my art background I approached things visually rather than phylogenetically, hence the Peterson field guide system was born." In 1934, Peterson created the first field guide that would allow people to identify birds from a distance, rather than relying on capture. He had some trouble finding a publisher, however, and when Houghton Mifflin finally agreed to publish *A Field Guide to the Birds,* he agreed to give up his royalties on the first 1000 copies sold. The book became a runaway success, selling out its first 2000 copies in fifteen days. Peterson's guides are my favorites—because of the art. More recently, Peterson's successor, David Allen Sibley, has contributed field guides that illustrate birds in various stages of maturity, extremely helpful books for identification.

I admire several contemporary wildlife artists who each portray something different about birds in their work. Canadian J. Fenwick Lansdowne, a self-taught artist, painted sensitive portraits of North American birds, often in a style that reminds me a bit of Asian art—the bird portraits are vignettes with simple yet convincing surroundings. Another Canadian, Robert Bateman, paints more completely rendered landscapes for his realistic portraits of birds. The brilliant geometrical interpretations of birds in Alaskan artist Charley Harper's work distill the essence of species. Fellow Washingtonian Tony Angell has made the study of wildlife his life's work; in his sculptures and illustrations he captures the sense of play that is so much a hallmark of many wild creatures. There are also many contemporary printmakers who make birds the subject of their work. Among them are Katrina Cook, Robert Greenhalf, Andrew Stock, and Greg Poole.

All of these artists, from the earliest cave painters to contemporary practitioners, have responded to birds with an attitude of wonder, curiosity, and reverence. As Roger Tory Peterson once wrote, "Birding is just a game. It's what comes after that is important." When we make art about birds, we accord them a respect that amounts to much more than simply adding them to our life lists.

Why Make Bird Art?

I feel that a real living form is the natural result of the individual's effort to create the living thing out of an adventure of his spirit into the unknown—where it has experienced something—felt something—it has not understood, and from that experience comes the desire to make the unknown—known—By unknown—I mean the thing that means so much to the person that he wants to put it down—clarify something he feels but does not clearly understand . . .

—**Georgia O'Keeffe,** from a September 1923 letter to Sherwood Anderson

Georgia O'Keeffe believed that we want to make art of things that have moved us deeply, even if we don't know exactly why or understand the meaning of what we feel. It is only by recording it, writing about it, or making art about it that it becomes clearer to us what it all means and why it is so important to us. I have found this many times, with every medium.

Great horned owl *(Bubo virginianus)* • WATERCOLOR SKETCH

One spring, my husband and I were walking in a city park in the small town of Klamath Falls, Oregon. We heard a strange plaintive cry and looked up about forty feet above us into a huge ponderosa pine and saw a great horned owl fledgling. Suddenly the mother flew in, probably worried when she saw us. We thought she was there to reassure and protect, not to deliver food, which seemed to be what the fledgling wanted, because it never ceased its begging cries. The many minutes we spent quietly observing, from a safe distance, gave us a respect for the lives of those two owls, mother and baby—the attachment, the mother's care, and the young owlet's need.

The encounter made me want to honor, with my art, the importance of that interspecies, intergenerational meeting. I felt it almost as a privilege—those minutes were given for a reason—and I was keenly aware, both during and after, that maybe a generation or two ago I could have had that experience in my Seattle neighborhood, but not now. Even though we've restored a few wetlands and there's some forest cover remaining, with every new house that's built, trees and understory plants are removed—the trees necessary for owl nesting and as shelter for their prey.

Understanding how special the encounter was, I knew I was going to make art about it, though I wasn't sure exactly how I would tell the story. I knew only that I felt a sharp poignancy both during the experience and while I was making the art, an awareness of the privilege and the loss, a reminder of all that we've given up because of human population growth and the destruction of habitat. According to John Berger, "art . . . is an affirmation of the visible which surrounds us and continually appears and disappears. Without the disappearing, there would perhaps be no impulse to paint, for then the visible itself would possess the surety (the permanence) which painting strives to find." It's exciting to see a new bird or a new species, but it's not enough to check it off a list and move on in search of the next new thing. It's important to pursue in our imaginations the wild creatures we encounter and further explore their value and beauty as we try to sketch and paint them.

When I'm in the middle of an arduous painting or printmaking effort, I often mentally return to the time of the encounter, to my memory, to help me if my enthusiasm for the project begins to flag, but also to re-experience my initial surprise and excitement in order to convey that to anyone who looks at my art. This helps so much when I'm doing something really difficult. Sometimes I feel I'm at the end of my patience, and then I ask myself: "How many eons of evolution did it take for nature to shape this bird?"

Although every artist has her own aesthetic goals, I don't belong to the art for art's sake camp. I want to make art about birds that is accurate about the ecosystem and true to the bird's anatomy, characteristic gestures, and plumage colors. Although I admire artists who exhibit technical virtuosity and create intriguing conceptual art, I don't choose to represent an imaginary bird just to fulfill my artistic purposes. I want my art to be in the service of the living, existing bird. That's not to say that mere representation is all I aim for—photorealism can drain the life out of a subject. There's a place somewhere between the representational and the conceptual that expresses all the meaning that I've found in watching birds.

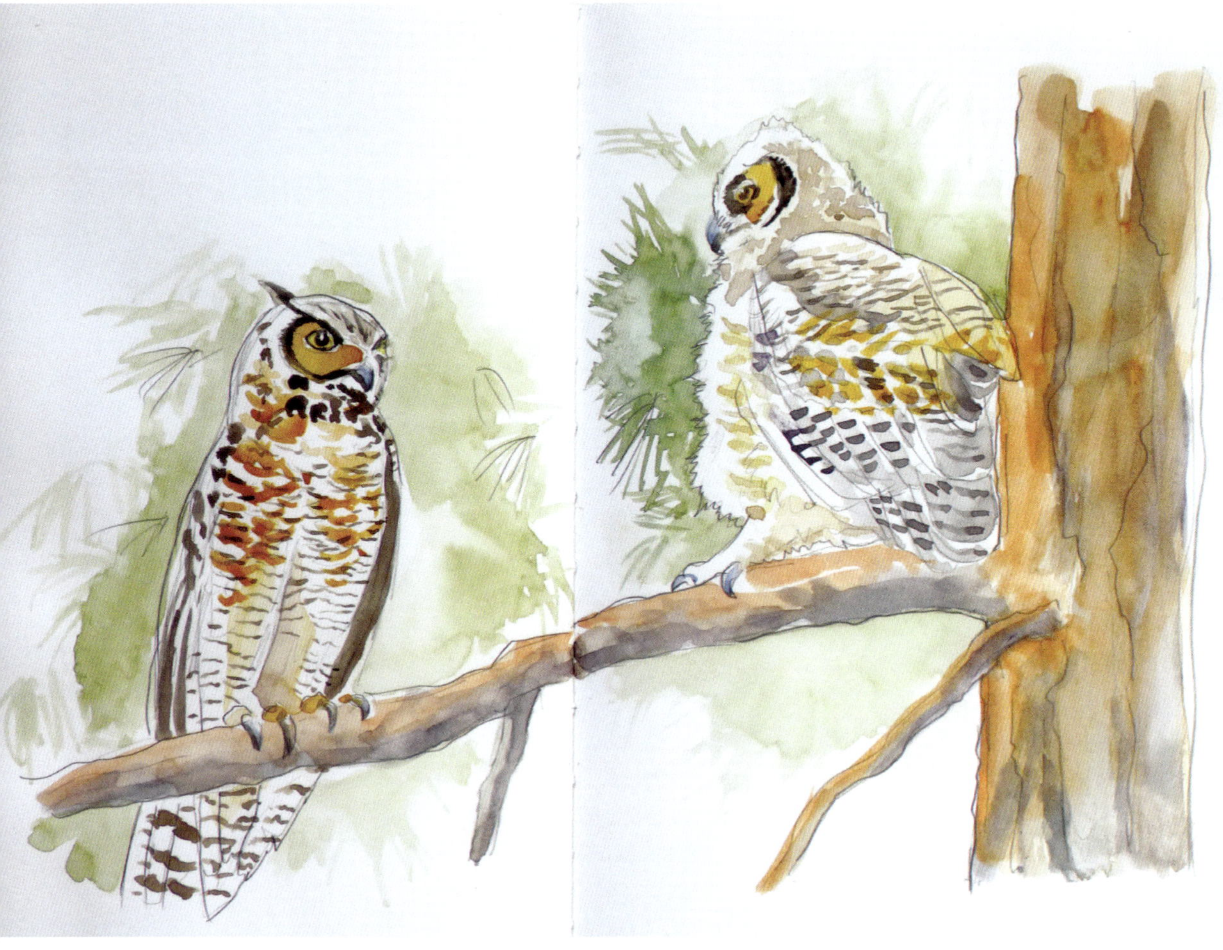

I also make art for the sake of connection and to inspire an ethic of stewardship. Philosopher Andy Clark believes human thought develops through what he calls "scaffolding." The scaffold can be a piece of paper on which we write something, a sketchbook where we draw, a book, a work of art, or a smartphone on which we record a photo or note or call or text someone to tell them about what we've seen. These devices extend our minds beyond the boundaries of our skulls. The scaffolds also connect us to other people, other minds. My publishers have helped me reach a fairly wide audience through my books, cards, and calendars. People write to me to say they saw a bird doing exactly what I pictured it doing in a print or painting. Our minds and our past experiences join in a sense. We belong to a community. When we share the value we place on birds, we make choices: to speak up, vote, educate the young, and contribute time and dollars to organizations that save habitat for them.

Which Art Medium Is Best for Birds?

The impulse to paint comes neither from observation nor from the soul (which is probably blind) but from an encounter: the encounter between painter and model.

—**John Berger,** *The Shape of a Pocket*

I usually begin to create my art using a series of photos that I've taken, because I get more of an idea of the movement and gestures of a bird with a whole set of photos. Although I do draw in the field, it can be difficult—the birds are constantly moving, and the drawn shapes can be awfully crude when you're in a rush. With the aid of photos, I can sift through the images, sometimes synthesize them, and create something that helps me get back to my feelings of excitement—the feelings I have when I'm outdoors. I'm not always sure what it adds up to, but if I sense there's something there to be uncovered or revealed, I decide to make art from it.

I've approached creating art about birds in many different media, including quick sketching methods such as pencil and pen drawings, acrylic ink, and light watercolor washes. (By washes I mean very thin applications of paint, nothing too saturated or thick, in order to let the strength of the pencil or pen line shine through.) I've also created more carefully rendered work in watercolor, relief prints, egg tempera, and intaglio etchings, all of which I describe in this section. You may wonder why I don't just focus on one. Curiosity and a desire to explore new media play a large part, and also at times a frustration that any one medium cannot express the beauty, or energy, or essence of a species. Birds have many different characteristics, and each species exhibits a unique personality. Every medium has a way of revealing distinct aspects of the birds. Etching utilizes fine lines that can precisely describe the elegant contours and feather groupings of birds; watercolor, with its wide-ranging hues and many technical options for indicating trees, shrubs, grasses, rocks, and all the components of an ecosystem, displays the manner in which they live and make use of their habitats. Sketches in pencil or pen, with and without added watercolor, convey, through their gestural quality, the attitude, demeanor, and movement of birds. Egg tempera, a centuries-old medium used in icons and altarpieces, can express the reverence I feel for birds and other animals. Relief or block prints, with their dramatic values contrasts and bright colors, help me share the surprise—sometimes even the shock—of encountering a new species. As composers work with many different types of instrumentation, with widely varying timbres and colors, such as full orchestras, smaller string groups, or choral ensembles, I use different media to express a range of moods and ideas.

SKETCHING

Black-capped chickadee *(Poecile atricapillus)* • PENCIL SKETCH

When sketching with a pencil, I like to use a smooth paper or one with not too much "tooth," or texture. Paper labeled "cold press" is bumpy; "hot press" is smooth. It's best if the pencil doesn't encounter too many bumps in the road, which can make for a broken line. I want to choose when to break the line, not have the paper do that! If you're planning to add watercolor later, select a hot press watercolor paper or a sketchbook with smooth paper.

To do a loose sketch, try making several tentative marks on paper with an HB pencil. "HB" refers to the degree of darkness—H pencils are harder, B are softer; so HB is in the middle range. (The full spectrum goes from 7H to 7B. The higher the number of H, the lighter the value; conversely, the higher the number of B, the darker the value.) Don't feel as if you're committing to the line, just put it down quickly, making a series of marks or strokes that feel loosely connected. Once you've completed the perimeter of the bird shape, stand back and see if your proportions look right. It often takes standing back to see that perhaps the head is too big—a common mistake for beginners. The broken line used in sketching can create a lot of energy and give a sense of movement and life to your bird. Feel free to erase (I like a white plastic eraser) and reposition lines if necessary. Then, once you're satisfied, use a slightly darker pencil, like a 2B, and go over the lines. Finally, if you choose, add some watercolor, but not too carefully. The whole idea with a sketch is that it's free and loose and not totally finished. That unfinished quality is what makes it so lively.

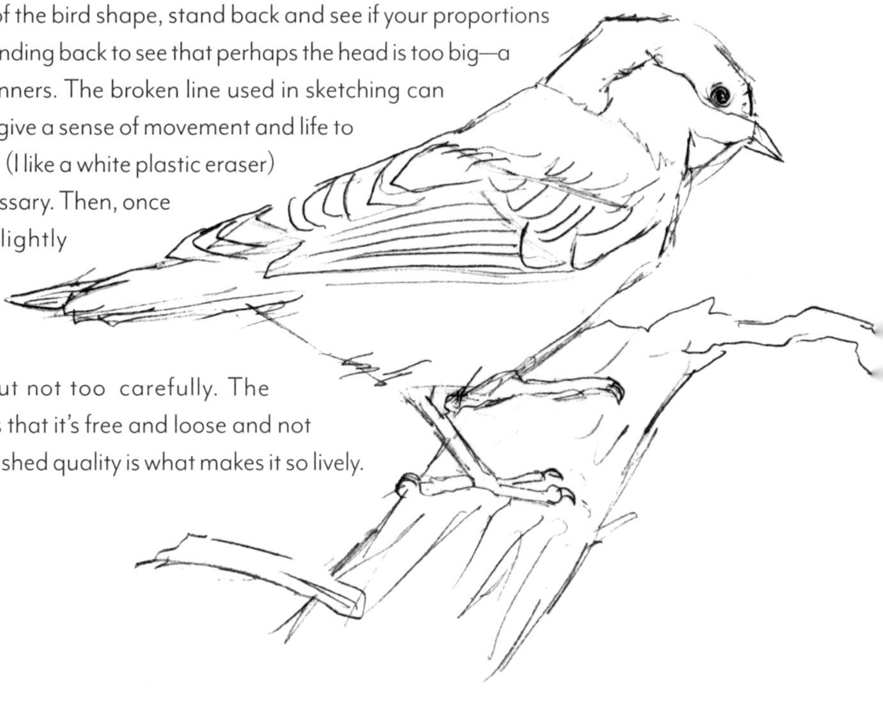

WATERCOLOR

Artists have long made studies in chalk and charcoal, but it became common practice to use watercolor in the sixteenth century, when Albrecht Dürer first showed its potential with animal, bird, and plant studies. In the eighteenth century, British artists chose it for many of their landscape views, as well as for travel sketches. Watercolor has continued unabated in popularity since that time, finding brilliant practitioners in England and the United States, including J. M. W. Turner, James McNeill Whistler, and Winslow Homer. This medium is not just for "professionals"—children and inexperienced adults can use watercolors with ease because the materials are inexpensive and easy to clean up. One of my favorite things about watercolor is its nontoxicity. Also, even though it's now becoming more common to clean up oil paints with oil—a practice of Renaissance painters—oil paints are usually cleaned up with solvents. (In the eighteenth century, painters quickly switched to these new inventions, a by-product of the Industrial Revolution, since they made cleaning so easy,

Creating a Watercolor Palette

For a basic watercolor palette, you need pigments in the three primary colors—yellow, red, and blue—in both their warmer and cooler versions, plus a few neutrals. The primaries I usually use are hansa yellow medium, hansa yellow deep, permanent alizarin crimson, pyrrol scarlet, phthalo blue red shade, and phthalo blue green shade. Then you can add a few neutrals, such as yellow ochre and quinacridone burnt orange. Each primary color has a bias toward warm or cool: hansa yellow medium leans toward blue; hansa yellow deep leans toward red; pyrrol scarlet leans toward yellow; permanent alizarin crimson leans toward blue; phthalo blue green shade leans toward yellow; and phthalo blue red shade leans toward red.

Knowing just a few basics about color mixing will help you choose colors for your sketches and prints. Looking at the split primary color wheel, you can see two of each primary color, one on either side of the same line (these lines divide the wheel into thirds). Using these primaries, you can mix secondary colors: For a warm orange, mix hansa yellow deep and pyrrol scarlet. For a violet, mix permanent alizarin crimson and phthalo blue red shade. For green, mix hansa yellow medium and phthalo blue green shade.

Notice on the color wheel how many possibilities there are within each third of the pie. As each mixture approaches a primary hue, it leans toward that color. I sometimes add quinacridone burnt orange (a color much like burnt sienna) to neutralize some of the brighter secondary mixtures and almost always add a bit of quinacridone burnt orange to green mixtures (see the color chart in "Technique: Watercolor Studio Painting" on page 25). Most greens in nature are not quite as vivid as pure secondary hues and need to be neutralized just a bit. Another way to achieve neutrals is to cross a line on the but solvents are very hard on the environment and painters alike.) Watercolor, on the other hand, rinses clean in water and cleans up in minutes.

You can do a multitude of things with watercolor—quick sketches, finished paintings, add it to pen and acrylic, and tint prints and etchings with it. I've included many examples in the book of casual pencil sketches that are hand-colored with watercolor in a fresh, unlabored way. But watercolor also lends itself to more carefully executed paintings, such as the green heron painting in "Technique: Watercolor Studio Painting" (see next page) which was done with a combination of techniques, including wet-into-wet and carefully applied brushstrokes on dry paper. Watercolor can help achieve more accurately rendered landscapes.

If a bird is the same basic color as the background landscape, just wet the paper first with clear water and, using a large brush, lay in a light wash of color everywhere. To suggest foliage or plant life in the background, add successive colors while the paper is still wet, using the wet-into-wet technique.

color wheel into the next third of the wheel—anytime you mix by using a color across a line, you'll get something a little more neutral. So I use hansa yellow medium and phthalo blue red shade (rather than phthalo blue green shade, which would give me a much brighter green). Another way to get a neutral green is to add a very small amount of permanent alizarin crimson to your mixture of hansa yellow medium and phthalo blue.

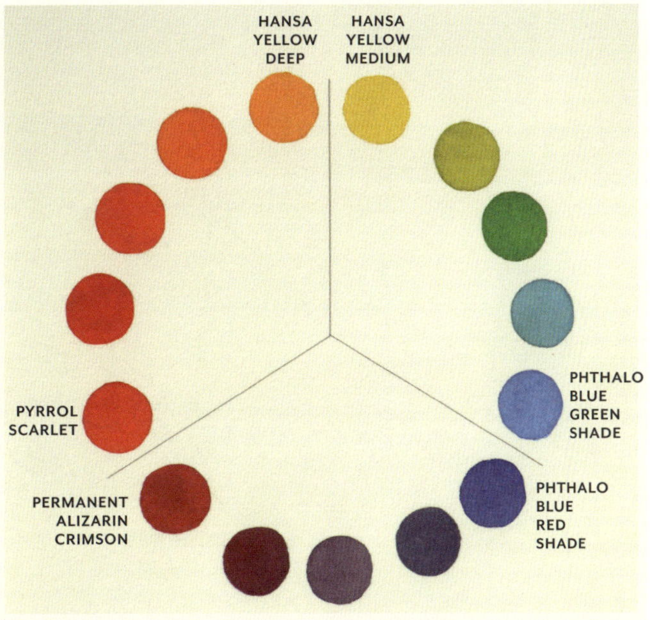

Colors that are adjacent to each other on the color wheel are called harmonious or analogous colors. Mixing them gives you clean, bright mixtures. Colors opposite each other are called complementary colors. You definitely cross the line when you mix complementaries, but there's no law against it, because mixing them gives you some very interesting neutral hues—try this and you'll discover intriguing grays, browns, and muddy greens. There are no rights and wrongs in color mixing. Try everything and make notes about which colors you used; those notes will come in handy for future painting sessions.

TECHNIQUE
Watercolor Studio Painting

Notice the background vegetation in the green heron (*Butorides virescens*) painting, where the colors are green-gold, chartreuse, and bluer greens. To achieve this, begin with the green-gold, proceed to the chartreuse, and then finish with the deeper blue-greens. Use a brush to stroke in these hues in long reed- and grass-shaped marks. Don't worry about being too precise, since you'll want to switch to completing your subject bird portrait before doing any more fussy work in the background. I always want to be sure my portrait is convincing before doing additional work on the landscape.

To paint the bird, start with the overall colors. If the colors are meant to merge into one

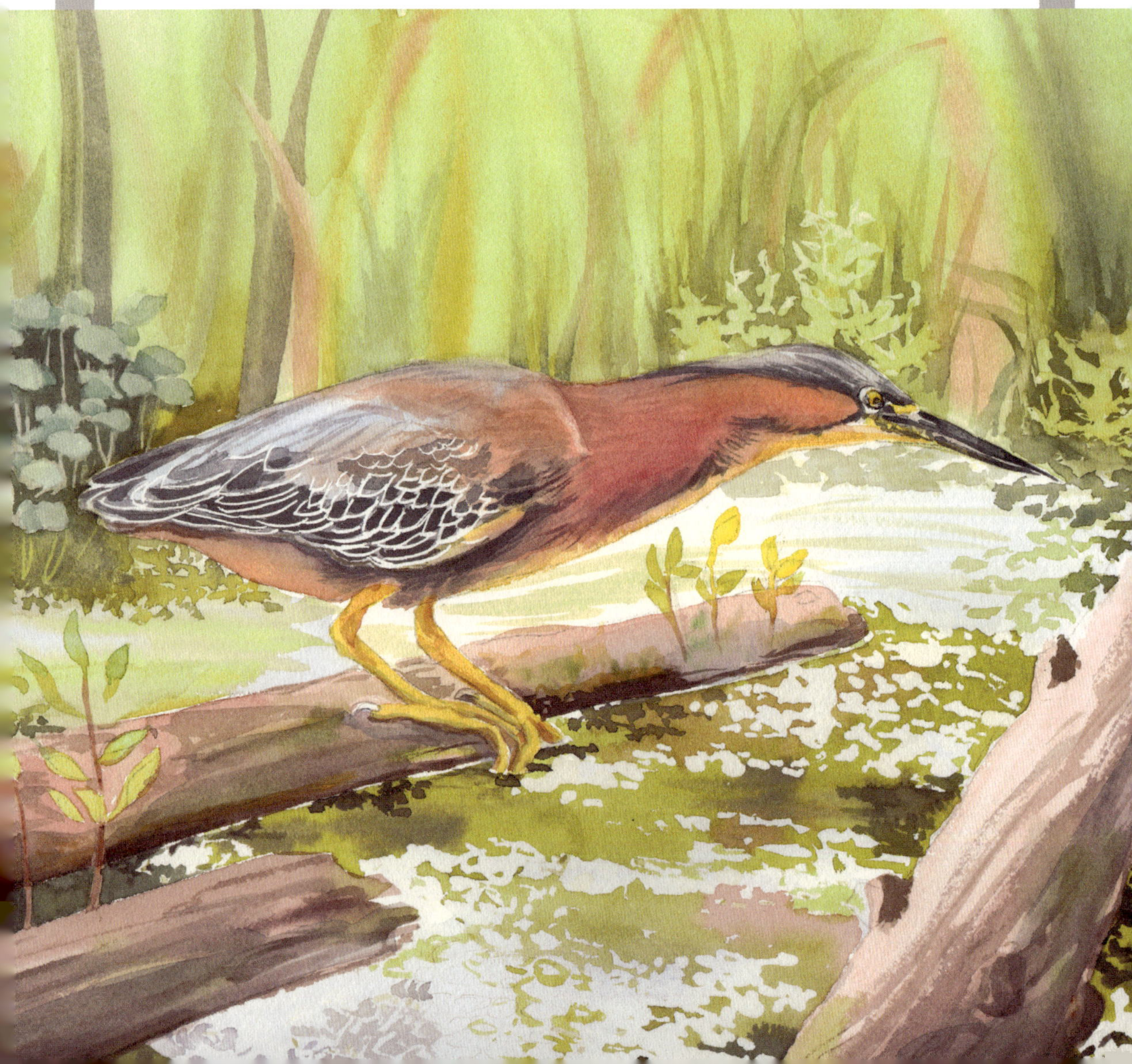

another, you can wet the bird shape and paint all of the colors onto the wet paper. If not, you need to paint the areas of color separately and allow each area to dry—this is more of a jigsaw-puzzle method. When the larger areas of color are dry, begin to add smaller details—such as feather groups, eyes, and beak or bill—on top, with carefully applied brushstrokes. If your bird doesn't turn out well, you can always start over—much better than if you spent hours developing the landscape first.

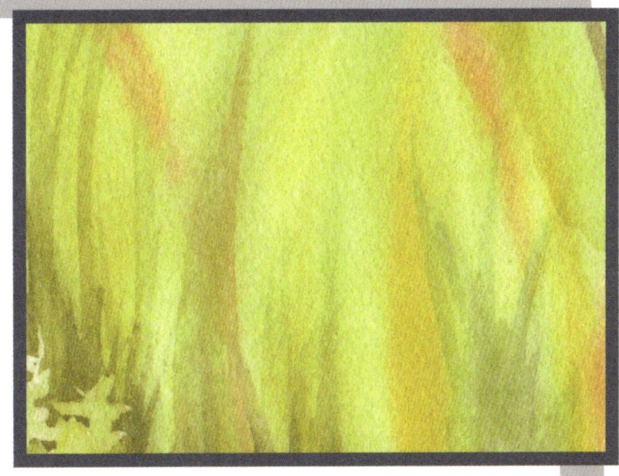

Follow the same plan for your landscape when you return to it. Add foreground reeds, leaves, and shapes that will be in greater focus. Background plant life can be left hazier, and that first-stage wet-into-wet method does a good job of suggesting that.

The first two columns in this chart show a sampling of the many shades of green you can create by mixing phthalo blue red shade and hansa yellow medium. The third column illustrates what can be achieved by adding a little quinacridone burnt orange to mixtures of the other two colors. Just these three colors give you endless possibilities. I used many of them in the green heron painting.

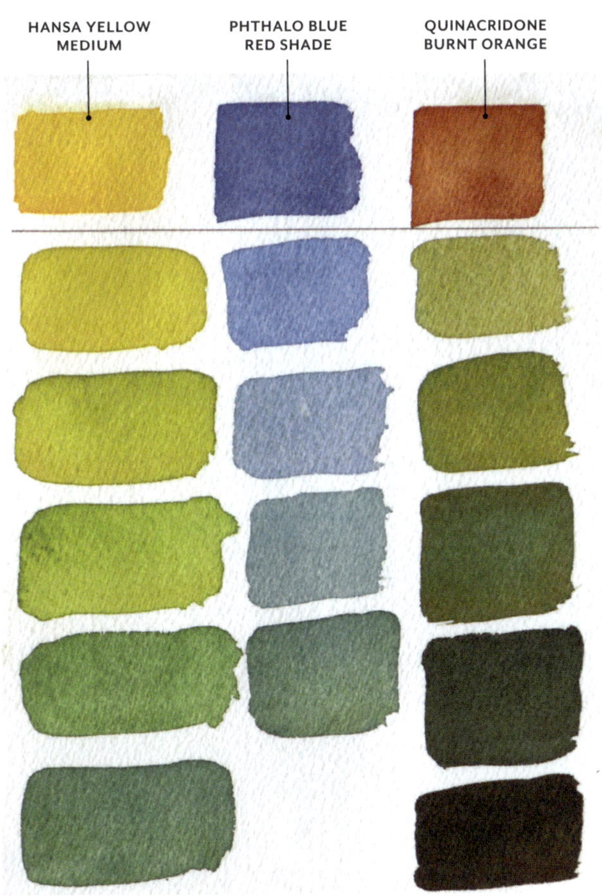

BLOCK PRINTING

When paper was introduced to Europe in the eleventh century, woodcut printing became an economical way to reproduce multiple pictures for the marketplace, making images and texts affordable for a larger segment of the population. In this art form, images are drawn directly or transferred onto a block, originally wood; then the material surrounding the outline (imagine a pen line) is carved away, in reverse, which can be a little confusing, especially when words are part of the design. The outline of the figure or the letter remains, raised, or in relief, so that a brayer or brush loaded with ink that is rolled or brushed across the block will leave a residue on the raised line. When paper is laid on the block, only the raised line prints. In the twenty-first century, images can be carved into linoleum (known as linocuts), wood, rubber, or any soft material—even a bar of soap. The resulting print is called a relief print. (The terms *block print* and *relief print* are interchangeable and can refer to any material.)

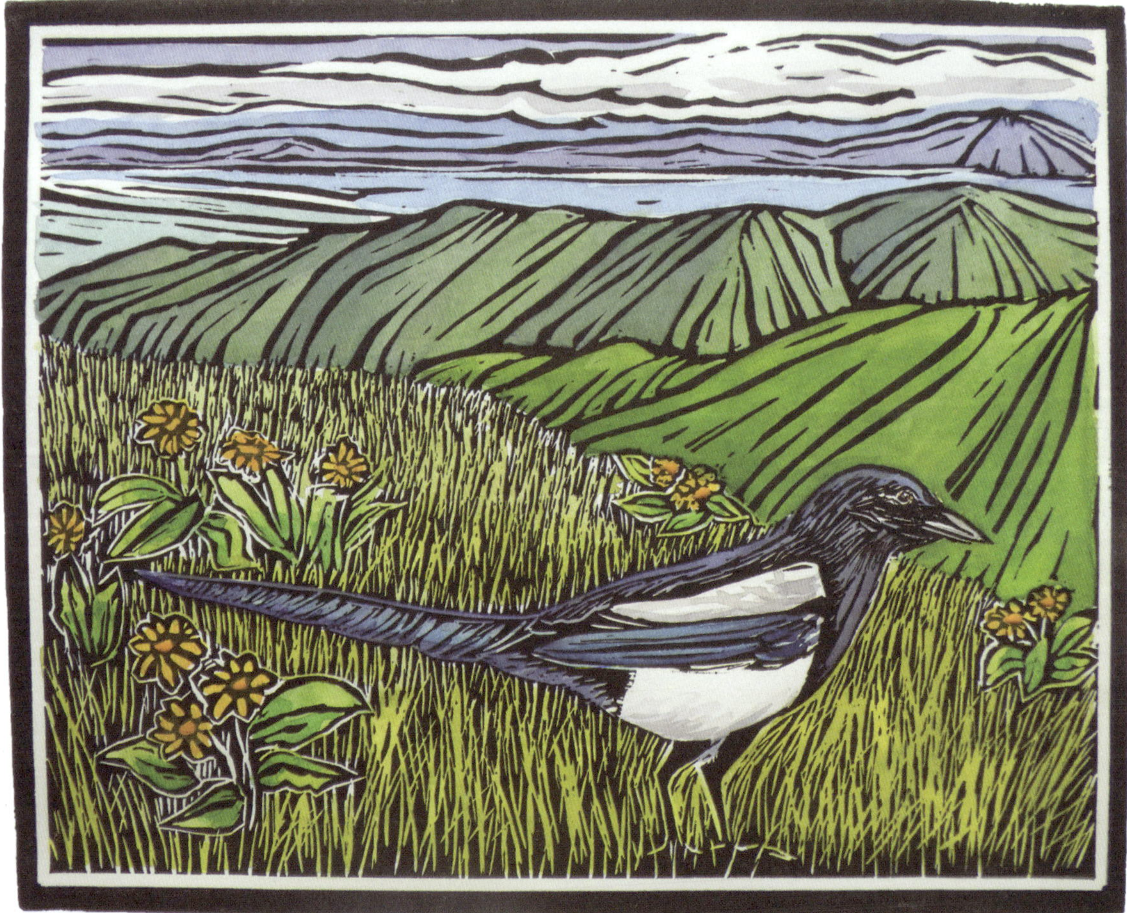

BLACK-BILLED MAGPIE (*PICA HUDSONIA*) BLOCK PRINT

Carving Tools and the Marks They Make

The tools for carving relief prints are called gouges, and they come in different shapes and numbered sizes. With the five tools shown here you can make a variety of marks. The #1, a V-gouge, makes thin lines. The #2, a larger V-gouge, makes wider lines. The #3, a U-gouge, creates broad lines. The #4 is a square gouge; the other gouges make more rounded marks, so use the #4 whenever you need 45-degree angles or sharp edges. Finally, the #5 is the largest U-gouge and clears out large areas; sometimes you may wish to have a lot of white space without any marks, or areas that are just colors (you'll tint those later). It's very difficult to completely clear out the block. Raised areas always remain, no matter how much you carve away, and the remaining raised areas often print as lines. Those lines are called chatter marks and are very useful for indicating linear subjects, such as skies, clouds, and fields (horizontally) and tree trunks and bark fissures (vertically).

In addition to easily carved rubber blocks, I've worked on wood and linoleum, though I rarely use the latter because it's very hard on the wrist and takes a lot more time. To color the prints, I've used both oil-based inks and watercolors in the Japanese *moku hanga* (*moku* means "wood"; *hanga*, "print") style, which typically relies on water-based media and rice paste for the color, although some Japanese printmakers have made use of oil-based inks. You can read a more specific description of the oil-based method in my discussion of the harlequin duck woodblock print in "Shoreline & Beach." Because I've produced so many relief prints over the years for calendars and note cards, the easily carved rubber blocks have been my mainstay—I've probably made more than sixty prints that way. There's always some new bird I want to try, and if I work only in the more labor-intensive media, such as woodblocks and etchings, I'll never get to experiment with new designs and bird species.

Finally, even though it's common practice to use a press for all printmaking, I've found a way to make block prints without the use of a press. It's possible for people without a press or access to one to create prints in their home studios.

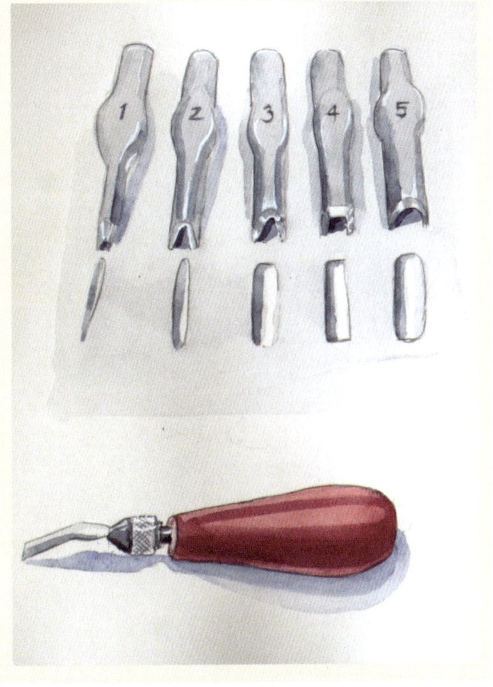

Editioning a Print

Many printmakers make an entire edition, or set of prints, at once; twenty-five is considered a standard edition, but you can make anywhere from 5 to 500. Printmakers often label their prints below the actual artwork with the title, signature, and a set of two numbers—for example, 1/25. The first number refers to the number of the print in an edition, the second to the total number of prints in the edition. If you make all twenty-five prints at once, you number them up to 25/25. If you're not sure what additional artistic touches you'll add to finish the print, you can label it AP, which stands for "artist's proof." Usually you make no more than five of those, eventually making your final artistic decisions. If you think the edition is going to be quite variable because of many factors you can't control, such as maintaining a consistent hue, you can label the print EV, which stands for "edition variable" and still need to number all the prints.

Because my hand-tinted prints are so very handmade, I generally print only a few at a time. It can be wasteful to use twenty-five pieces of paper to make prints that may never sell, since you never know how the public will respond to a print. Many artists do the same—there's no rule that says you have to print an entire edition at once. But I decide at printing time how many I'll eventually be making, and I cannot increase that number later—even if the print proves to be very popular—for the sake of the collectors who buy my prints. It would be unfair to them to decide later that I'm going to make more prints from a block, because generally, the smaller the edition, the more valuable the print. Also, the closer to the end of the edition the print is—for example, 24/25 or 25/25—it becomes obvious that all the other prints have been sold; thus the remaining ones may be seen as worth more.

The earliest woodcut prints—images of saints and other religious figures—came from Germany and were sold as pilgrims' souvenirs at shrines and fairs; travelers collected mementos from their trips, very much as we do today. But early pilgrims also carried them as amulets on their journeys, to protect themselves from the plague or other misfortunes, and often kept them at home as well. Many of the earliest woodcut images have been found pasted into small travel chests. These simple figures were crudely carved, though full of strong line work, and contrasted notably with the high art achieved by later wood engravers such as Albrecht Dürer. The images were powerful objects of devotion and were invested with spiritual properties of great significance to those who owned and carried them. Today, art still has a kind of talismanic power. In common with ancient cave artists, aboriginal peoples, and pilgrims, we keep images of birds and the natural world close to us as we decorate textiles with them and make paintings and prints of them to display in museums and in our homes. This reassures us that we have not lost our place in the world; we are still part of a sacred natural order.

I draw inspiration in my own woodcuts from two of my favorite twentieth-century artists, Russian Vasily Kandinsky and German Ernst Ludwig Kirchner, both of whom created many woodcuts early in their

TECHNIQUE

Making a Block Print

The hairy woodpecker (*Picoides villosus*) is about nine inches long and eats wood-boring beetles and their larvae, ants, and other insects. The bird is so named because of the hairlike feathers above its bill. I heard one tapping on a lodgepole pine quite early one morning in the North Cascades. The tapping is one of the easiest ways to identify that you're in the neighborhood of a woodpecker.

The process of creating block prints requires a number of steps but is relatively simple.

Quick sketch with marker and watercolor: I created this sketch very quickly using a waterproof bold marker and watercolor on Bristol paper, a heavyweight smooth paper strong enough to absorb a light wash without disintegrating. The pen is black and bold, so it makes heavy lines like you'd see in a finished carved print, and the Bristol paper is inexpensive—this is, after all, just a sketch to try things out.

Drawing a block print: The drawing refines the concept I explored in the quick marker and watercolor sketch. Once I'm happy with the drawing, done in an HB pencil, I use a very dark pencil (a 5B) to redraw over the lighter pencil lines. Then I flip the drawing onto the carving block and rub it with a heavyweight kitchen spoon to transfer the image onto the block.

Carved block: Here you see the finished block with the areas that will be painted, or will remain white, carved away. The outline is now in relief,

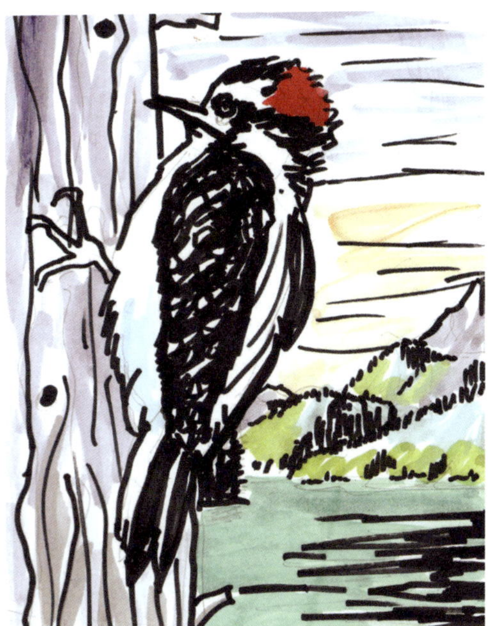

QUICK SKETCH WITH MARKER

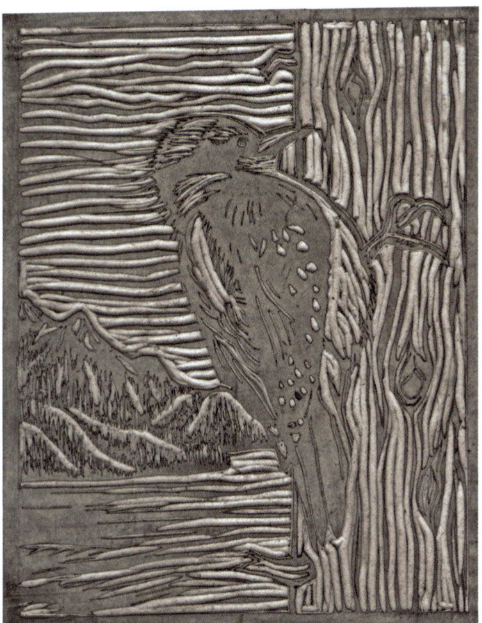

CARVED BLOCK

ready to print. The carved contours help to describe both the markings on the bird as well as the movement of water and texture of bark.

Inking the block: In printing, I don't use relief inks, since they don't come in the beautiful range of colors I like to choose from. Instead, I use high-quality oil-based etching ink (soft black, ivory black, or carbon black), which will resist—i.e., not bleed into—the watercolor I'll use later to tint the print; as the saying goes, oil and water don't mix! I like to thin the etching ink with a bit of a tack reducer. Tack refers to the stickiness of the ink. You roll out an ink that is fairly gooey, not stiff. If the ink is an etching ink (as opposed to a relief ink), and depending on the color, as different colors have different degrees of viscosity, you may need to add some burnt plate oil to thin it out a little. I use ½ teaspoon of tack reducer to 2 tablespoons of ink, and then 1 tablespoon of burnt plate oil to 4 tablespoons of ink/tack reducer mixture.

Using an ink knife, I spread the ink on a piece of glass or plexiglass (plexi is nicer because you don't have to worry about it breaking) to about the width of the brayer. Then I roll the brayer back and forth on the plexi until I obtain a thin layer of ink sufficient to cover the brayer but not completely overload it. Next I roll the brayer onto the block, first horizontally and then vertically. Going in both directions ensures good coverage.

Printing: I place a good-quality hot press watercolor paper on the block and then rub vigorously with a heavyweight kitchen spoon. I gently lift up one corner of the print to see how well the image is transferring to the paper. If coverage is too light, I hold down the upper

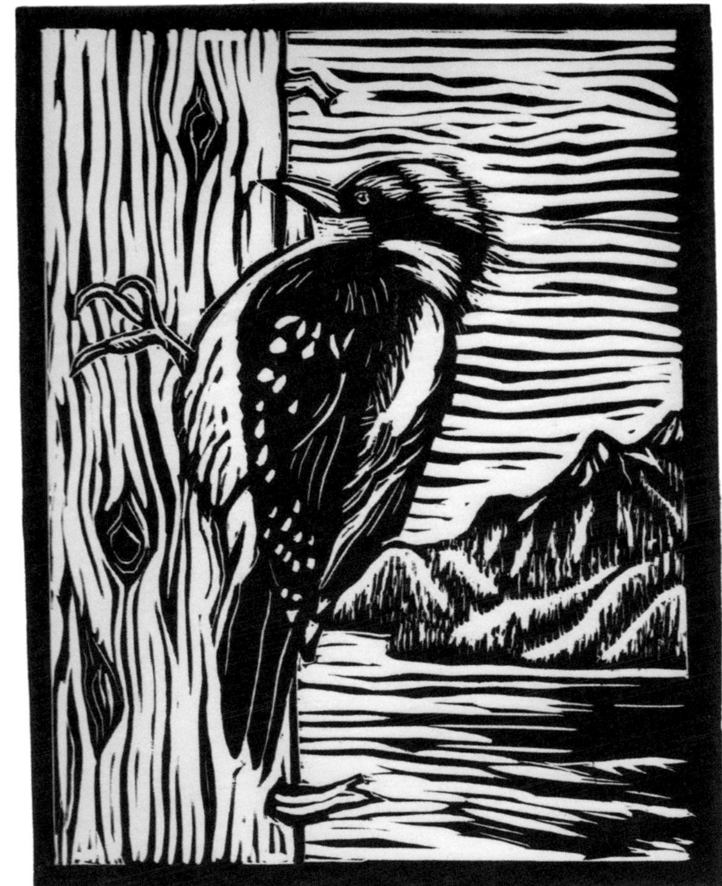

UNPAINTED PRINT

half of the print firmly, lift up the lower half, and reapply ink. I reverse this process for the upper half.

There's no need to clean the block between prints; you can leave the ink on and reapply with the brayer for each additional print.

Unpainted print: Notice how the print is a mirror image of the carved block.

Tinting the block print: There are a number of ways to introduce color into a print. The block can be printed with oil-based black ink and then tinted by applying watercolor with a brush (see "Watercolor" section above). Or the block can be printed with a colored ink. If only one color is chosen, then one block is sufficient, but if areas with different colors are required, then it's necessary to carve multiple blocks, with each block dedicated to a specific color. (To get each block to line up, or "register," you create a registration template and lay the block on it before running it through the press; for more information, see *The Encyclopedia of Printmaking Techniques*, listed in "Further Reading.") When I tint with watercolor, I'm careful to accentuate the bright colors, since the strong blacks require intense color for balance. Often, leaving a few white, unpainted areas helps to dramatize the blacks and bright colors.

Cleanup of materials: Cooking oil removes the ink on all surfaces. I like to use a single-edge razor blade to remove the ink from the plexiglass before squirting it with oil to finish cleaning it. Unless you pay for a laundry service to clean your supplies, it's best to use paper towels, as washing oil-soaked rags and then putting them in your dryer can cause a fire.

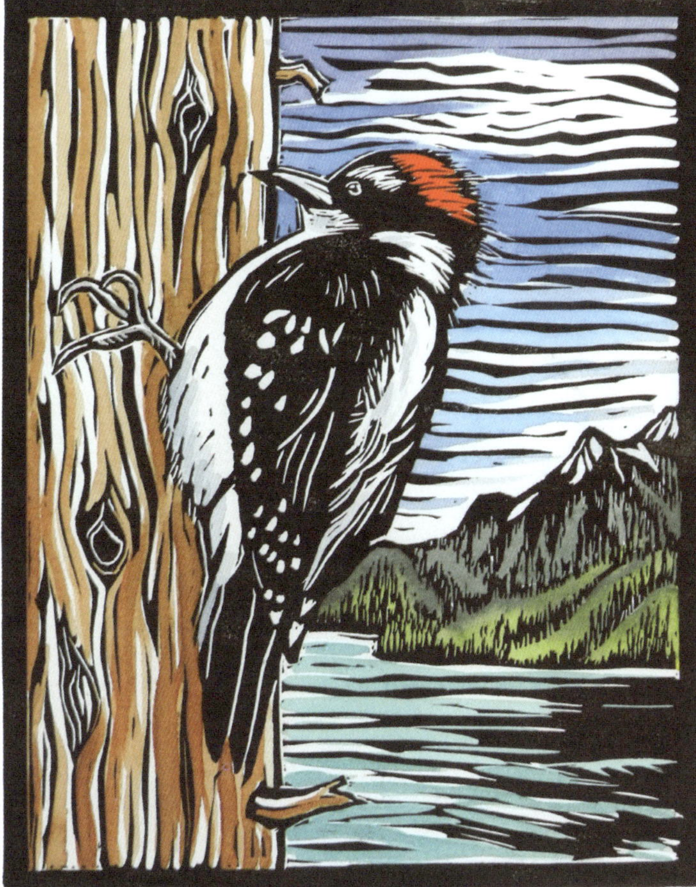

TINTED BLOCK PRINT

careers. Kandinsky was much impressed by the folk art of the Vologda region of Russia, later producing art that was very decorative, featuring bright colors contrasting with dark backgrounds. Kirchner's woodcuts dramatically employ expressive line work that is deliberately rough and crude, calling to mind some of the earliest German woodcuts. Both artists were drawn to the dynamic interplay of dark and light, as well as to intense color. In my block prints, I've tried to capture something of what I admire in these two artists: the folk art craftsmanship of Kandinsky and the energy of Kirchner's carved lines.

After working as a watercolor artist for years, I tried carving rubber blocks (a soft material very similar to linoleum but much easier to carve) as an introduction to printmaking and fell in love with it after my very first carving. I found it was a way to create art with high values contrast, something not easily achieved in watercolor. With watercolor, edges are blurred, much is based on subtle gradations, and color can be somewhat weaker. With a block print, lines have clearly defined edges, and when black is used as one of the colors, the contrast between it and other colors is even greater. I also appreciate the very tactile three dimensions of the carving block itself and the carving tools—it's as close to sculpting as I've yet come, and it's deeply satisfying.

ETCHING

Etching is also called *intaglio* printmaking; the word derives from the Italian verb *intagliare*, which means "to engrave" or "to cut." The lines you see in the final artwork are created by incising lines in metal plates. These incised lines will fill when ink is applied. The process is exactly the opposite of relief printmaking in which the lines themselves stand out in relief from the wood. Nineteenth-century artist James McNeill Whistler actually brought his plates outdoors and drew *en plein air* (French for "in the open air"), quite an accomplishment with a studio technique like etching—few other artists have had the nerve to try that! Venice was a favorite subject, and Whistler captured all the beauty and drama of its canals and architecture.

Copper is the most common material for etching plates. After the etching process is complete, the plate is inked and wiped so that the only ink remaining on the plate is caught in the incised lines. Next, damp paper is laid on the plate, and finally the plate and paper are run through a press with a fairly tight pressure setting. The paper picks up the ink that remains in the incised lines. I love the precision that I can achieve with etching—the crispness of markings on a great horned owl's breast, or the lovely silhouetted form of a bluebird or dowitcher. Although etching materials and techniques are a bit more complex than those used in sketching, watercolor, or block printing, they're easily understood once you take a class; see "Resources" to find places you can take classes. After you get the basics in a classroom, consider joining a printmaking cooperative or a studio with a large press on hand, because you need to have access to a press for etching. All the other media I cover in the book can be done by hand at home.

Great horned owl *(Bubo virginianus)* • ETCHING

Birds are endlessly fascinating, often at the same time familiar, yet difficult to know. I almost always think that with just one medium I haven't fully explored the meaning of those meetings that are so important to me. The summer after coming upon the great horned owls I mentioned above, I had access to an etching press, so I decided to try the adult great horned owl with a focus on line. As I worked, I discovered

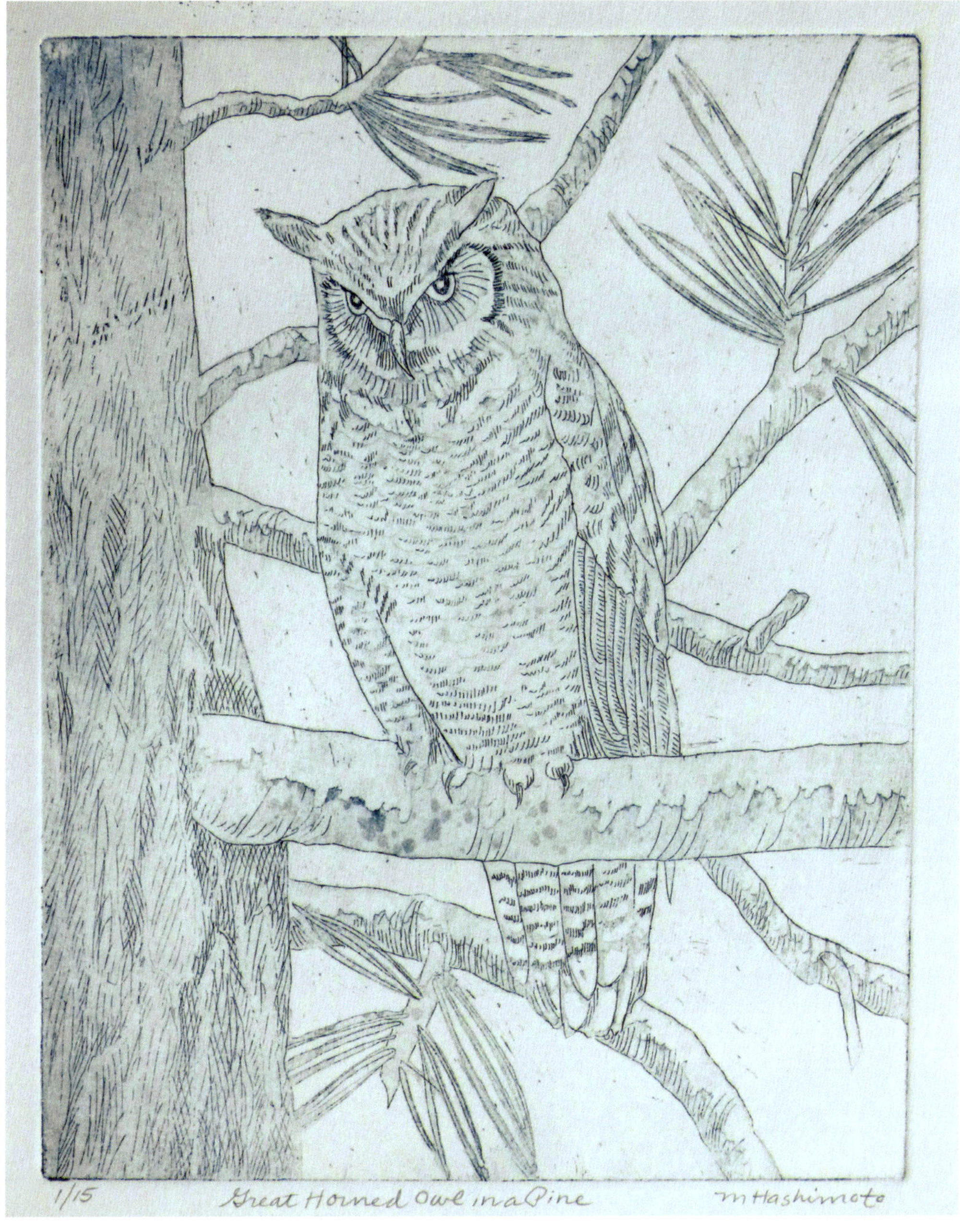

that this medium, through its multiple hatch lines, captured the mother owl's barred plumage as I saw it from below, looking up into the pine. The hours I put into the etching helped me render the markings of this amazing creature. It tells a different story about our encounter than my sketch of the owls, (page 19), which, with its more tentative strokes and brighter colors, captures the relationship between the begging baby and its mother—and how incongruous it is that the fluffy fledgling is even larger than the adult bird. The colors help enliven the sketch, even adding a touch of comedy. The etching, on the other hand, has a gravity that a medium like a watercolor sketch does not have. The mother owl is serious; perhaps wishing us away from her home, she is beautiful, dignified, and threatening. It took me hours and hours to tell that story, and it's entirely possible that the owls haven't had their last word with me!

EGG TEMPERA

Byzantine icon painters worked in egg tempera, and the practice continues today in Greek and Russian Orthodox churches. The medium was used everywhere in the medieval and Early Renaissance art of Italy and northern Europe, both in altarpieces on gessoed wood (gesso is any material used to prime a surface such as wood, canvas, or paper; when dry, it lies between the surface and the painting medium) and in manuscript illuminations on vellum. Twentieth-century artist Andrew Wyeth renewed the medium's relevance with his work, which focused on his Chadds Ford, Pennsylvania, home, as well as seascapes at his summer home in Maine. He used egg tempera to create the rich textures of beach, dry winter grasses, farm fields, architecture, stone, and interiors.

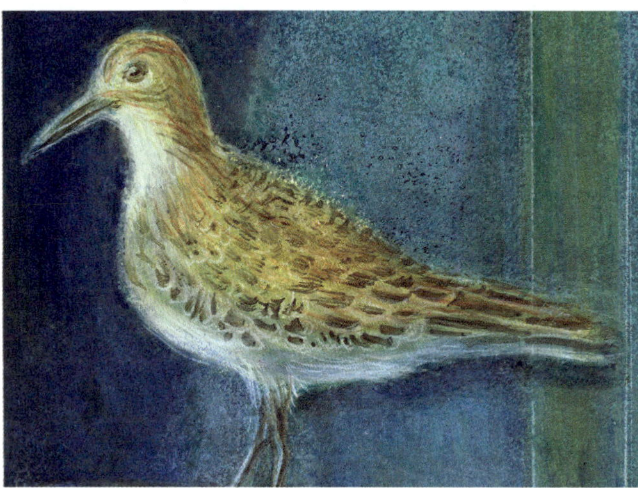

WESTERN SANDPIPER *(CALIDRIS MAURI)* EGG TEMPERA

For this medium, dry ground pigments are mixed with egg yolk and water and then applied in thin layers onto gessoed board or wood. Egg tempera dries quickly, and broad areas of color can be built up in very thin layers like oil glazes or can be spattered and sponged to create spotted and speckled textures. The egg yolk mixture creates a luminous sheen. In my own work with the medium, I like to add the design motif of arches that were so popular for religious subjects in the Early Renaissance, something I learned from contemporary artist Koo Schadler. The arches help to express the dignity of the bird subjects, harkening back to the reverence manifest in those Early Renaissance religious paintings.

Bird Habitats: Part of the Picture

I seldom passed a day without drawing a bird, or noting something respecting its habits.

—**John James Audubon,** "Myself"

Birds need four basics—food, water, shelter, and nesting sites—and species evolve to make the best use of whatever each ecosystem can provide them. To ensure their success in mating, waterfowl have evolved as the most colorful and flamboyant of North American birds. They don't hide out as much as birds of other habitats, which makes them so much more accessible to us. Many forest fliers have short wings that help them maneuver between branches, while woodpeckers and sapsuckers have strong tail feathers that help prop their bodies on tree trunks, with long beaks and tongues for reaching the insects found in trees. Desert inhabitants are often perfectly camouflaged in browns and grays.

This book is divided into chapters organized by habitat, and each chapter opens with an appreciation of that habitat. As much as I enjoy seeing the birds themselves, without the surrounding landscapes those experiences would not be so complex and satisfying. The silence of the desert, the sound of wind through the high branches in a coniferous forest, the complex patterns of reflected color in ripples on a pond, the crashing surf, the austere beauty of alpine heights—all of these contribute to the great pleasure that comes with watching birds. In these locales and moments, we are sharing an environment with the birds, which gives us, earthbound as we are, a deeper connection with our fellow creatures.

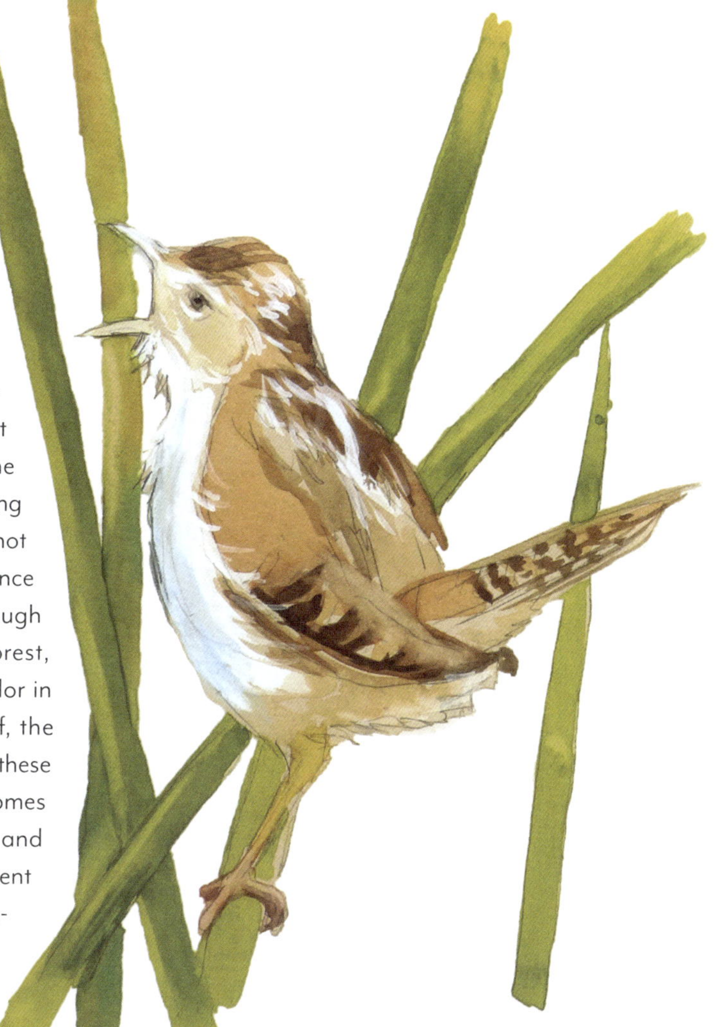

MARSH WREN (*CISTOHORUS PALUSTRIS*) WATERCOLOR

Tips for Viewing Birds

For the best bird-viewing opportunities, find the locations they're most likely to frequent. Some of the key places to look are boundaries, edges, and transitional zones, such as areas between forest and field, hedgerows, watery edges, and coastlines. There's a great variety of food in those places, plus cover for protection. Look for birds in sheltered areas, such as the lee sides of ground structures and windbreaks. Water is crucial to birds; the more arid the surrounding landscape, the more likely there will be birds at any water sources, including desert oases, which can be visited by huge numbers of migrants for a few weeks in spring and fall.

One of the best times to see birds in any location is at first light—the first two hours after sunrise—when insects are warming up in the sun and birds are hungry from a long night without food. During breeding season, birds sing earlier in the morning, establishing their territorial boundaries. The hours before dark are a good time, too, since the birds need to feed for energy overnight. You may also see birds in the heat of midday in summer as they visit birdbaths to cool off. Peak migrations in fall and spring are optimal times to view birds at beaches. You'll see most shorebirds during low tides, when receding waters expose more food sources.

The book begins with the most easily approached habitat: our own backyards, neighborhood parks, and urban wildlands. Birds accompany us daily with their songs, bright colors, and energetic activity. Some are familiar, like robins and mallards, and others rarely seen, like Townsend's warblers and sharp-shinned hawks. The best thing about backyards is their proximity to us: daily observation can yield amazing results. If you go somewhere else just once—for example, to a foreign country—you have only a single, short opportunity to view that country's wildlife. In your own backyard or neighborhood park, you can go every day of the year and are guaranteed to see something different on many of those visits. Checking off new species is not always the most profound experience; learning something new about a very familiar bird or place can be more significant.

Next I visit wetlands, one of the richest and most populous habitats, and consequently one of the longest chapters in the book, followed by beaches and shorelines, also teeming with birds. Meadows and grasslands, covered in the subsequent chapter, attract many compelling species, including birds of prey. Deserts and sagebrush steppe come next. Although deserts are less hospitable to birds than are other habitats, there are some appealing inhabitants, such as roadrunners and burrowing owls. The deserts I've visited are the sagebrush areas of the Great Basin, which includes most of Nevada, northeastern California, eastern Oregon and Washington, southern Idaho, southwestern Montana, much of Utah, western Wyoming, and the foothills and valleys of northwestern Colorado. Thus most of the birds in this chapter are limited to those types of dry terrain, although there are a few species from the Sonoran Desert of California, Arizona, and northwestern Mexico. The following chapter covers woodlands and forests, which are filled with some of my favorite birds—woodpeckers and owls. Finally, I share the birds I've seen in alpine habitats, a well-known world for me after many years of hiking.

Of course, some species travel easily between various habitats and are widespread. Others are much more limited to specific regions and plant life communities; these include chickadees and woodpeckers, which don't travel far. Some birds are present only during breeding and nesting seasons, whereas others visit us only during the winter. Field guides provide helpful information about the seasonal ranges of birds.

In each chapter, I write about my encounters with numerous species and offer some information on their names and habits, as well as quotes about the birds from authors and poets. I explain why I've chosen certain media to express aspects of the birds—and why, for some birds, I've worked in multiple media. I also include tips and technique sections in which you'll learn how to use various media and techniques to achieve expressive bird art. My hope is that this book inspires you to create your own art and gives you even more appreciation for the beauty of birds. Just putting up a feeder will draw birds to you, and walking in your own neighborhood will acquaint you with all your local species. You don't need to travel to exotic destinations to find fascinating subject matter!

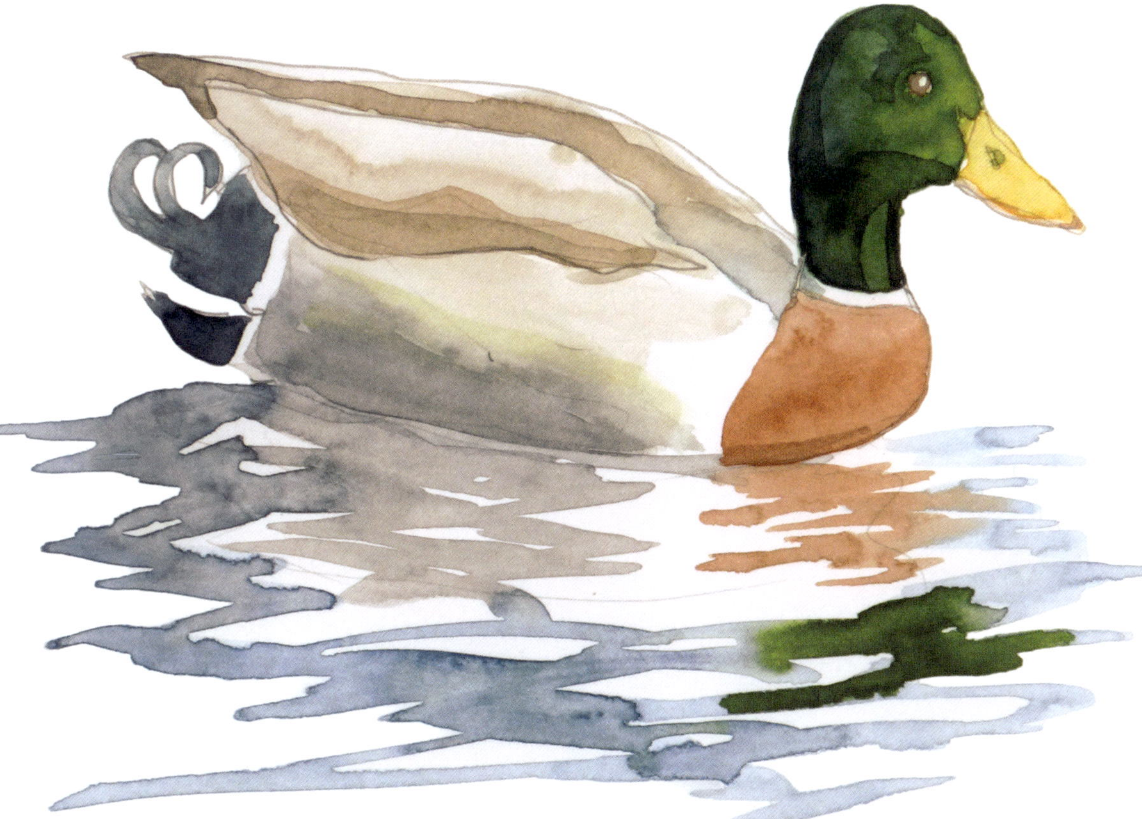

MALLARD (*ANAS PLATYRHYNCHOS*) WATERCOLOR SKETCH

Backyard & City

suburbs

city parks

urban wildlife refuges

golf courses

waste areas

parking lots

industrial sites

birdbaths

brambles

snags and stumps

feeders

fences

flowers

lawns

mosses

lichens

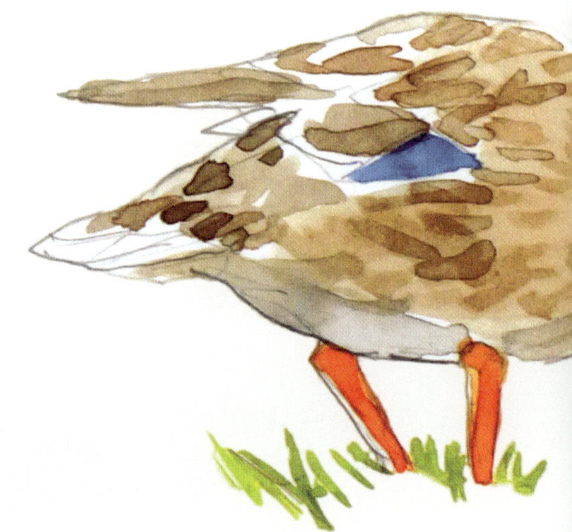

Though relatively tame and constructed mostly from human hands, subirdia is not a zoo. There are no confining bars to isolate species or moats to separate humans from wild beasts. In subirdia, birds and humans share an ecosystem in which they are connected by fibers that define the web of life.

—**John Marzluff,** *Welcome to Subirdia*

In spring and summer, Anna's and rufous hummingbirds fill the backyard air with their buzzing calls, wild aerial battles, and plunging dives. Dapper Bewick's wrens, tails erect, perch on a fence and give life to a cold winter's day. Warblers, both Townsend's and yellow-rumped, appear in the snow and cold, singly and in groups, to feed on suet. Even in winter, when most birds are silent or absent, crows entertain us with their noisy family gatherings, foraging, and resourcefulness. Beginning as early as February, northern flickers hammer a rhythm on anything metallic to attract mates. Chickadees travel with bushtits in morning and afternoon and nest in boxes and backyard trees in spring and summer. Goldfinches visit thistle feeders and splash in birdbaths in the heat of summer when water is more scarce. Kingfishers fly low and fast over neighborhood ponds, so often heard before they are seen.

Of course, the backyard habitat is a relatively new one for birds. In *Welcome to Subirdia*, John Marzluff sorts the birds that surround us into three groups: The ones that have been threatened by rapid development and home construction in cities and suburbs are "avoiders." The second group, the "adapters," are birds that have managed to hold their own. The third group, the "exploiters," consists of birds that are downright thriving. In my neighborhood in Seattle, we're fortunate enough to count the occasional avoiders, such as hairy woodpeckers. We also have lots of adapters, among them, chickadees, corvids such as Steller's jays, and Anna's hummingbirds. Hummingbirds have expanded their territory northward because so many homes have feeders; Anna's stay all winter now in the Pacific Northwest. The exploiters are species that have enlarged their territory and gained in population during decades of rapid urban and suburban development, and in many cases they've crowded out the avoiders. They're able to make use of many of the by-products of human development, as you'll know if you've ever seen a crow dumpster-diving or dropping a nut in the middle of the road in order to make use of an oncoming car to crack it open.

All of these birds benefit from backyards and suburban fringes of forests that remain messy, with downed branches, dead trees, overgrown hedges, and the like. Perfectly manicured lawns are bad for birds, first of all because many such lawns require herbicides to kill weeds, and those chemicals run into streams, ponds, and lakes, which we share with wild creatures. Vast expanses of lawn also have no flowering plants for feeding or pollination, no protected places for nests, and a dearth of insects. And in formerly forested areas, Marzluff writes, "Dead trees, or 'snags,' are critical resources for many birds, but construction crews and homeowners concerned with safety quickly remove them. That many small snags remain in our forests may explain why both creeper and woodpecker populations are faring better than other development avoiders across the West."

To create welcoming spaces for birds in your own backyard, use diverse plantings, native plants, and plenty of undergrowth. All the unsightly places in our yard (areas with leaf litter and overgrown vines) support juncos, wrens, and towhees. Having many different types of plants with flowers of varying heights is a huge help to birds, enabling them to move safely from high blooms to lower flowers without exposing themselves to predators. The variety of plants is a boon to all pollinators as they bloom at different times of the year. It's also important to allow plants to go to seed in autumn because that leaves food for birds through the winter. All this makes for gardens that are interesting to look at, too.

American goldfinch *(Spinus tristis)* • **BLOCK PRINT**

One of the best ways to attract birds is by placing birdbaths in your garden. Sometimes water is even more important to birds than food, especially in summer in the Pacific Northwest, when rain is very scarce. I try to change the water frequently to keep it safe for the birds. In springtime, I often see crows using it as a kind of fondue dip for scraps such as chicken wings, chunks of dry bread, and waffle cones. My guess is that they're softening the food for their nestlings, but it also means I have to change the water several times a day.

In this relief print, one of the first bird prints I ever made, I attempted to express how moving it was to see the vivid colors of the male goldfinches visiting at the height of color in the garden, in May, with blooming poppies and clematis. Finch colors peak during their breeding season, in late spring and early summer. In winter, the males are drab brown with a few yellow streaks on their wings—you might not even know you're looking at the same bird.

Goldfinches

One of my father's gifts
was the joy that would light his face
when he saw something beautiful:

Goldfinches in the spring,
morning waves on a lake,
a sunset glimpsed through trees.

He smiled with his lips pulled back
as if the bright flash of beauty
had seared him with its sudden heat.

Then he would turn his head
to make sure
that we had seen it too.

—Saul Weisberg, from *Headwaters*

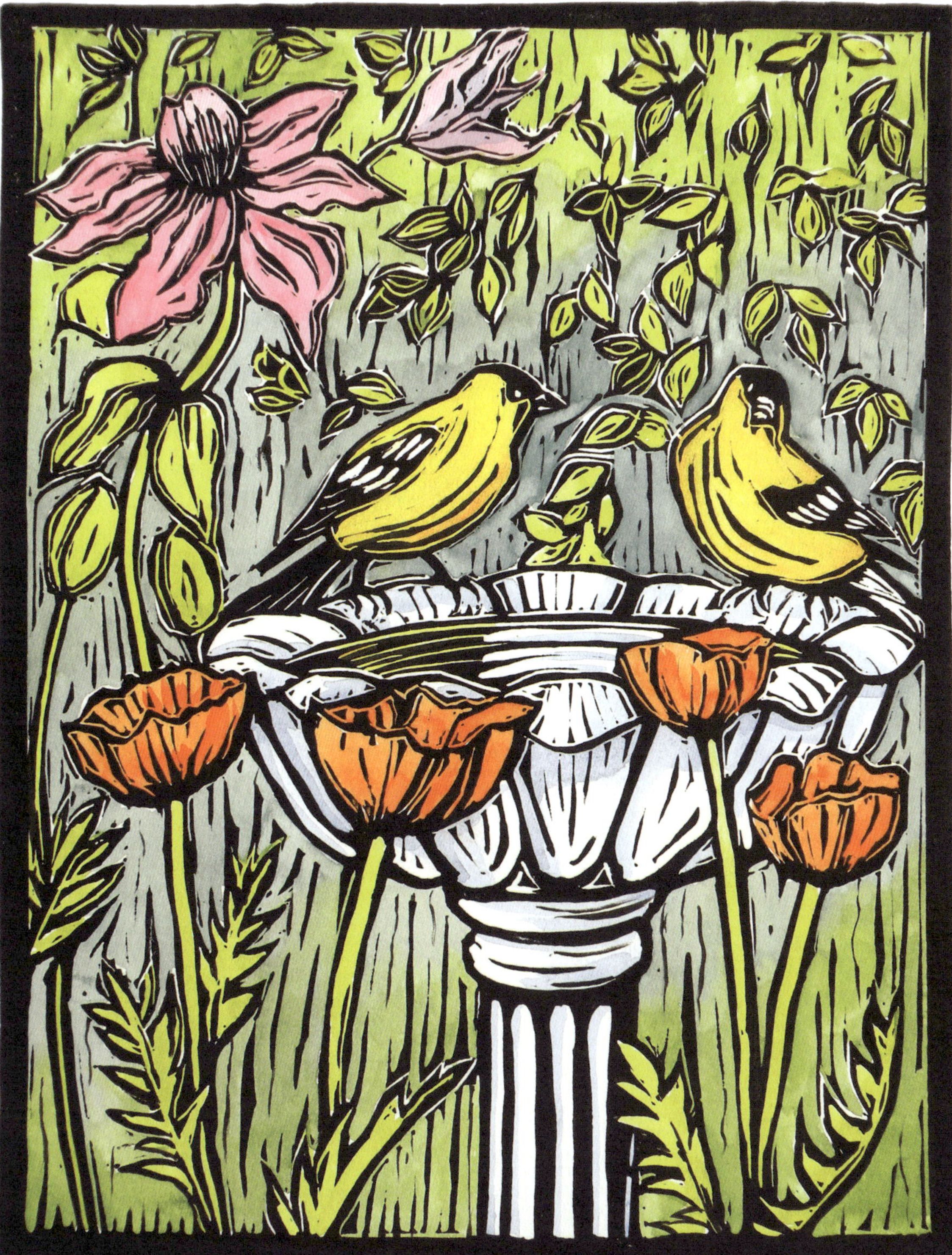

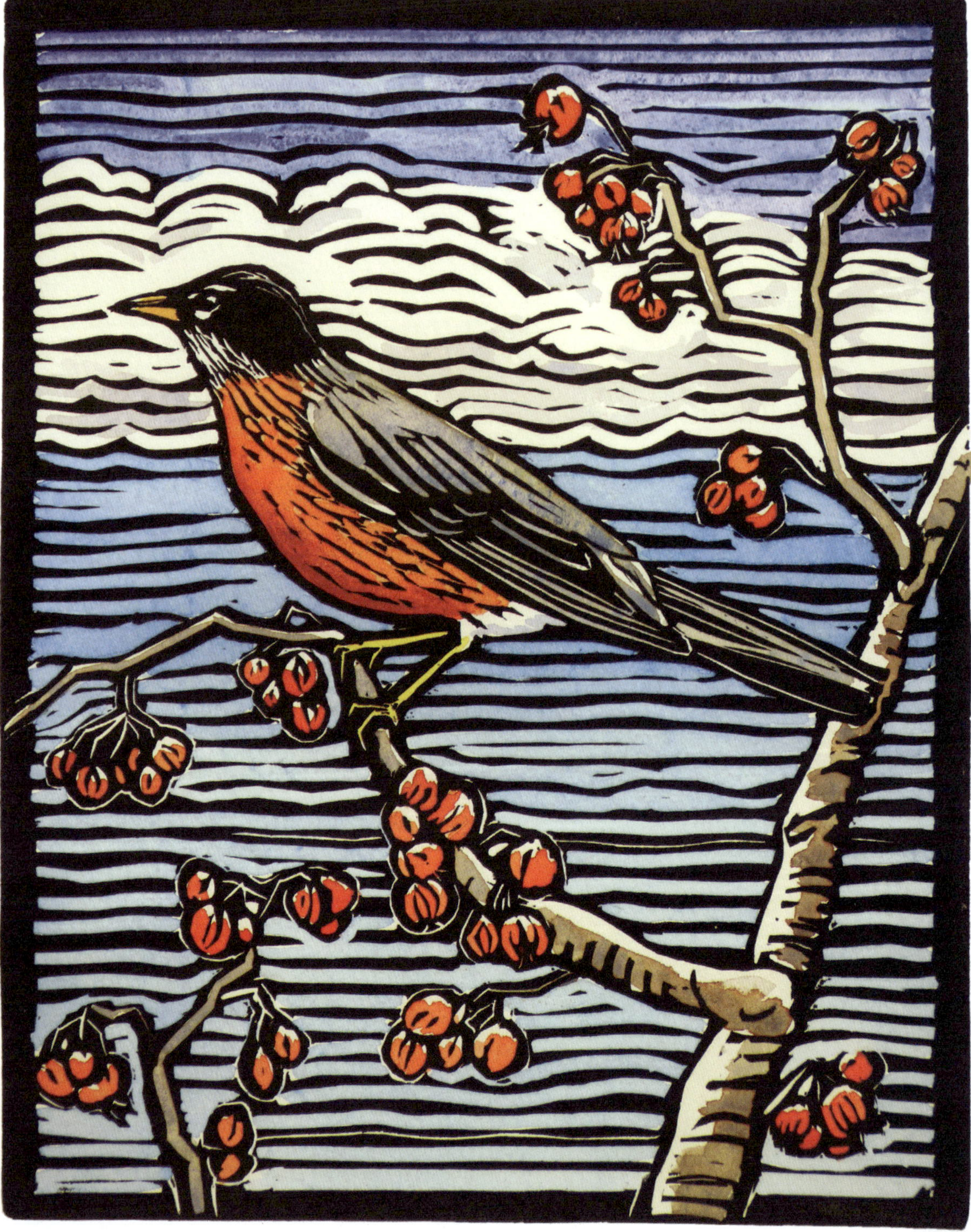

How admirable the constitution and temper of this cheery, graceful bird, keeping glad health over so vast and varied a range!

—John Muir, "Among the Birds of the Yosemite"

American robin *(Turdus migratorius)* • BLOCK PRINT

This robin was feeding in early winter at a tree in the park near our house. Robins flock in the wintertime in the Pacific Northwest, behavior that is not observed during nesting season. Seeing a whole flock of robins feeding on a green park lawn in winter can almost convince you that you're not stuck in the endless month of January! In winter, they find all the remaining berries, and sometimes dozens gather in a single tree. I loved the color of the breast of the bird paired with the color of the tree fruit; I'm not sure if this small tree was a crabapple, or a hawthorn. In the block print, I deliberately nudged the reddish berries toward orange so that the breast and berry color harmonized.

Sharp-shinned hawk *(Accipiter striatus)* • WATERCOLOR SKETCH

Both sharp-shinned hawks and Cooper's hawks (page 57)—members of the *Accipiter* genus—are woodland birds but are not rare in winter in backyards near bird feeders. Recently, a sharp-shinned hawk, about the size of a flicker, visited our feeder for nefarious purposes. It was a day of drenching rain, and perhaps the hawk had to take some chances, coming close to our house. Having no success in our yard, the hawk flew from our fence to our neighbors' tree, where they hang a thistle feeder. As I watched, I suddenly noticed a Bewick's wren crouching inside the cage of our suet feeder, utterly still for many minutes. The wren didn't take its eyes off the hawk in the neighbors' tree the entire time and began to move only after the hawk left the area.

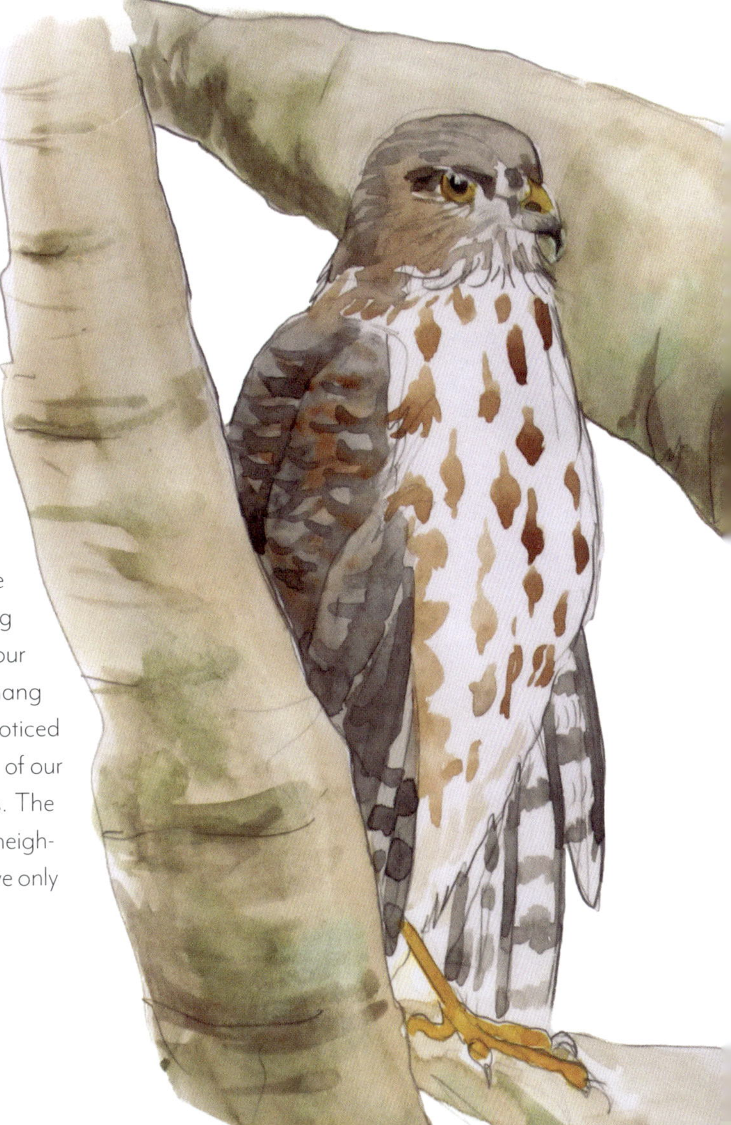

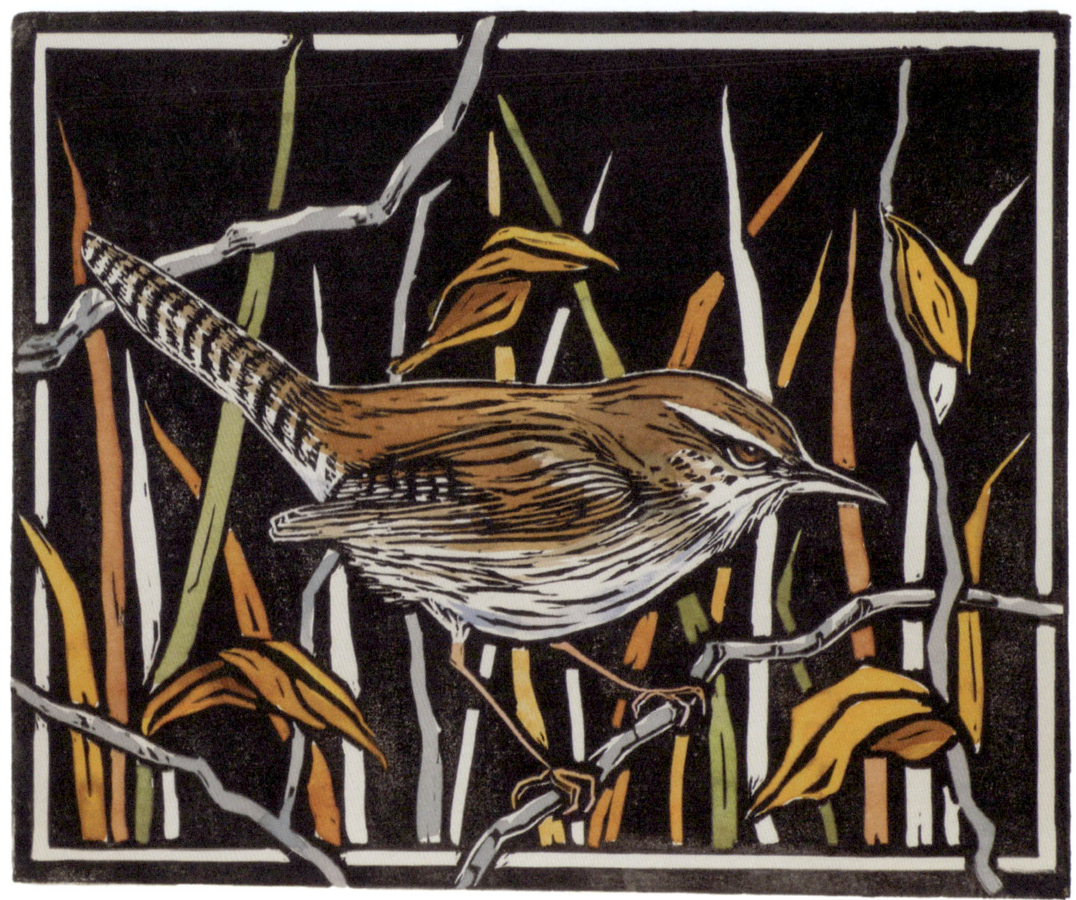

Bewick's wren *(Thryomanes bewickii)* • **BLOCK PRINT**

There's a resident Bewick's in our neighbor's garden shed—one spring the neighbor found a nest there and didn't disturb it. Another year, I discovered one inside the *Clematis montana* vine that creeps up our old grapestake fence, growing wildly every year, so I'm careful when pruning to leave the section where I found the nest. The nests are made of twigs, hair, leaves, and grasses and are fairly compact. Because we've welcomed the wrens this way, I observe them all year; in winter they're daily visitors to the suet feeder. The birds' upright tails and wagging strut across the fence add a lot of cheerfulness to gloomy rainy days in winter. In early spring their songs alternate between buzzing and warbling, and in our yard they seem to be among the first birds to be aware of the changing seasons, something birds recognize because of the length of the days. So even if it's still cold and plants delay their flowering, birds have an internal calendar.

In this print I wanted to express the Bewick's movement and gesture, as well as the beauty it brings to the muted colors of winter; notice the golden and pale withered grasses highlighted against the black surroundings. For me this was the perfect *wabi-sabi* subject, a Japanese concept that celebrates the imperfect, impermanent, and incomplete, based on Buddhist philosophy. *Sabi* means "chill," "lean," or "withered," and *wabi* suggests rustic simplicity and quietness. Modesty and austerity describe this aesthetic best.

Rufous hummingbird *(Selasphorus rufus)* • **BLOCK PRINT**

Years ago I grew a scarlet trumpet vine specifically to attract hummingbirds, and it really worked—until the vine overtook the fence and we finally had to cut it down since it threatened to collapse the old fence with its weight. I didn't replace the vine but now grow a yellow variety of crocosmia that the birds visit. The rufous still return every summer, and it's always amusing to see them, smaller than the Anna's, fighting for territory. They're known to chase away much larger hummingbird species and are so fearless that they've even been observed chasing chipmunks away from their nests. The loyal Anna's lives in the environs year-round, while the pugnacious rufous stays only the summer; yet the latter insists on domination, which from my human point of view seems entirely unfair! Rufous winter in Mexico and can breed as far north as Southeast Alaska, the longest range of any hummingbird.

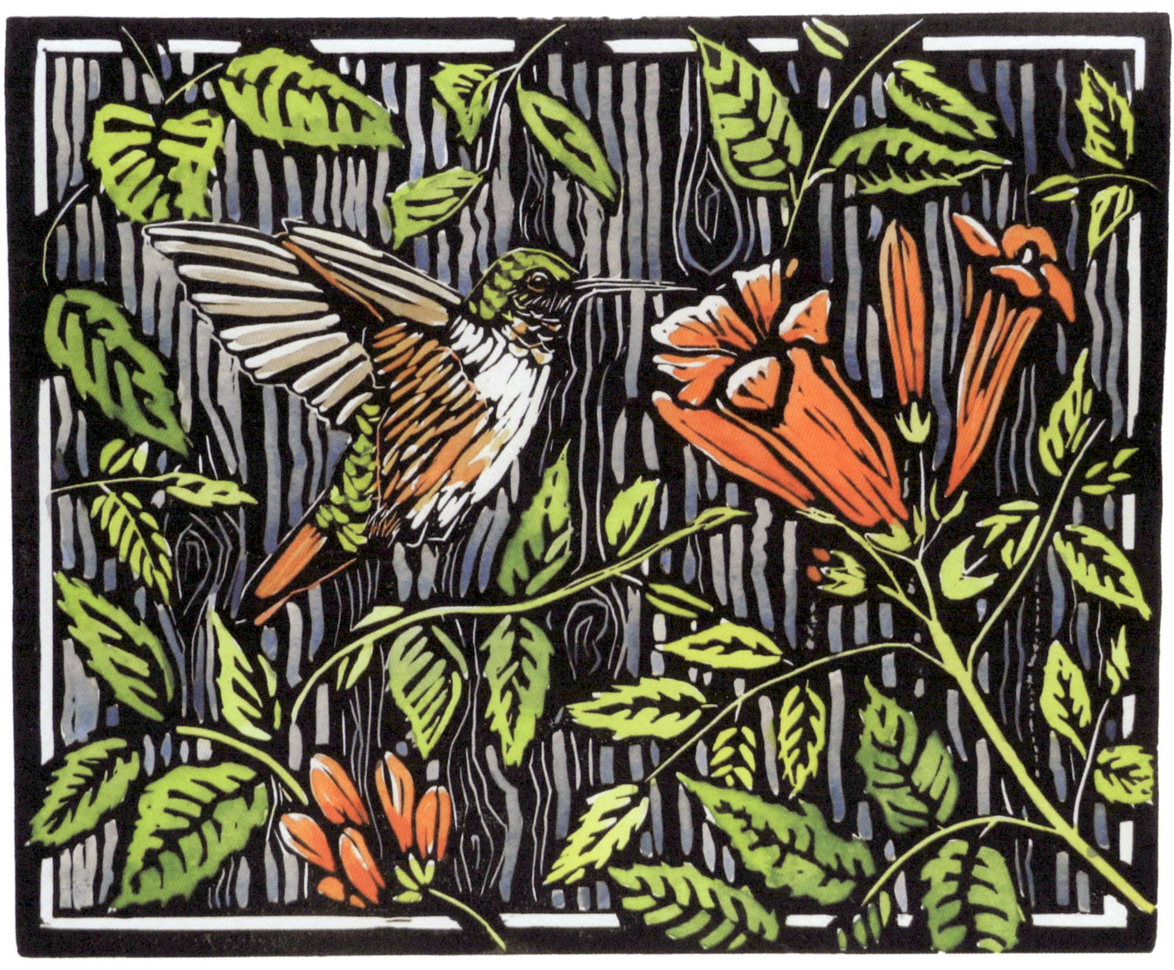

TECHNIQUE
Watercolor, White Gouache, and Toned Paper

It's possible the name *kingfisher* derives from the Arthurian legend of the Fisher King and stories of Percival and the Holy Grail. It may also be that the bird was referred to as the King's Fisher because of its great skill in fishing. Belted kingfishers (*Megaceryle alcyon*) are regal birds in appearance, with their dramatic colors, markings, and crowns. They thrive in urban areas along watercourses as long as there are embankments in which they can build their nests. Usually they're heard first, then seen, because of their very distinctive rattle cry, unlike any other bird's. The female is also remarkable; she has a rich sienna breast bar, a rare instance in the bird world of the female being more colorful than the male.

My husband (a frequent birdwatching companion) and I watched the juvenile shown in these sketches for many minutes as she perched in a snag above a pond in our neighborhood park, and I took about two dozen photos. The bird was still for at least ten minutes, concentrating on the water below and changing her head position frequently enough to strike many different poses. At home, I created this series of sketches in a sketchbook filled with gray-toned paper, beginning with a pencil sketch that was loosely drawn to capture the gesture of the bird's intense watching and tilted head poses. After I was satisfied with the

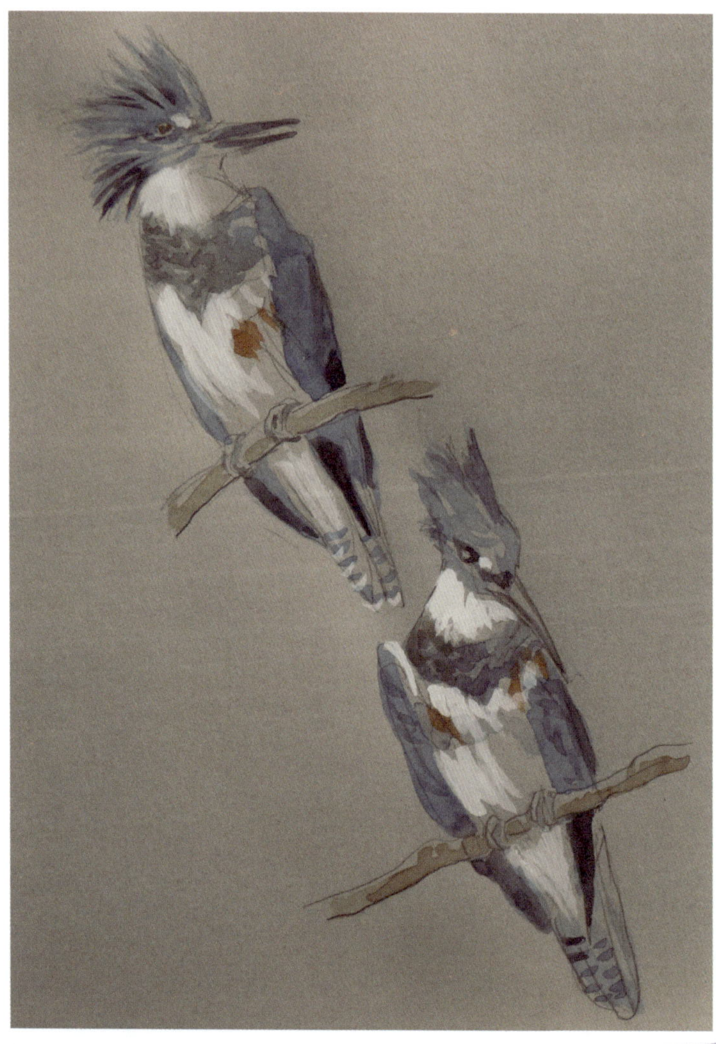

pencil drawings, I added watercolor, taking care to leave a lot of the gray paper unpainted—the toned paper often comprises the midtones of a sketch and the overall color of the subject. I painted darker areas next and then finally added a saturated white gouache in selected areas to dramatize the whites on her breast. ("Gouache" is a French word derived from the Italian *guazzo*, sometimes translated as "mud.") Gouache can be used alone or mixed with other watercolor pigments, but it's definitely muddy and opaque compared to transparent watercolor. Using gouache obscures the paper color, rather than letting it shine through, as is most often done in watercolor when painting on white paper. Some artists use it to fix mistakes in watercolors or, as in this example on toned paper, when trying to achieve whites. (For more on gouache, see "Technique: Watercolor, Gouache, and Gum Arabic on Illustration Board" in "Desert & Sagebrush Steppe.") I made the sketches on the very day I took the photos and found that I was able to capture more of the gestural quality of the bird by doing the drawings so close to the time of viewing. Sometimes sketches are more labored if too much time has passed since the sighting and no longer convey the energy of the birds.

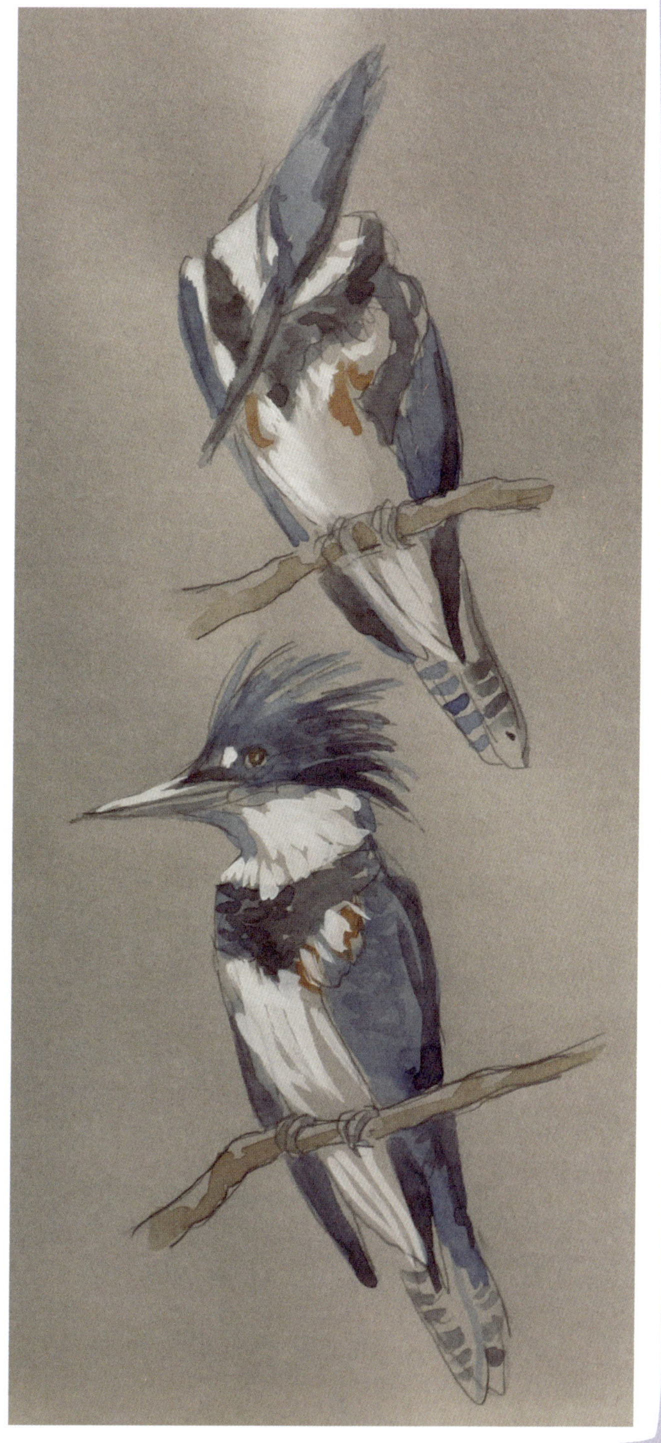

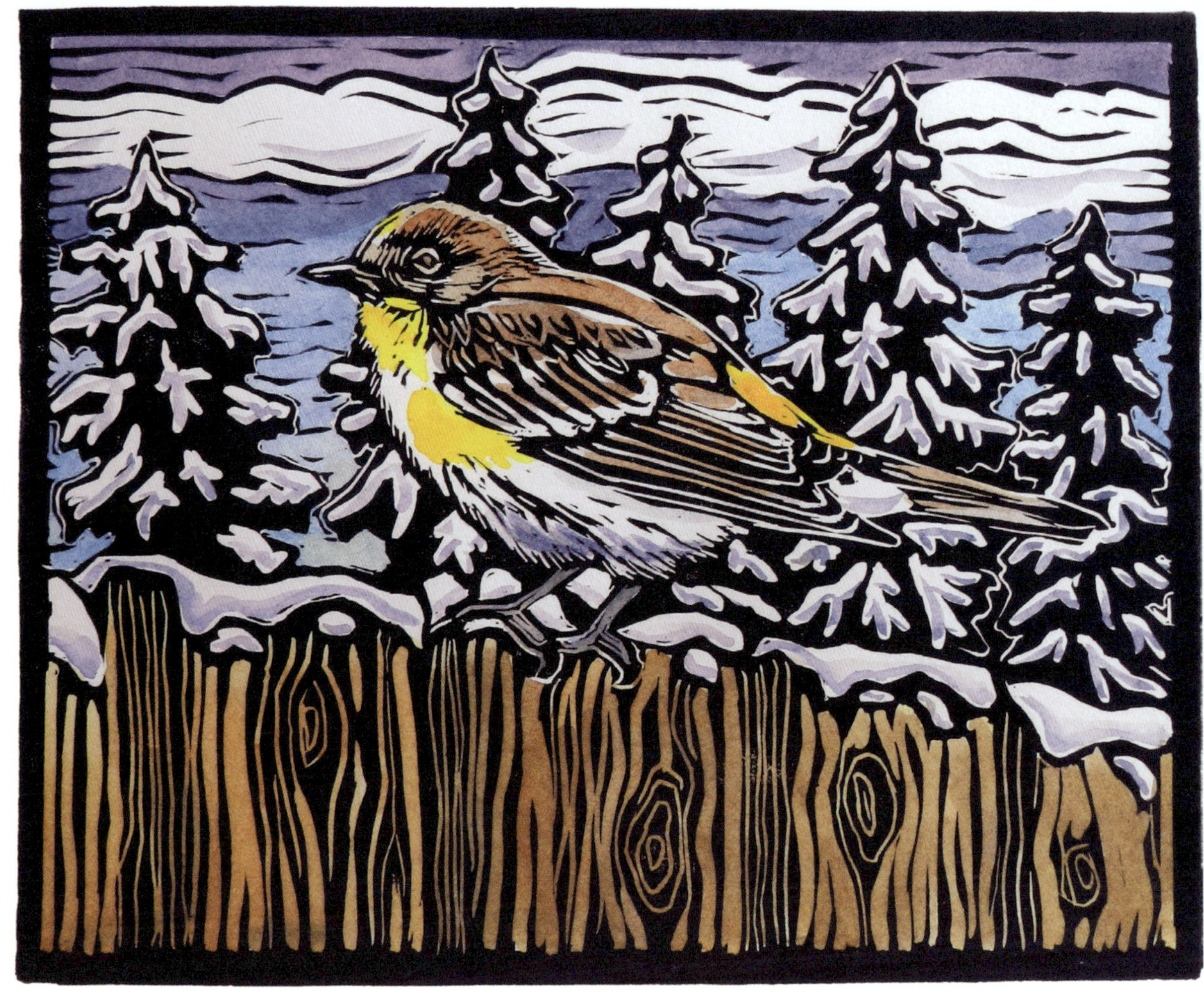

Yellow-rumped warbler *(Setophaga coronata)* • **BLOCK PRINT**

Once we placed suet in a feeder outside our kitchen window, the bird visitors to our garden became much more interesting, especially on the coldest days of winter. The cage-style feeders keep out starlings, crows, and squirrels. Unfortunately, rats still occasionally visit at night. I try to ignore that, figuring the birds of day-time are entirely worth it. The yellow-rumped warbler is a fairly common denizen of urban backyards in the Pacific Northwest, particularly in winter, but perhaps a little more secretive during other seasons, when many food sources are more plentiful. I once read that birds were the flowers of winter, and with its vibrant spots of color, the yellow-rumped warbler is one of those prized blooms. The bright yellow feathers that decorate the warbler simply demanded the block print medium because of the strong blacks and whites together with a lot of color. Our old grapestake fence created a dynamic pattern beneath its barred plumage.

Townsend's warbler *(Setophaga townsendi)* · **WOODBLOCK PRINT**

Yet another warbler visits our suet feeder in winter, this one with even more yellow decorating its feathers. Since birds tend to look rather imprisoned when pictured at the large squirrel-proof cage of the suet feeder, I prefer to show them unobstructed. In this woodblock print, I took some artistic license by posing the bird in spring with some yellow irises to harmonize with its beautiful yellow plumage.

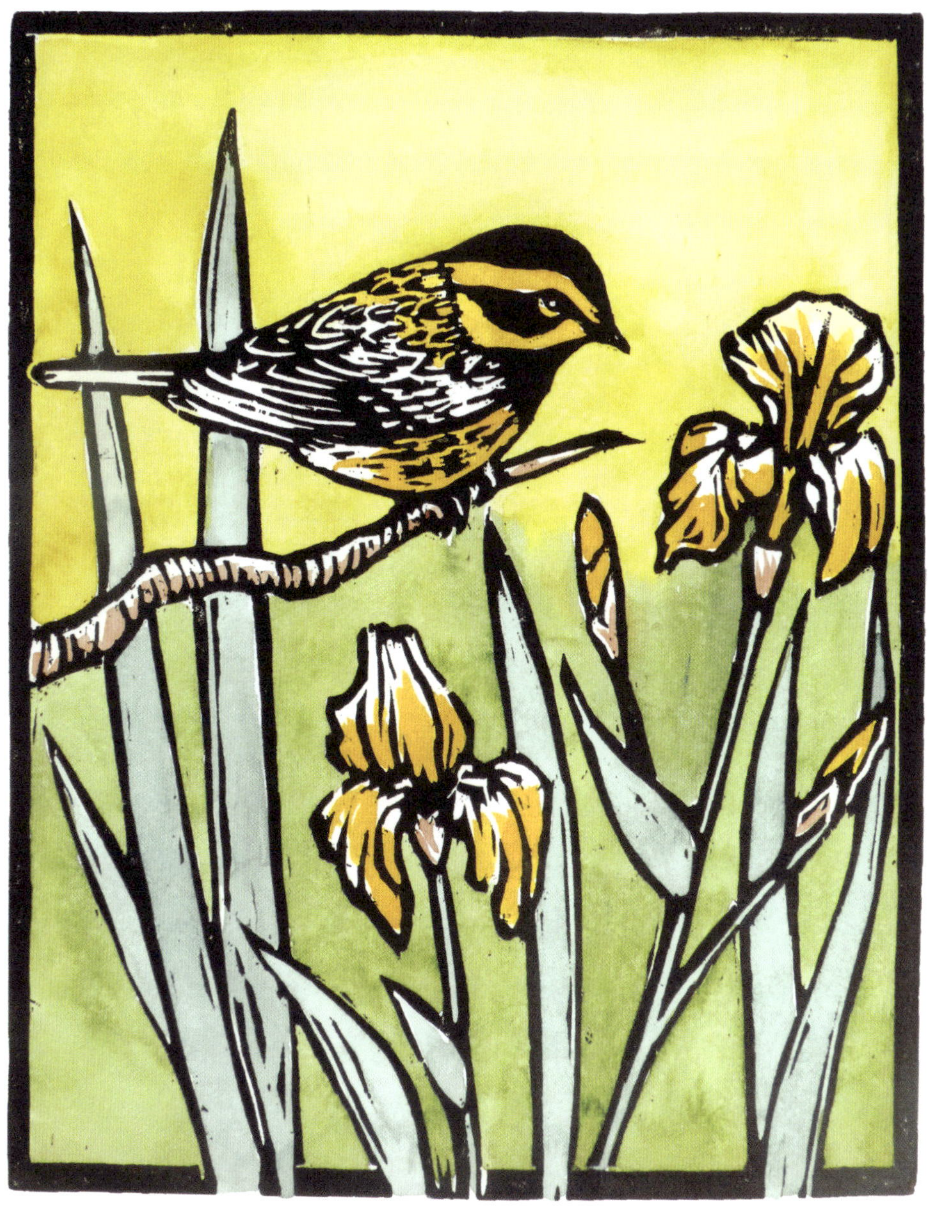

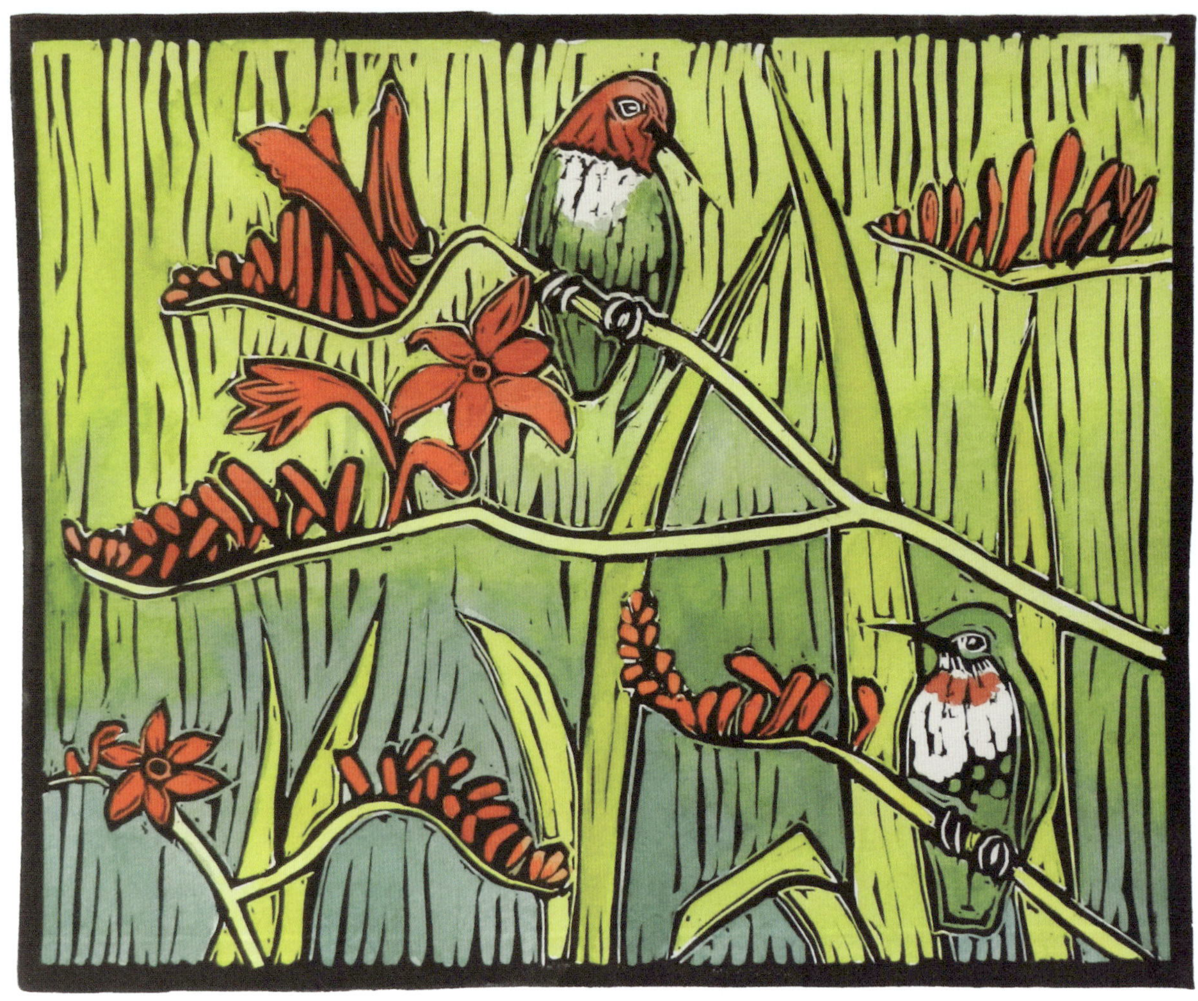

Anna's hummingbird *(Calypte anna)* • **BLOCK PRINT, WATERCOLOR**

Anna's visit our small backyard year-round. I keep a feeder full at all times but also make a point of growing flowers and shrubs that they like. *Crocosmia* 'Lucifer' has dramatic strappy leaves that grow almost five feet tall, plus elegant racemes of brilliant scarlet flowers in June and July that are irresistible to hummingbirds. The plants grow outside our bedroom window, and for a few short weeks I get to watch the hummers from indoors, where my presence doesn't seem to be noticed by the birds. I grow other crocosmia varieties in golds, oranges, and apricot hues that bloom later in the summer, and the hummingbirds seem to like them just as well. It's a delight to see these tiny fliers in every season. Sometimes in winter when I carry out their feeders in the morning (taken indoors at night to prevent them from freezing), they buzz me impatiently, as if to ask, "Where were you? Why are you so late?" And if I wear a bright color, they often come close to investigate.

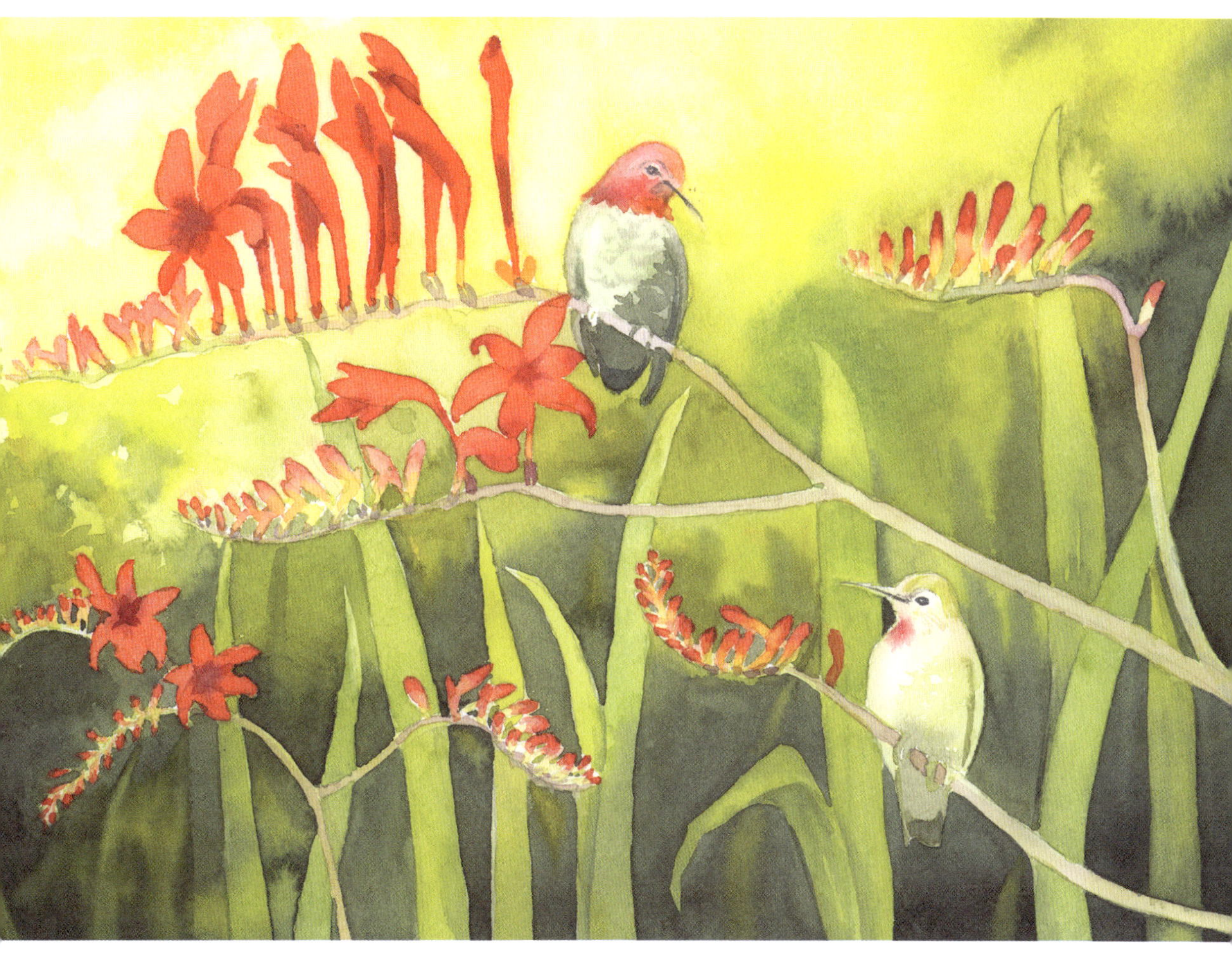

All summer long, tremendous aerial battles are waged in our backyard—sometimes between two Anna's and other times between an Anna's and a rufous. It's rare to find two hummingbirds calmly sitting together once they're independent and out of their nests, as I observed here. I'm not sure what their relationship was to each other. Perhaps they were siblings, newly fledged? Or, since they're male and female, maybe they were new mates.

"As long as the hummingbird had not abandoned the land, somewhere there were still flowers, and they could all go on."

—Leslie Marmon Silko, Ceremony

Mallard *(Anas platyrhynchos)* • **WATERCOLOR SKETCH**

How charming it is to see mallard pairs wandering around the neighborhood through the winter and spring, far from their potential nesting sites near ponds and other bodies of water. They often appear to be grazing in the wet grass, like cows or sheep, searching for insects that form part of their diet. Like livestock, they also eat grain! Only mallards seem happy about the endless rainy season, when small puddles just right for bathing form even in backyards. The drakes are among the most dazzling of waterfowl, with their iridescent green heads; yet because they're so common, it's easy to overlook them as we search for rarer birds.

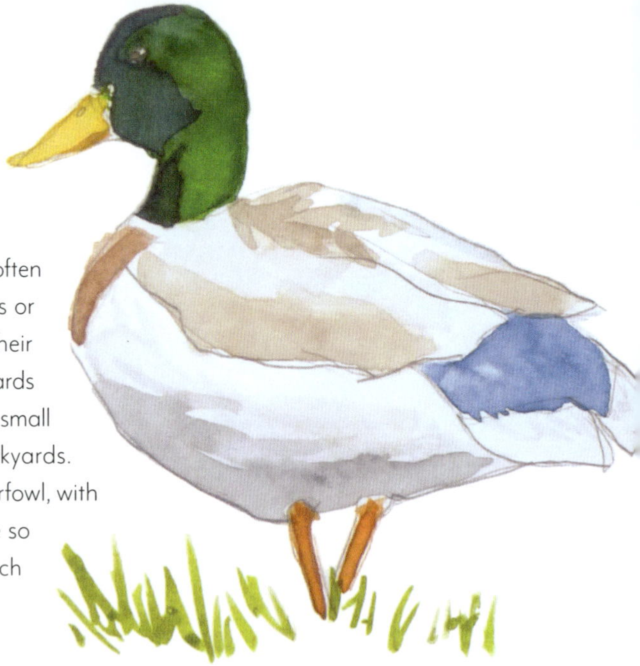

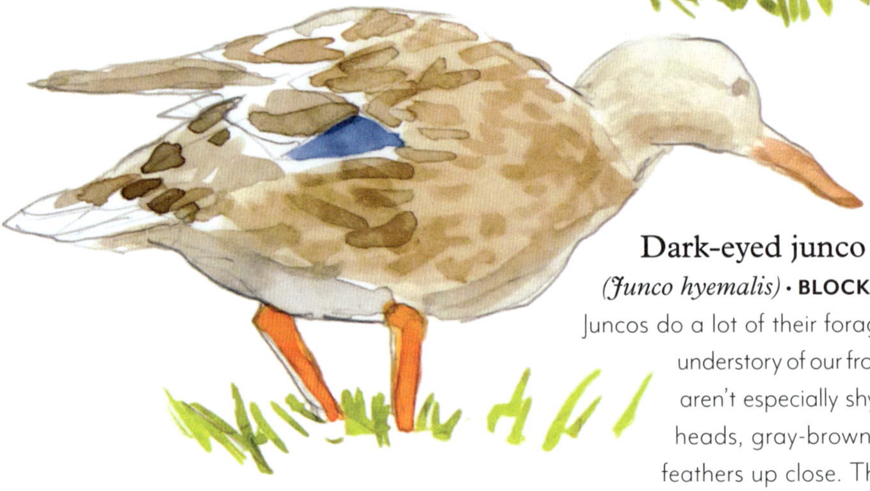

Dark-eyed junco *(Junco hyemalis)* • **BLOCK PRINT**

Juncos do a lot of their foraging and nesting in the understory of our front and back yards. They aren't especially shy, so I've seen their dark heads, gray-brown bodies, and white tail feathers up close. Their tail feathers are an adaptation that helps the small groups stay together as they fly—the flash of white is not unlike the rump patches on elk herds. The bright signal seen from behind is a feature of many animals that travel in flocks and herds for safety. Staying in groups protects many animals from predators, which seek out lone, weak targets. Predators can be easily confused by many individuals banding together in groups. Year-round residents, the juncos are welcome inhabitants. They seem to love the garden environment and frequently hop around underneath large flowering shrubs, where they feed mostly on fallen seeds. One of their favorite plants in our backyard is a hydrangea, which is spectacular for many months of the year. This variety, 'Glowing Embers,' ranges from magentas to violets to blues, and even though it grows huge every year and needs major pruning at the end of autumn, I can't bear to part with it.

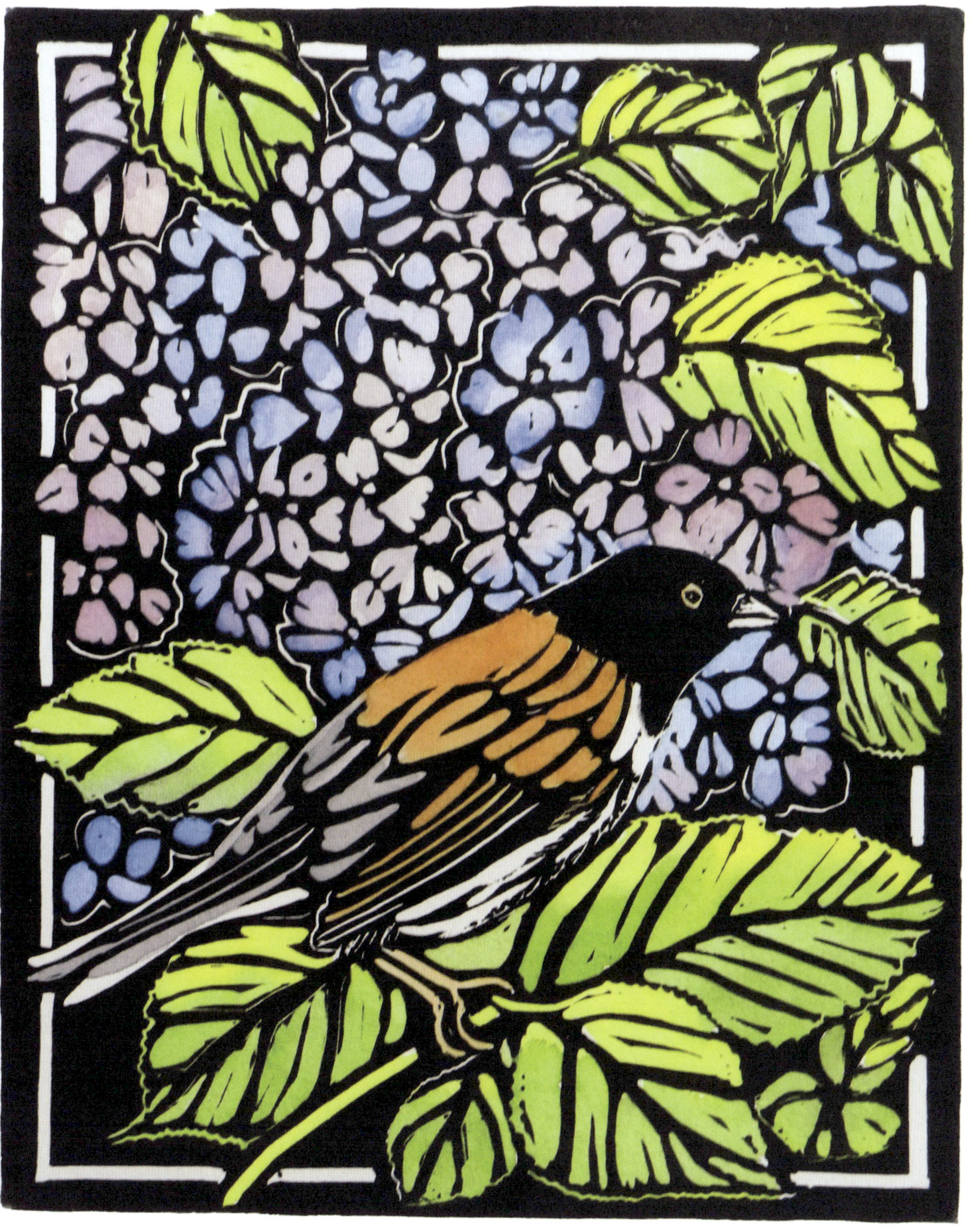

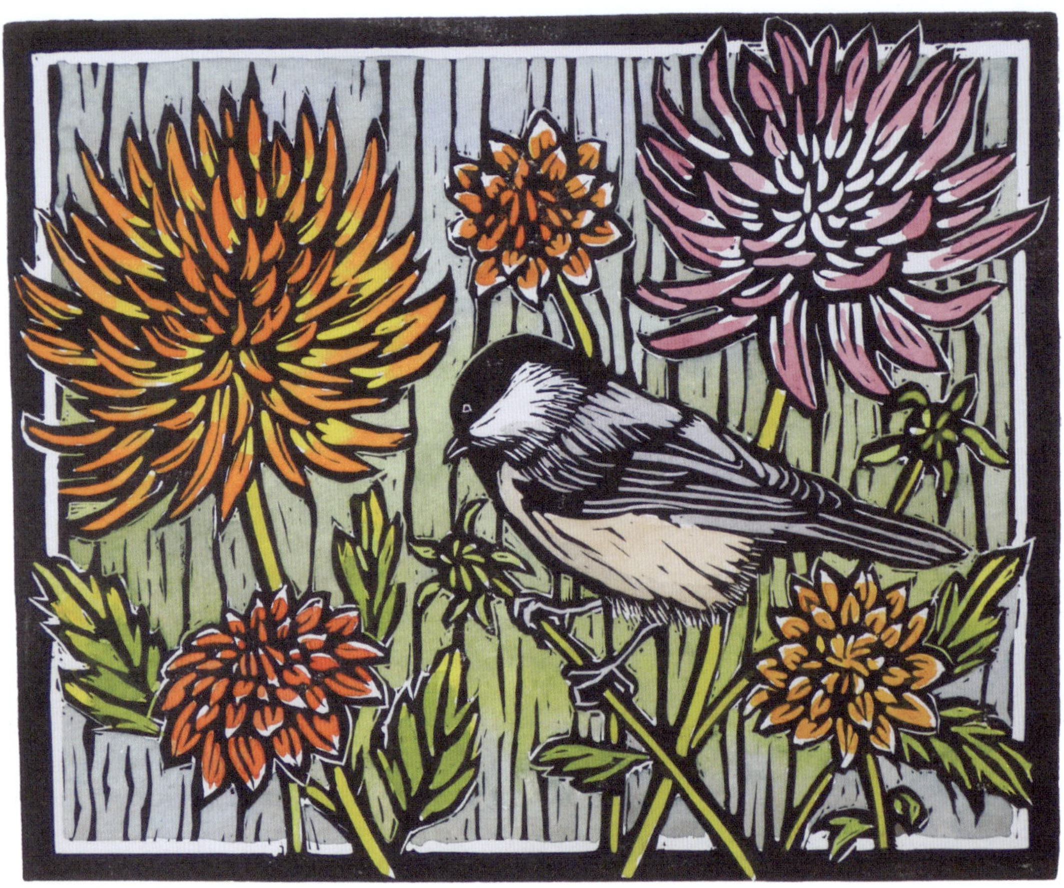

Black-capped chickadee *(Poecile atricapillus)* • **BLOCK PRINT**

Chickadees are acrobats; here you see one clinging to the frailest of dahlia stems in our backyard garden, looking for aphids and other tiny insects on a warm late-summer afternoon. The busy activity of the chickadee was a fitting counterpoint to the cactus variety of dahlia, with its emphatic furled sharp petals. Chickadees are fairly tame and seem very well adapted to humans, frequently visiting our suet feeder in winter along with other small birds such as bushtits and warblers.

Northern flicker *(Colaptes auratus)* • **BLOCK PRINT**

Perhaps it's surprising to find this woodpecker in the backyard chapter, rather than in the woodland chapter, but the species is very common in our Seattle neighborhood and is thriving. As one of the adapters, flickers haven't suffered from development in Washington State, even though nationwide their numbers declined more than 49 percent between the 1960s and 2012. In late winter, the males land on our chimney cap and make an incredible racket as they pound on it to mark their territory and attract females, often way too early in the morning. This behavior is common to other woodpecker species in more rural, woodland, and alpine areas; you'll see and hear them land on lampposts and other metal stands and posts, banging away like carpenters.

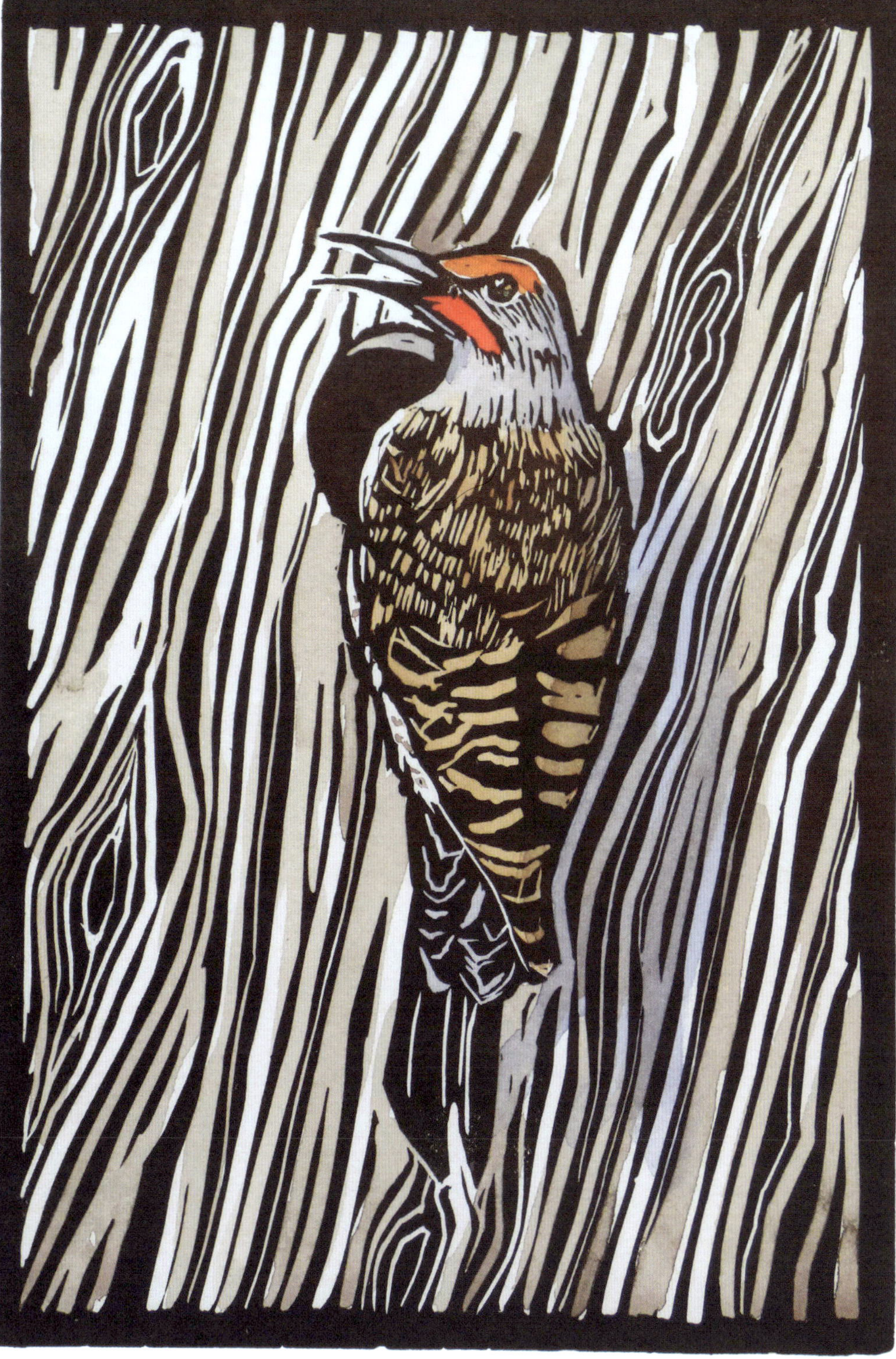

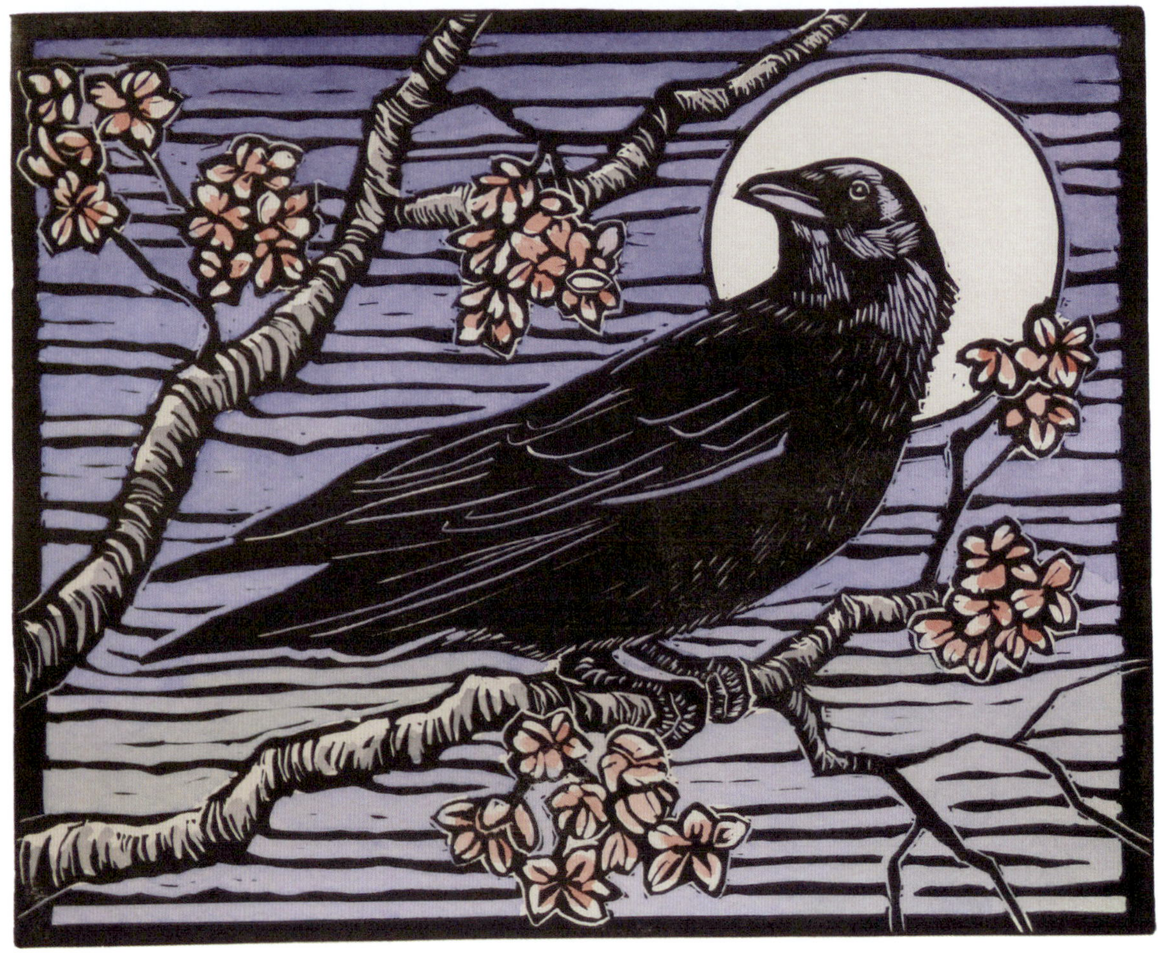

American crow *(Corvus brachyrhynchos)* • **BLOCK PRINT**

Crows are the most common birds in the city in wintertime, and I appreciate them more during that season, when fewer birds are around. In our neighborhood, they gather in flocks in late afternoon to begin their journey northward to their roosting spot, where thousands congregate. I enjoy watching the crows gang up on predators, joining forces to keep their family members safe. Birdwatchers know that a crowd of noisy crows is almost a sure sign that there's an owl or other raptor nearby. One afternoon I saw two crows chasing a neighborhood cat down the sidewalk. The pair took turns dive-bombing the cat, squawking all the while. Running away, the cat anxiously turned around to look at them, as if to ask, "What did I do wrong?" Oh, cat—beautiful as you are, living outdoors makes you a menace!

It may be uncommon to consider crows beautiful, but seeing one on the branch of a cherry tree in earliest spring was a stunning sight. The black of its feathers contrasted startlingly with the soft pink of the cherry blossoms.

Cooper's hawk *(Accipiter cooperii)* • WATERCOLOR SKETCH

Cooper's hawks hunt in the urban wetland park near our house, and in winter they're easy to observe as they perch on snags looking for prey, both small birds and rodents that inhabit the wetlands. They're also known to visit bird feeders for the easy pickings. The Cooper's is much larger than the sharp-shinned, topping out at twenty inches long, as opposed to the sharp-shinned's fourteen inches maximum length; they're often confused, and this size difference is the main way to distinguish them. One summer a Cooper's dropped out of the sky like a missile right into our feeder, where house sparrows were enjoying a late-afternoon snack. Our aging cat, about the same size as the hawk, was sitting on the fence, thoroughly entertained by the sparrow show, when the hawk plummeted out of nowhere. There was a flurry of feathers, and the cat literally jumped two feet into the air, totally gobsmacked. I've never seen another house sparrow at our feeder.

> *Hawks are beautiful objects when on the wing I have often stood to view a hawk in the sky trembling its wings & then hanging quite still for a moment as if it was as light as a shadow & could find like the clouds a resting place upon the still blue air.*
>
> **—John Clare,**
> English poet, journal (1820s)

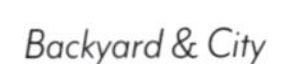

Wetland & Pond

marsh

fen

muskeg

slough

swamp

bog

reed

sedge

rush

cattail

water lily

bulrush

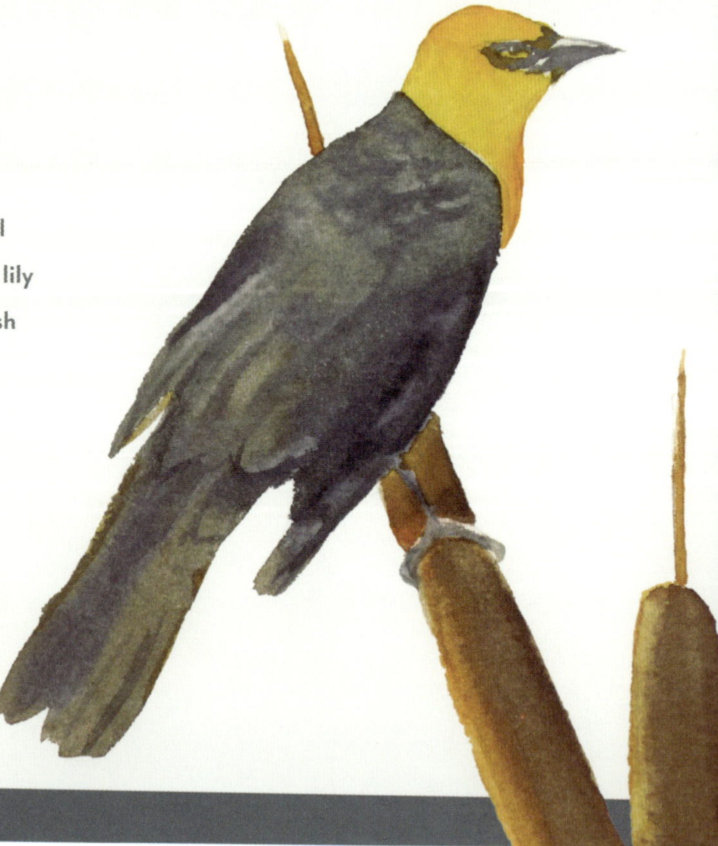

I enter a swamp as a sacred place, a sanctum sanctorum . . . I seemed to have reached a new world, so wild a place . . . far away from human society.

—Henry David Thoreau, "Walking"

In his classic book *The Natural History of Puget Sound Country*, botanist Arthur Kruckeberg describes "the post-Pleistocene topography that produced lakes, ponds and streams studding our lowland landscape." These places include seasonally flooded basins or flats, wet meadows, marshes, and swamps with tree or shrub cover. Where I live in Seattle near Lake Washington, there are two wetlands within walking distance, near the University of Washington: Union Bay Natural Area and Magnuson Park. Around Puget Sound, there are also saline wetlands and estuaries that include marshes and tidelands with eelgrass beds, as well as countless freshwater wetlands. Many of the birds that have inspired my art were first observed in wetlands, both near my home and farther afield. Waterfowl don't hide in trees, as many other avian species do, so they're easy to see, and many of them are with us year-round. Best of all, waterbirds have the most color and dramatic markings.

At Union Bay Natural Area, just north of Seattle's Husky Stadium, you might observe wood duck pairs paddling in harmony, the drakes gloriously attired in ruby, emerald, and sapphire hues. Trumpeter swans sparkle in the wider spaces of the bay on a sunny February day. Great blue herons, pied-billed grebes, and northern shovelers are ever present in winter, adding movement to the quiet world of the reclaimed wetland. In March, red-winged blackbirds trill out the earliest notes of springtime; a ring-necked duck punctuates the pale water with its dark head. Later in the year you might see a green heron if you're lucky, or a Wilson's snipe.

If you travel far enough north in the state, you'll see loons nesting and fledging on lakes in summer. One evening I saw a pair swimming in Diablo Lake in North Cascades National Park, and though I've only seen them once, I've heard them several times on early summer mornings there. In wetlands far to the east, sandhill cranes gather in spring at Blacktail Ponds in Yellowstone National Park, preening in the thawing sloughs. Clark's grebes perform their exquisite courtship dance on Lower Klamath Lake in Northern California, while white-faced ibises there decorate the marshes with their exotic flamingo shapes and iridescent copper and verdigris plumage.

Such places, along with Washington deltas including the Nisqually, Stillaguamish, Nooksack, and Skagit, create major habitat for waterfowl. In his book *Against the Grain*, James C. Scott writes about the importance of wetlands to birds, particularly migratory ones: " . . . the most common route for a great many of these migrations has been via the wetlands, estuaries, and river valleys of major waterways, owing to the density of nutritional resources they offer. Bird migration routes favor marshes and river valleys, as do, more obviously, the movement of anadromous salmon . . . Any watercourse is itself a nutrient trough with its own flood plains, back swamps, and alluvial fans."

Watercourses are a habitat requirement for us humans as well. Scott explains that the patterns of hunter-gatherer societies were "governed by the natural pulse of migrations that represent much of their most prized food supply." Throughout history most of our larger population centers were founded on estuaries, river hubs, and waterways. We feel most at home in these places, where there is adequate food and water for us and a diverse web of plant, bird, and mammal life that also supplies endless subjects for our imaginative life. The rhythms of nature continue to govern us, even as we have evolved, some say, beyond our hunter-gatherer beginnings.

Wood duck *(Aix sponsa)* • **BLOCK PRINT, WATERCOLOR**

The opulently colored male wood duck I painted in the watercolor nests with his mate just behind the University of Washington's Husky Stadium, a surprisingly quiet little backwater of Union Bay. I've seen them there in winter many years. My artist eyes are drawn to the iridescent green feathers and white markings that set off the maroon breast so dramatically. The male wood duck is perhaps the most beautiful of North American waterfowl. In his book *The Evolution of Beauty*, Richard O. Prum describes how male beauty and elaborate courtship displays give female ducks a kind of sexual autonomy, as they choose the most beautiful plumage and extravagant courtship displays instead of having to succumb to coercive male

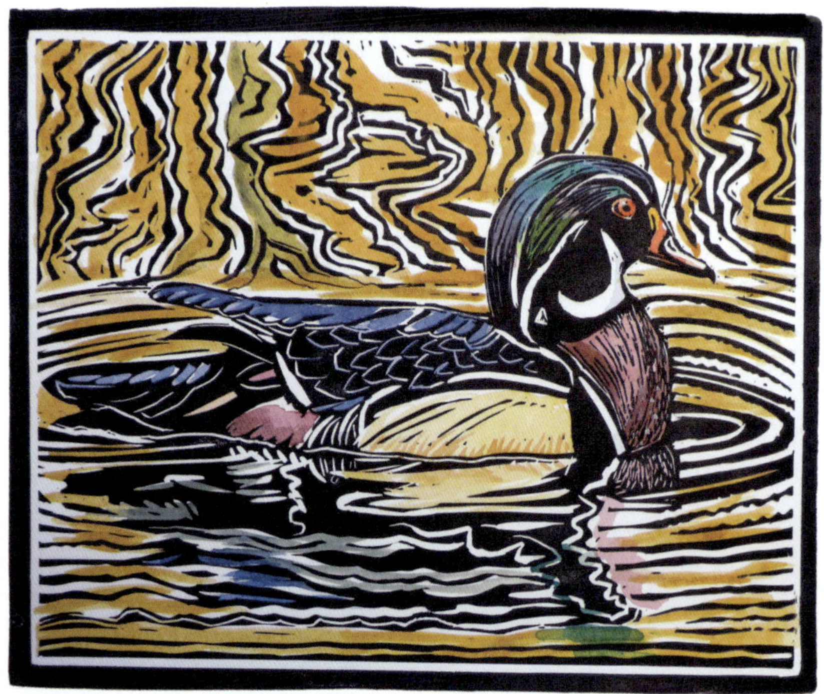

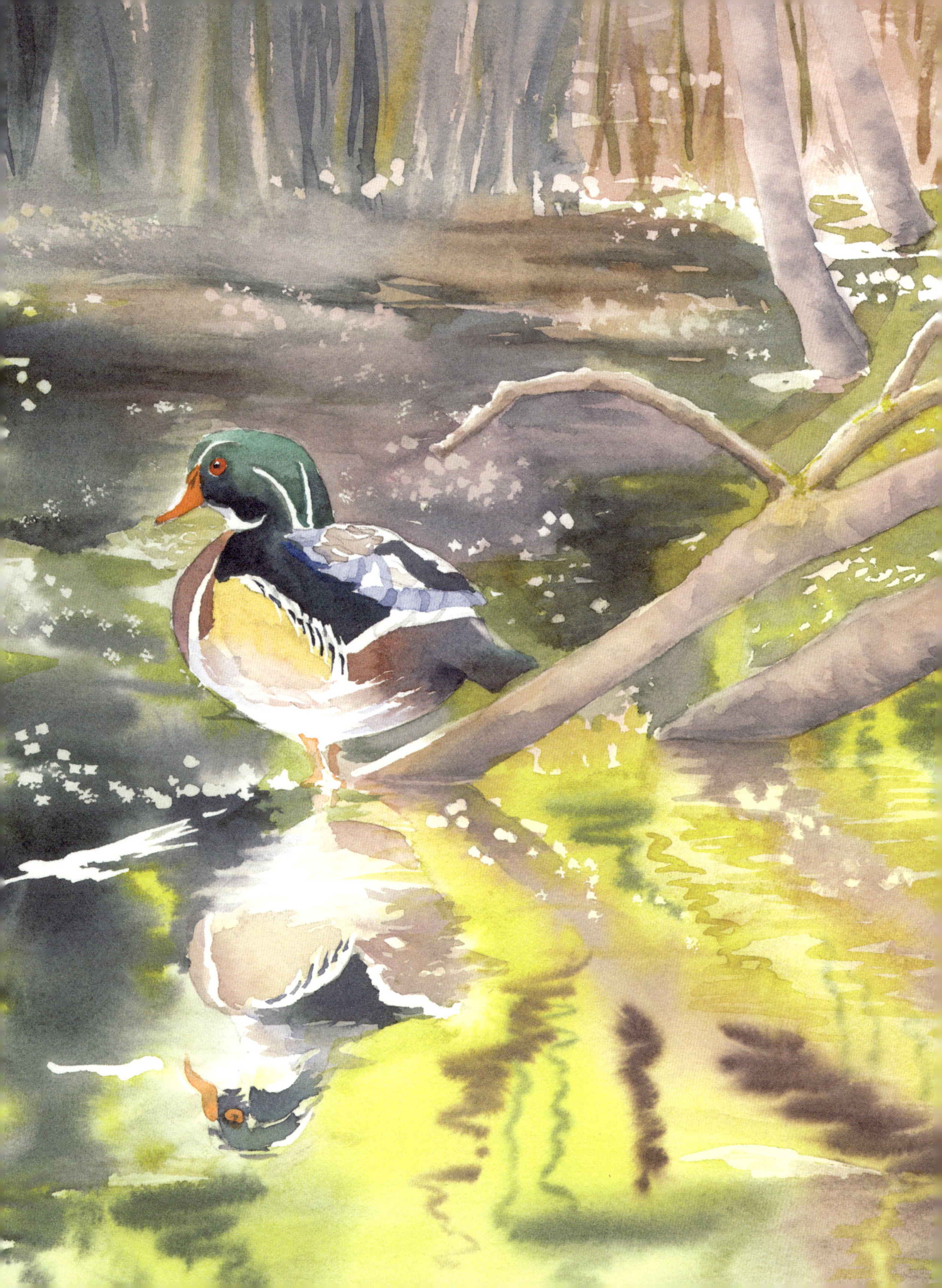

behaviors. He explains that coercive sex may not be useful for a species' survival—the death of the female can happen as a result, so it is in both the females' and the species' interest to choose beauty over strength and dominance. The courting male wood duck swims before a female with wings and tail elevated and tilts the head backward for a few seconds. At times the males may also drink, preen, and shake in a ritual fashion. The block print celebrates a drake that I saw swimming on an autumn day when the cottonwoods and maples on the east side of the Cascades were at the peak of their golden color display.

TECHNIQUE
Wet-into-Wet Watercolor Reflections

Northern shovelers (*Anas clypeata*), unmistakable because of their long spatulate bills which are used for straining water, inhabit both of the wetland ponds near our house. These three ducks were resting beside the big pond at Union Bay Natural Area. In order to show a little motion in the water as well as the reflections of the plants onshore and the ducks themselves, I painted the water first in a light blue wash and then brushed the duck colors and the plant colors directly into the blue wash and added a darker blue to show ripples. I used a ½-inch flat brush, damp but not too wet, to stroke horizontally across those areas while they were still wet to suggest the movement of water.

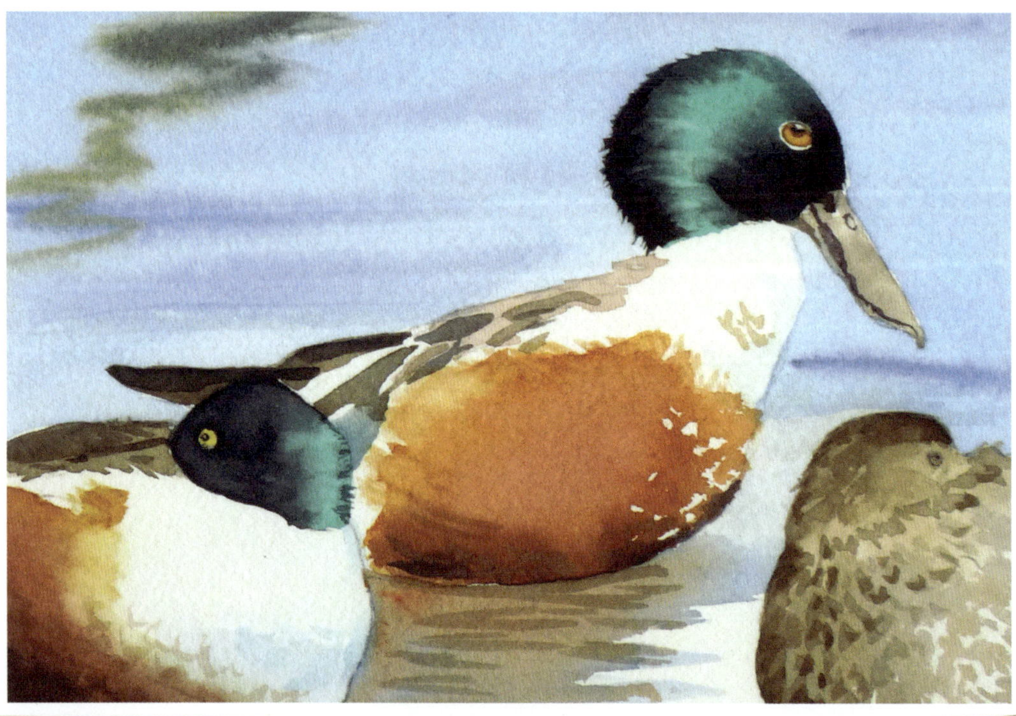

Common loon *(Gavia immer)* • **WATERCOLOR**

Wildlife abounds in North Cascades National Park, but loons are rare. One summer evening when I was teaching a watercolor workshop for the North Cascades Institute, my students and I were graced by this pair swimming in Diablo Lake on the brink of Diablo Dam. The patterns of the loon plumage beside the choppy water (winds pick up there as the day wears on) created an indelible image, which I photographed, in order to paint later. The color of Diablo Lake becomes nearly turquoise in later summer, when the glaciers high above begin to thaw. Earlier in the season the water is mostly snowmelt, which shows up in the lake as a clearer greenish color. By August, the rock flour in the glacial melt appears in the lake so that the water hue becomes a more opaque teal color. People have questioned me about the color in my North Cascades lake paintings, thinking that I make it up, but I assure them the color is really just like that in late summer.

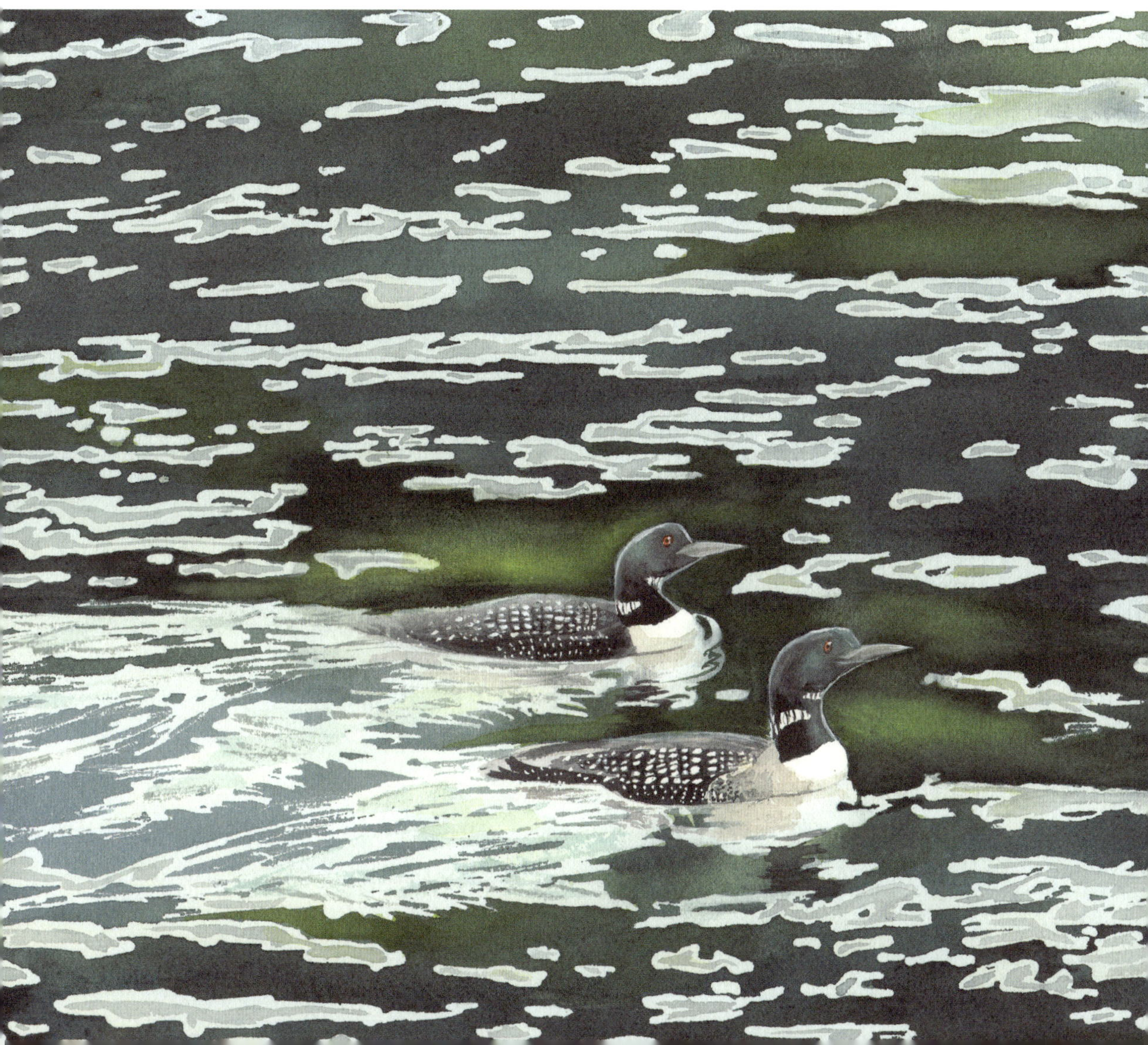

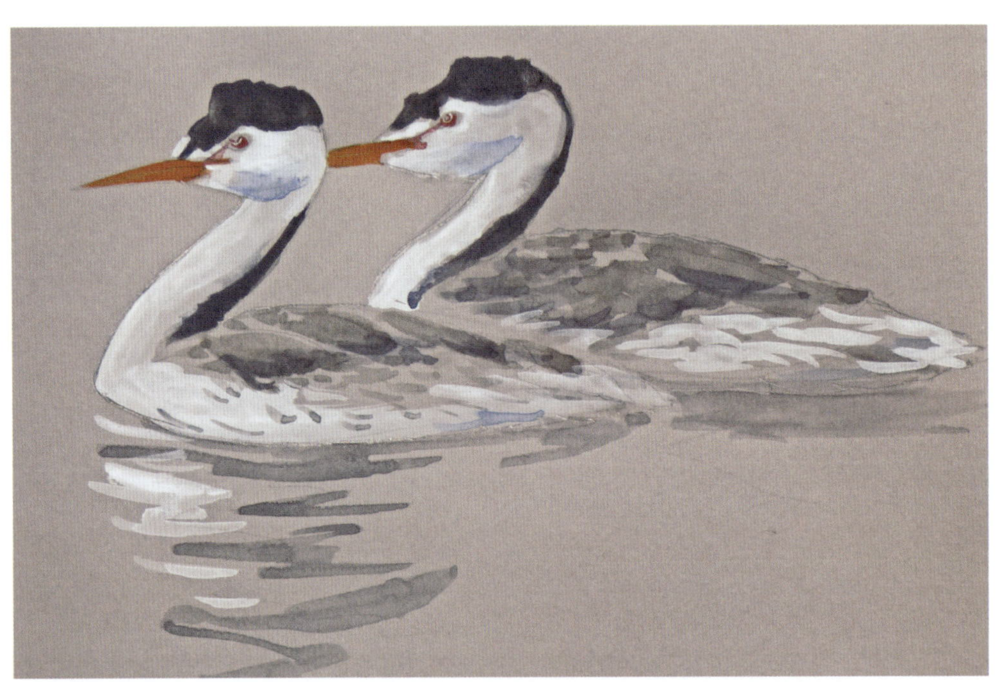

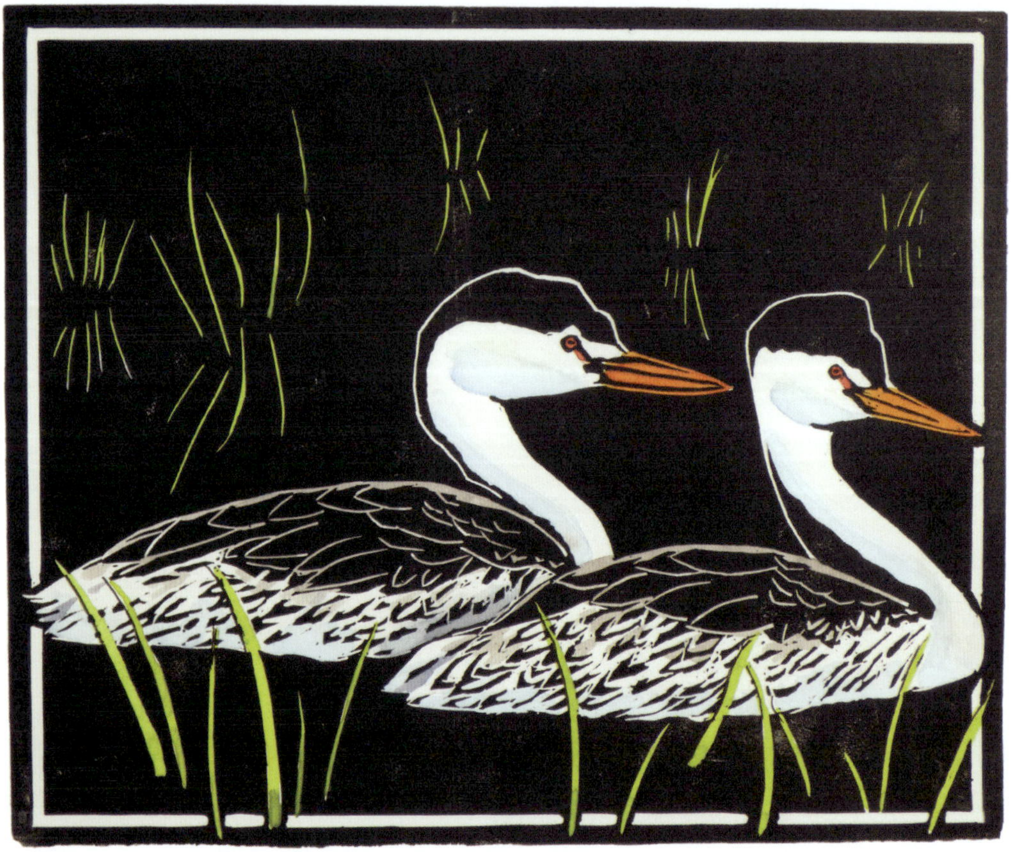

Clark's grebe *(Aechmophorus clarkii)* · **WATERCOLOR SKETCH ON TONED PAPER, BLOCK PRINT**

In the early twentieth century, Clark's grebes and their cousins, western grebes, were nearly extinct due to the harvesting of their white breast feathers for women's hats and clothing. Lower Klamath Lake was established as a preserve in 1908, by presidential order of Theodore Roosevelt, to save these Pacific Northwest residents. This was one of the earliest victories of the Audubon Society, which sponsored the trip that documented the frightening decline of the species. Nowadays, both Clark's and western grebes are present there in large numbers in spring and summer, and you can see countless graceful duos pairing up in May. Both species are famous for their courtship dance, in which the birds race in a long sprint above the water in perfect levitating unison.

I began to explore making art about the Clark's grebes with a sketch on toned paper to see how their white would look against a darker background. I was very taken with the stunning contrast of their white plumage against the water. The result inspired a block print with an even darker background—the black of the inked paper. To me the birds are the quintessential pair, and the print references the Chinese tradition of using the mandarin duck to symbolize marital happiness, since that species mates for life.

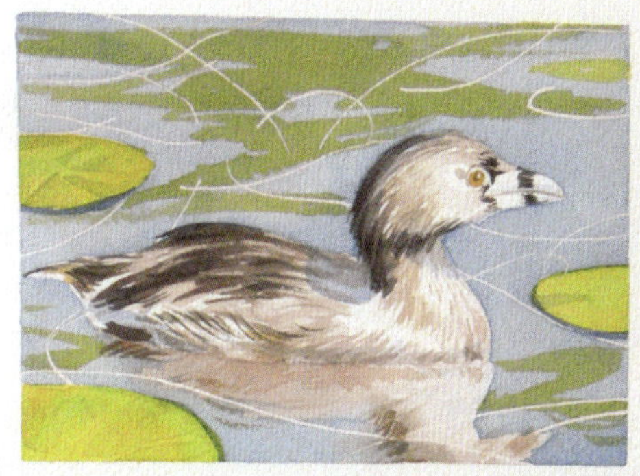

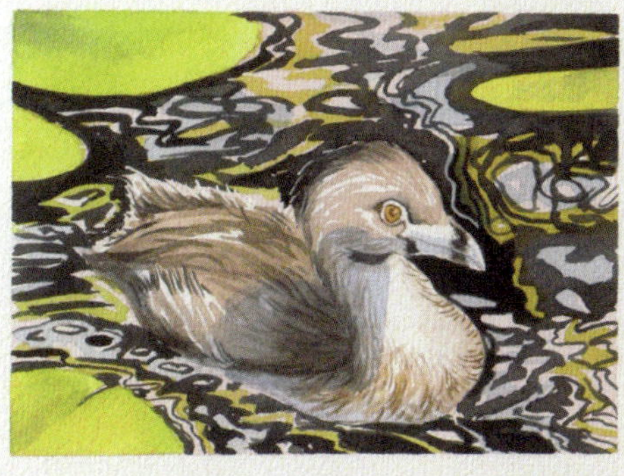

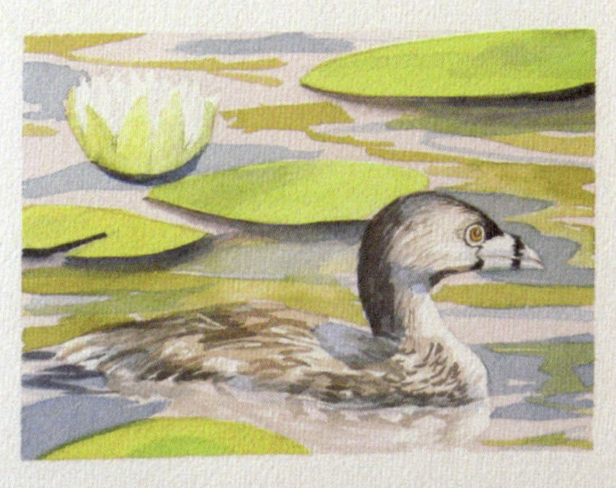

Pied-billed grebe

(Podilymbus podiceps) · **WATERCOLOR**

The grebes in our wetlands build nests of decaying vegetation in the middle of ponds, and it's exciting to observe them and patiently await the hatching of the eggs, often in clutches of four to seven. Last summer it seemed to take forever, as we walked down there to check day after day, but finally, in late June, the chicks emerged. All those days of watching gave me an appreciation for the colors: the brown, black, and white plumage of the adult birds contrasts beautifully with the pale blue of the water and the green of the water lily leaves. I decided to try a small triptych to celebrate different views of the bird.

Trumpeter swan *(Cygnus buccinator)* • **WOODBLOCK PRINT, WATERCOLOR**

The trumpeter swan is the largest waterfowl in North America, standing on average four feet tall, with a wingspan of seven feet. Trumpeters breed in Alaska, and a large contingent of one of North America's three populations, the Pacific Coast swans, winters in Washington's Skagit Valley. According to Martha Jordan of the Northwest Swan Conservation Association, only fifteen trumpeters were reported in Skagit County in the early 1960s due to widespread hunting that nearly wiped them out. Since that time, hunting trumpeters has been prohibited nationally, and the trumpeter is one of conservation's greatest success stories: 11,000 were counted in the Skagit Valley in January 2017. One major task left in protecting this magnificent species is the cleanup of agricultural fields and ponds that still contain residue of the lead shot used for hunting ducks and other species. An effort is being made to identify and remove the toxic shot in those areas.

The white of a swan in winter is one of the purest colors you'll ever see, inviting endless artistic interpretations. With the watercolor, I attempted to capture the low light and soft grays of winter in the Skagit Valley of Washington; with the woodblock, the stunning contrast of the swans' white bodies with the water surrounding them.

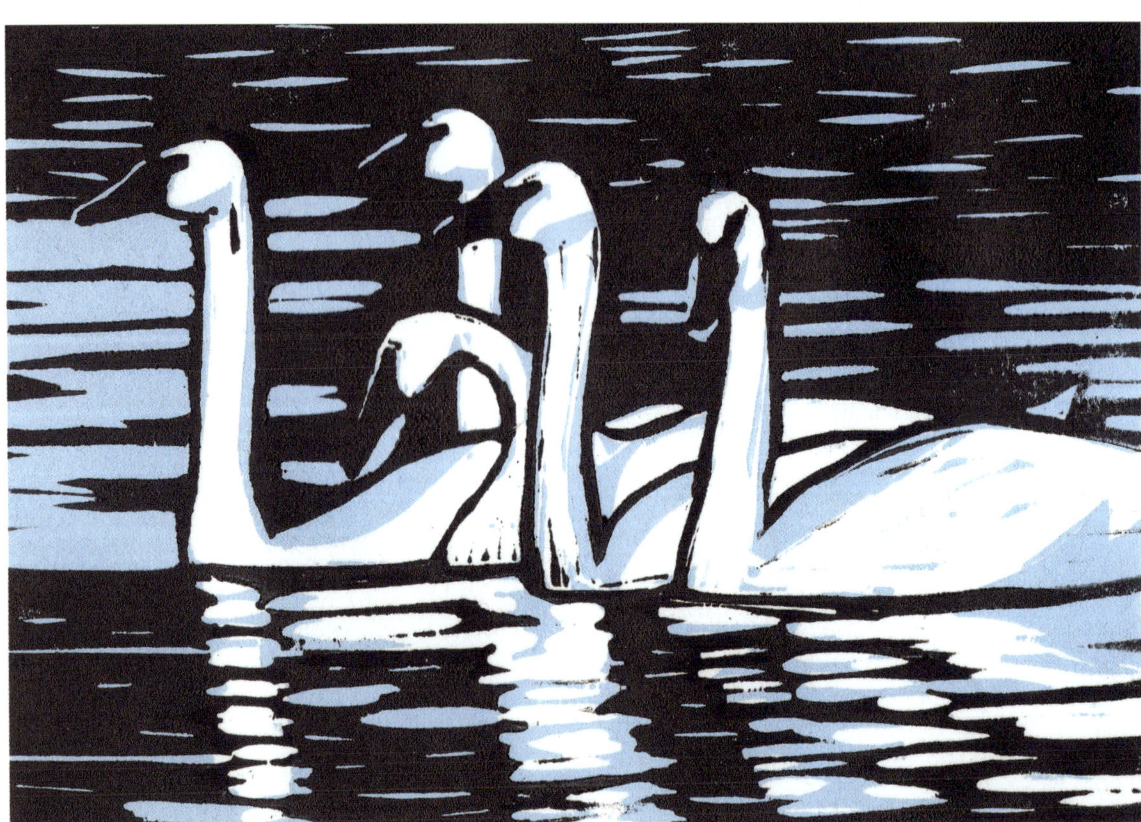

Imagine . . . that a flock of fifty swans are thus sporting before you . . . and you will feel as I have, more happy and void of care than I can describe.

—**John James Audubon,** *Birds of America*

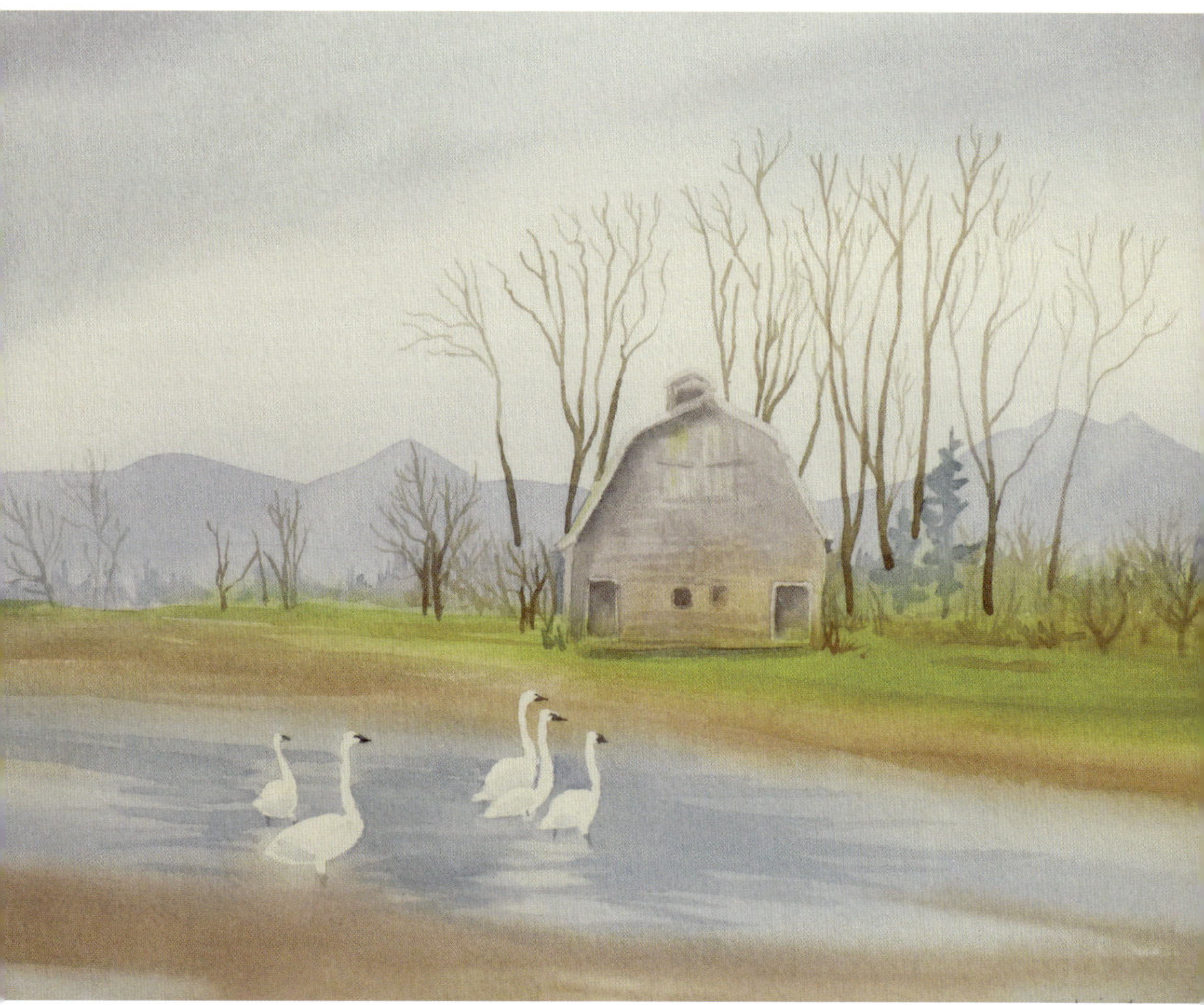

Red-winged blackbird *(Agelaius phoeniceus)* • **BLOCK PRINT**

Blackbirds are the first singers of spring in the wetlands near our house. Sometimes they begin to sing during their breeding season, as early as February, and it's surprising on cold days that still feel very much like winter. The birds' throaty arias are always welcome. Admittedly, I took a lot of artistic license in this block print, since the blackbird is shown in the fall—I like how cattails, common wetland plants, look in autumn, when the tails have developed fully, in rich dark browns, exclamation points among the reeds. In actuality, since much of the beautiful music of birds revolves around establishing and maintaining territories in springtime, the bird might not be trilling so lustily after the nesting season!

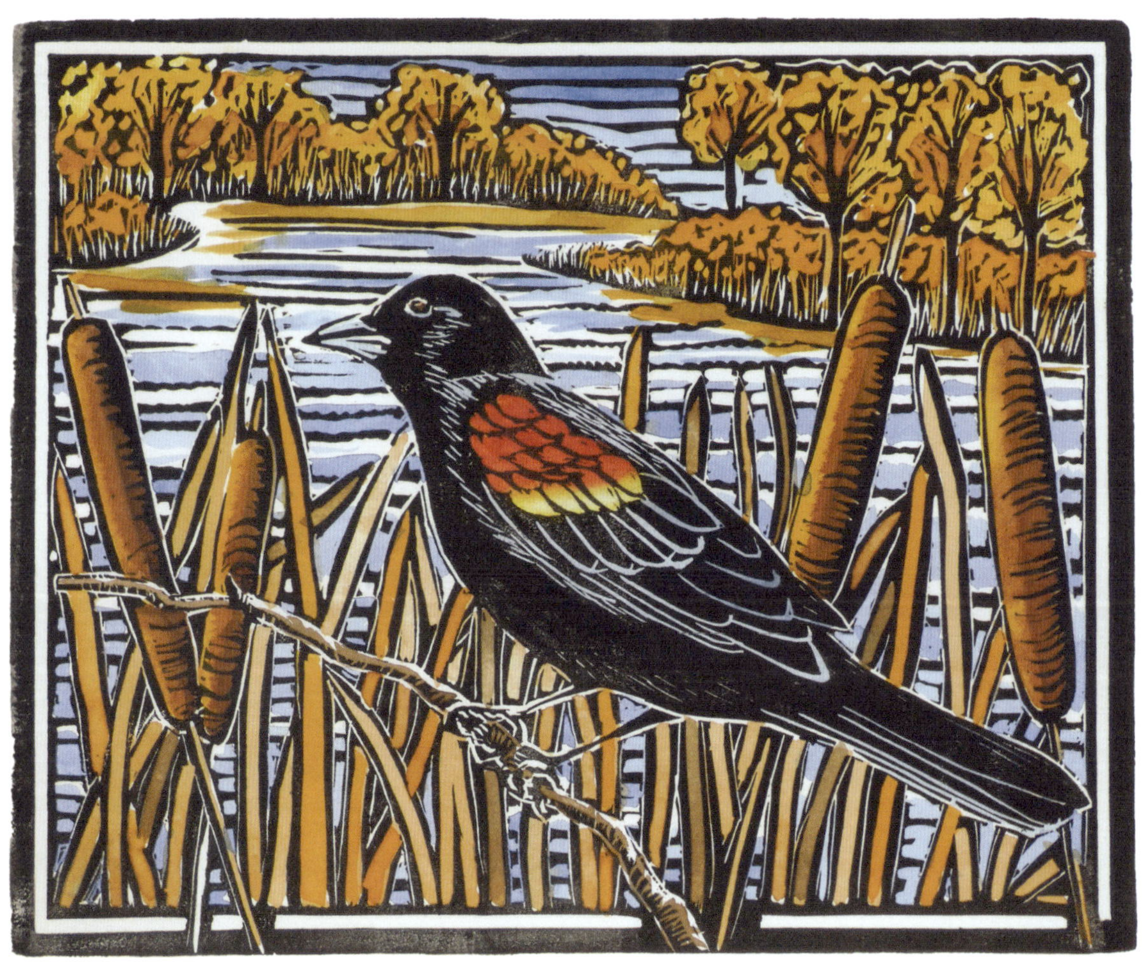

TECHNIQUE
Shading the Sphere

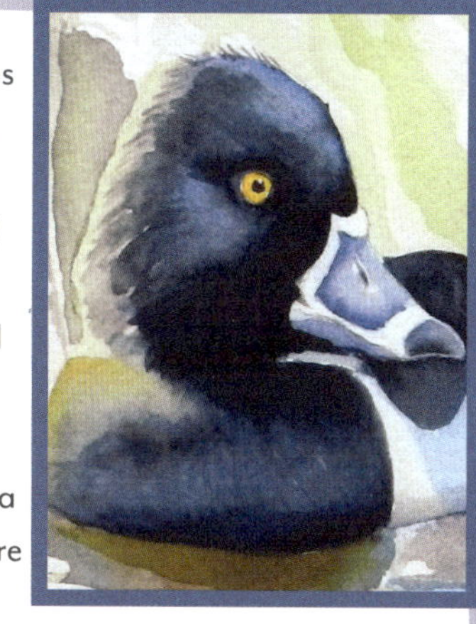

I observed this ring-necked duck (*Aythya fuligula*) in winter in our neighborhood wetland. I loved the dramatic blocky yet spherical shape of its head and the elegance of the patterns on its bill. In order to capture the three-dimensionality of the head, it's important to vary the degree of darkness on it. This is called gradation. Where light rays strike most perpendicularly, on cheeks and forehead, the area is the brightest. As the surface of the sphere (the head) falls gradually away on all sides from this point, the light strikes less directly and you'll find a gradation on all sides from the highest light. I often start with a bluish gray where light is striking, and then, while that lighter color is still wet, I add the darker values next to it so that they blend seamlessly.

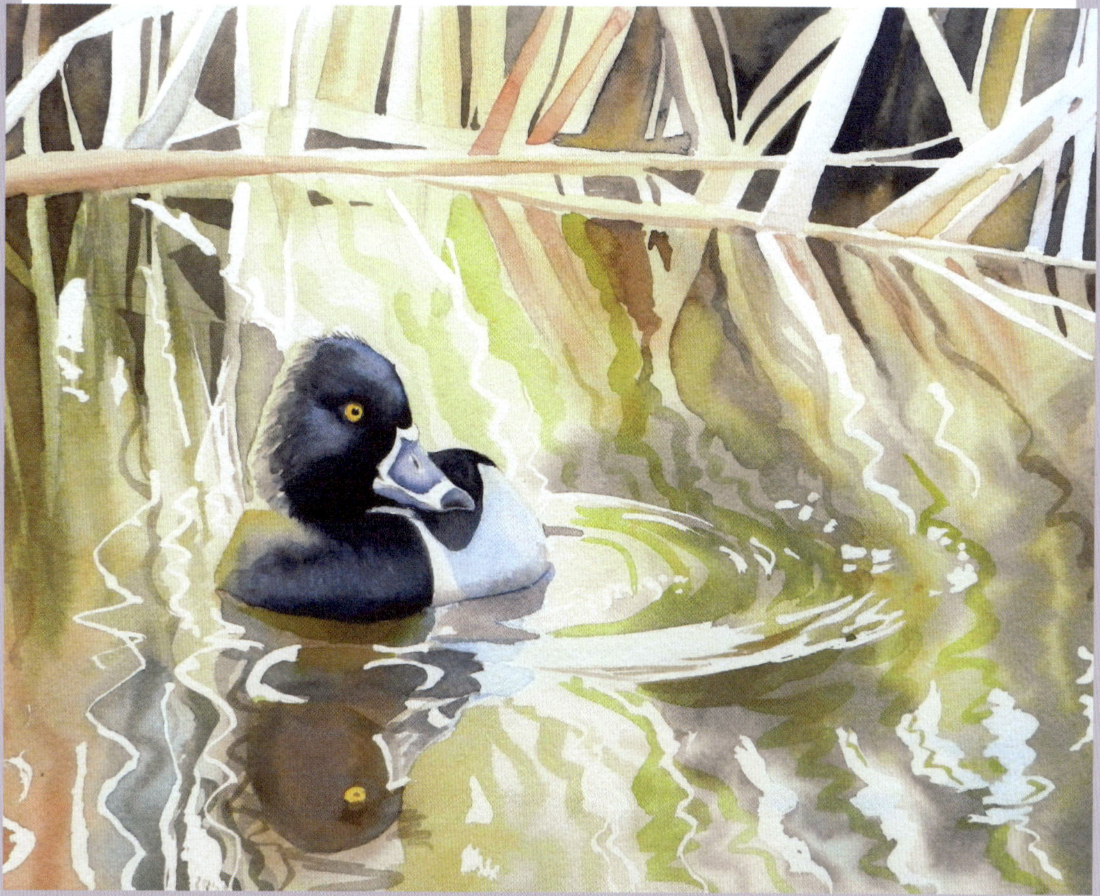

The snipe is a quite common bird even today, but the average person, lacking a taste for marshy ground and "snipe bogs," does not often see one.

—**Peter Matthiessen,** *The Shorebirds of North America*

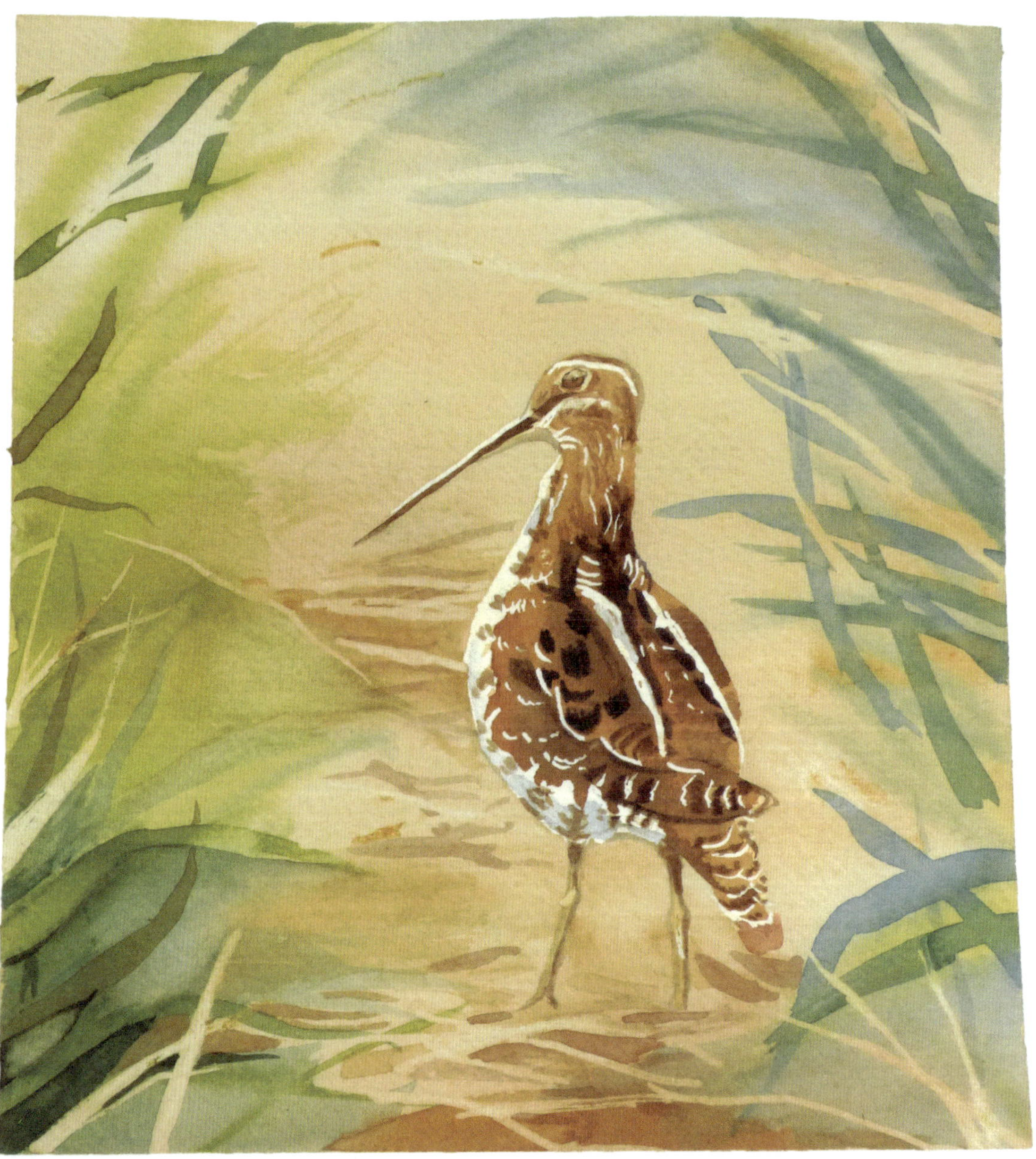

Wilson's snipe *(Gallinago delicata)* · **WATERCOLOR SKETCH**

I saw this bird in our neighborhood wetlands at the beginnings of my birdwatching days. In spite of what Matthiessen wrote, I think it's pretty rare to see this shy bird; I've visited countless bogs and seen one on only two occasions. I was thrilled, and determined to go home and immediately sketch the bird from my photo. The word snipe comes from the German *schnippeln*, meaning "to snip," implying the long, sharp scissors that may have been used to make delicate cuts. The snipe inserts its bill, which looks like a fantastically long drill bit, into the muck to uncover crane flies and other insect larvae, as well as frogs and mollusks. Snipes are difficult birds for hunters to target, and this is where the word *sniper* comes from.

Yellow-headed blackbird *(Xanthocephalus xanthocephalus)* · **WATERCOLOR SKETCH**

Yellow-headed blackbirds eat both wild seeds and cultivated grains most of the year, but in nesting season they feast on aquatic insects like dragonflies. Although they've been observed at Billy Frank Jr. Nisqually Wildlife Refuge near Olympia, they're much more common east of the Cascades. My husband and I viewed this pair in northernmost central California near Tule Lake. The female is quite beautiful, too, which is rather rare in birds, so I decided to honor her with a companion watercolor sketch.

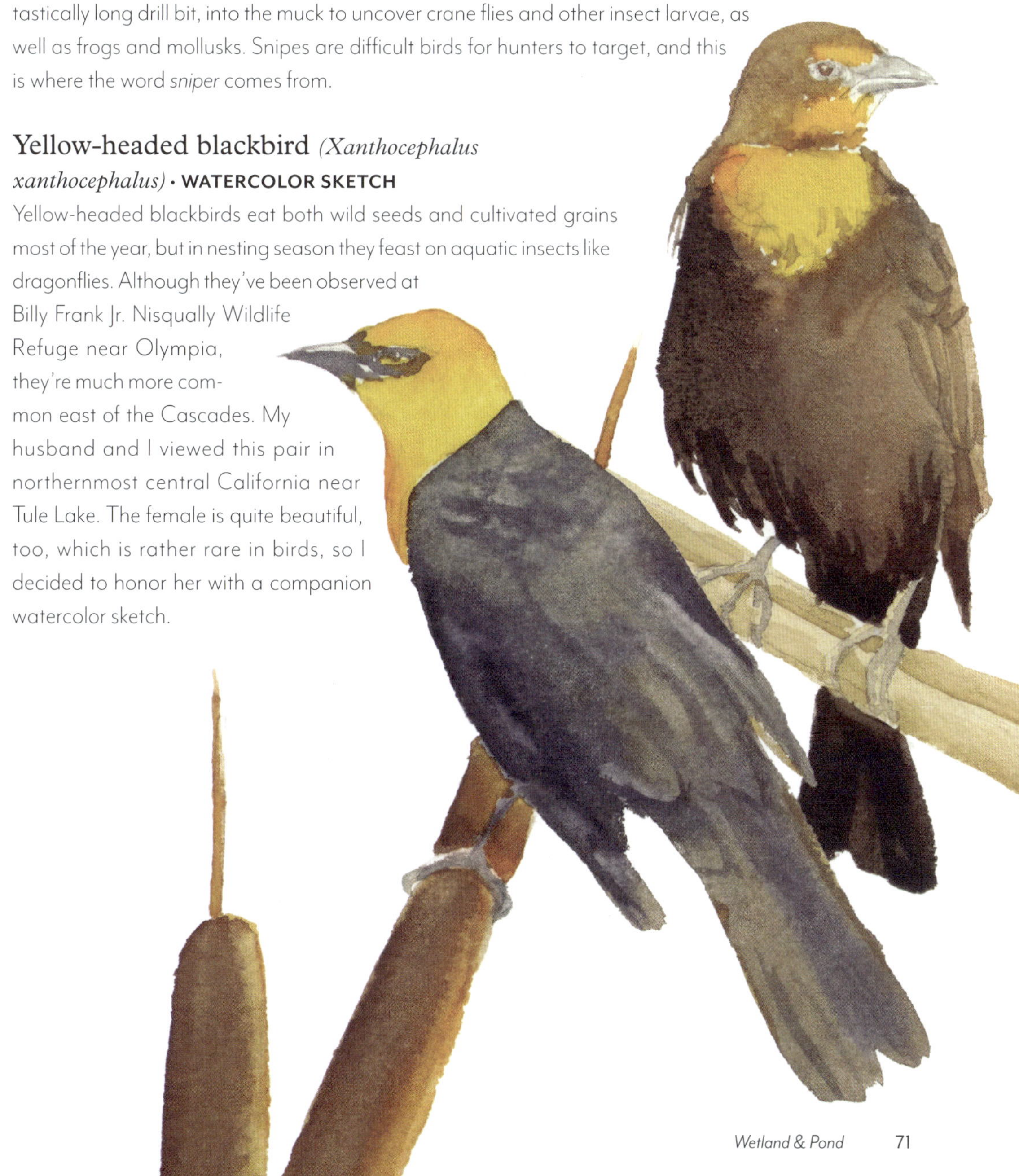

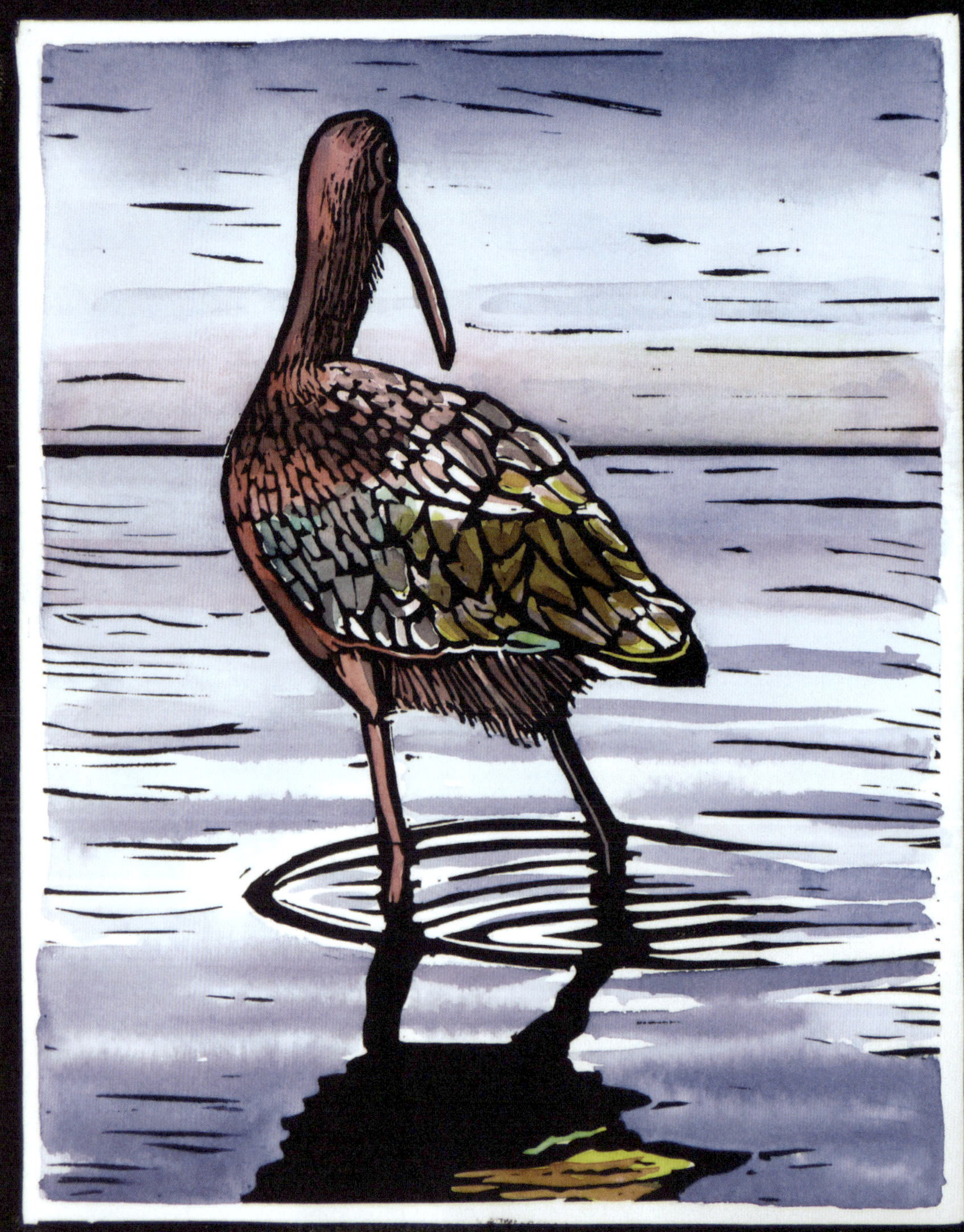

White-faced ibis *(Plegadis chihi)* • BLOCK PRINT

The ibis looks so much like a tropical bird that the first time you see one in the Pacific Northwest you doubt your eyes; its plumage colors are copper, wine red, magenta, and iridescent green. The birds flock and wade together throughout the West, but they aren't common, so I was very excited to see them in marshes at Lower Klamath Lake in Northern California. I thought the long neck and teardrop-shaped body invited a relief print because they're so unusual and graphically appealing. While watercolor is subtle, seeming to draw our eyes more to the overall surroundings and minute color gradations than to the actual forms of the birds, shape stands out in a block print.

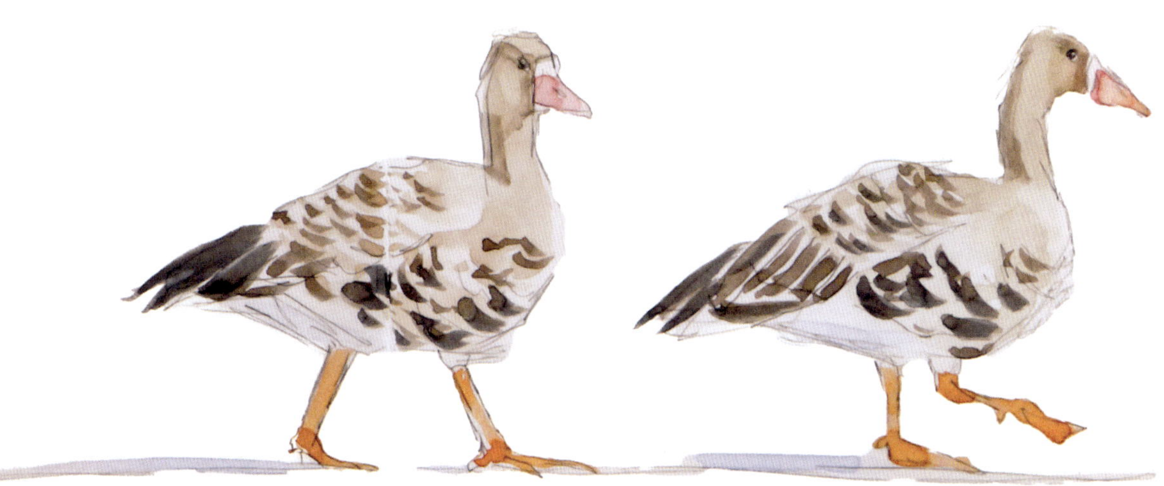

Greater white-fronted goose *(Anser albifrons)* • WATERCOLOR SKETCH

The gaggle walked along the pathway in single file at our neighborhood park alongside Lake Washington. I'd never seen them there before, among the countless Canada geese, but on researching, I discovered that greater white-fronted geese mix with Canada geese while wintering and in migration. Because their appearance was rare, I went home and sketched them right away while the winsome vision of their small column was still fresh in my mind.

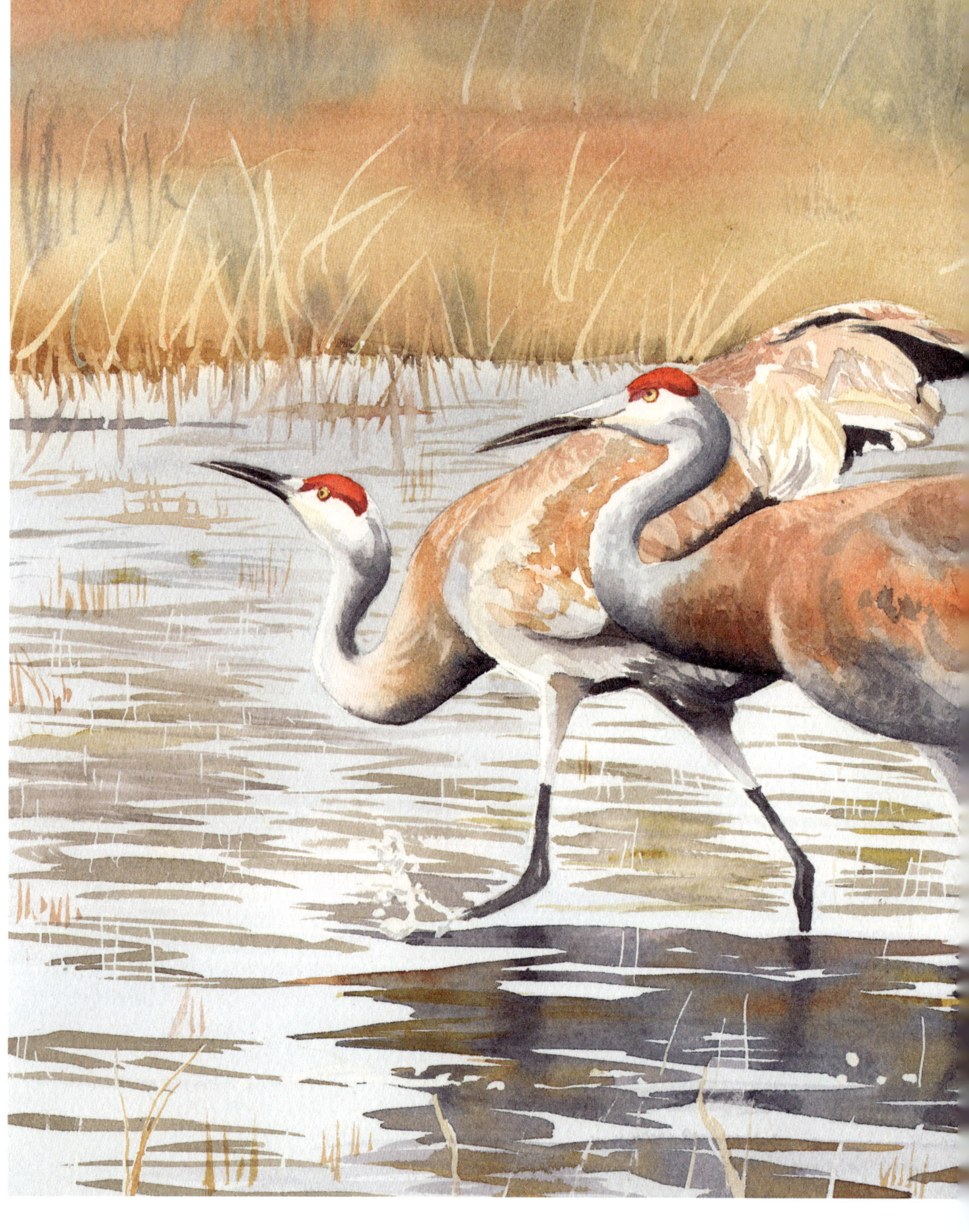

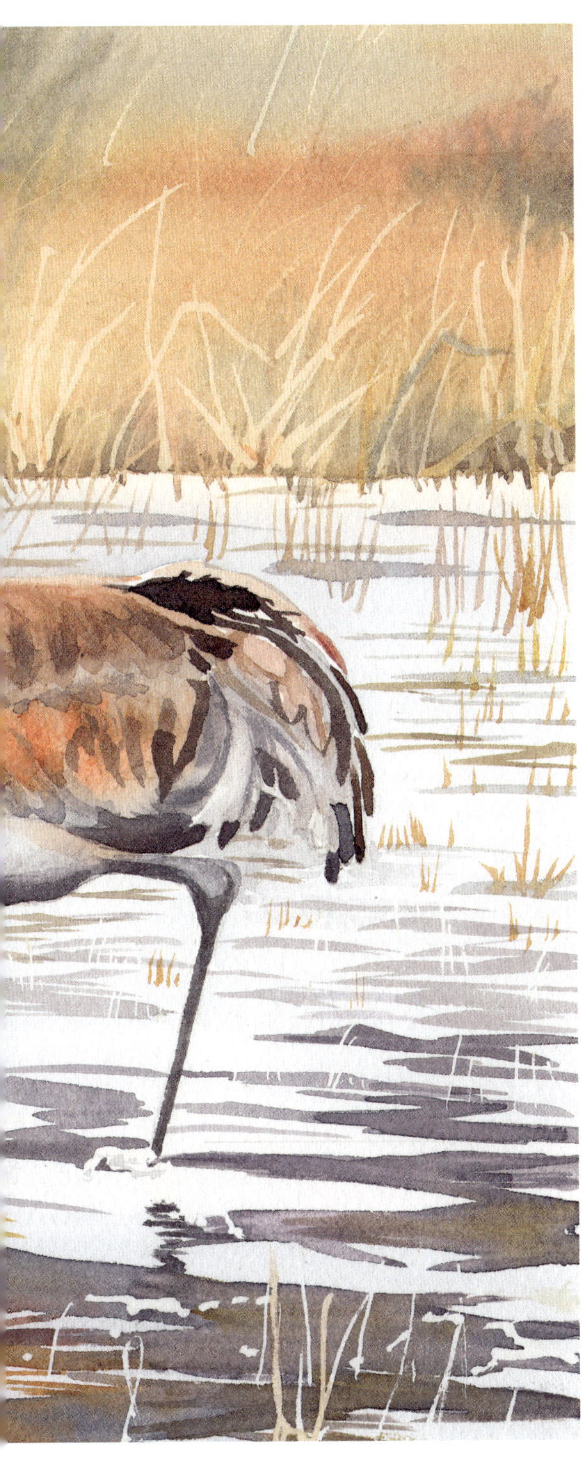

Sandhill crane *(Grus canadensis)* •

WATERCOLOR, EGG TEMPERA, BLOCK PRINT

Sandhill cranes nest at Yellowstone National Park in Swan Lake, as well as in Blacktail Ponds along the highway to the Lamar Valley, after wintering in the American Southwest and Mexico. Seeing them has always been a very powerful experience for me and calls out for explorations in multiple media. The Blacktail Ponds cranes in the watercolor were alternately preening and exhibiting their elegant bowing courtship behavior. The rust-colored feathers are the result of dipping their beaks in mud stained with iron, an element prevalent in the canyons and thermal areas of Yellowstone. I never before thought a mud bath could result in such beauty! Through the block print medium, I chose to express the grace of a lone crane with its neck extended in a landscape that had greened up for the summer. In the egg tempera painting, I chose the golden colors of latest winter verging on spring. The tempera is less transparent than the watercolor, with layers upon layers of paint. It's more like an oil painting and has a thicker, more substantial quality that is very unlike the other two media, providing a kind of opulence and richness that suited the plumage and golden colors of the wetland.

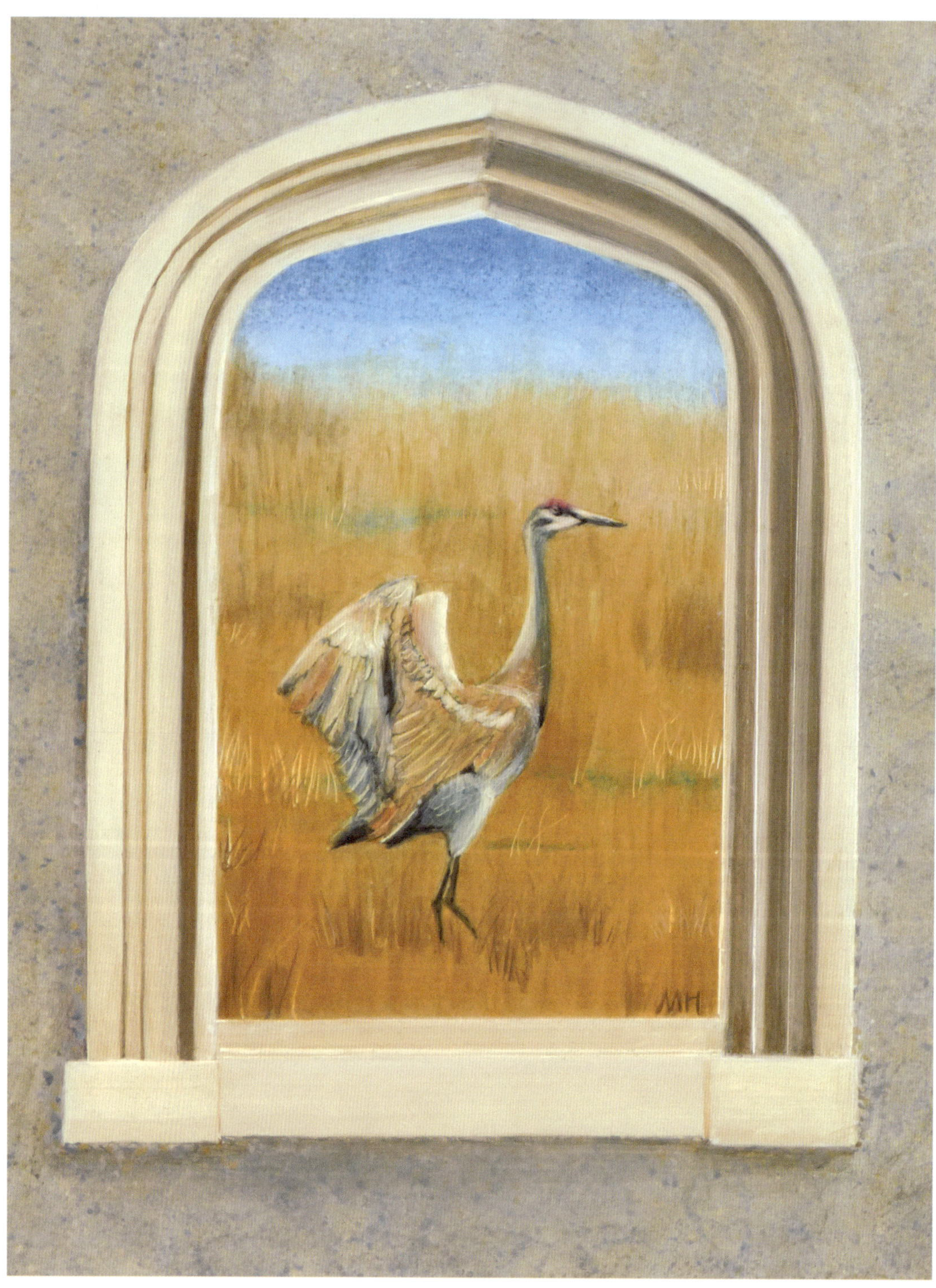
MH

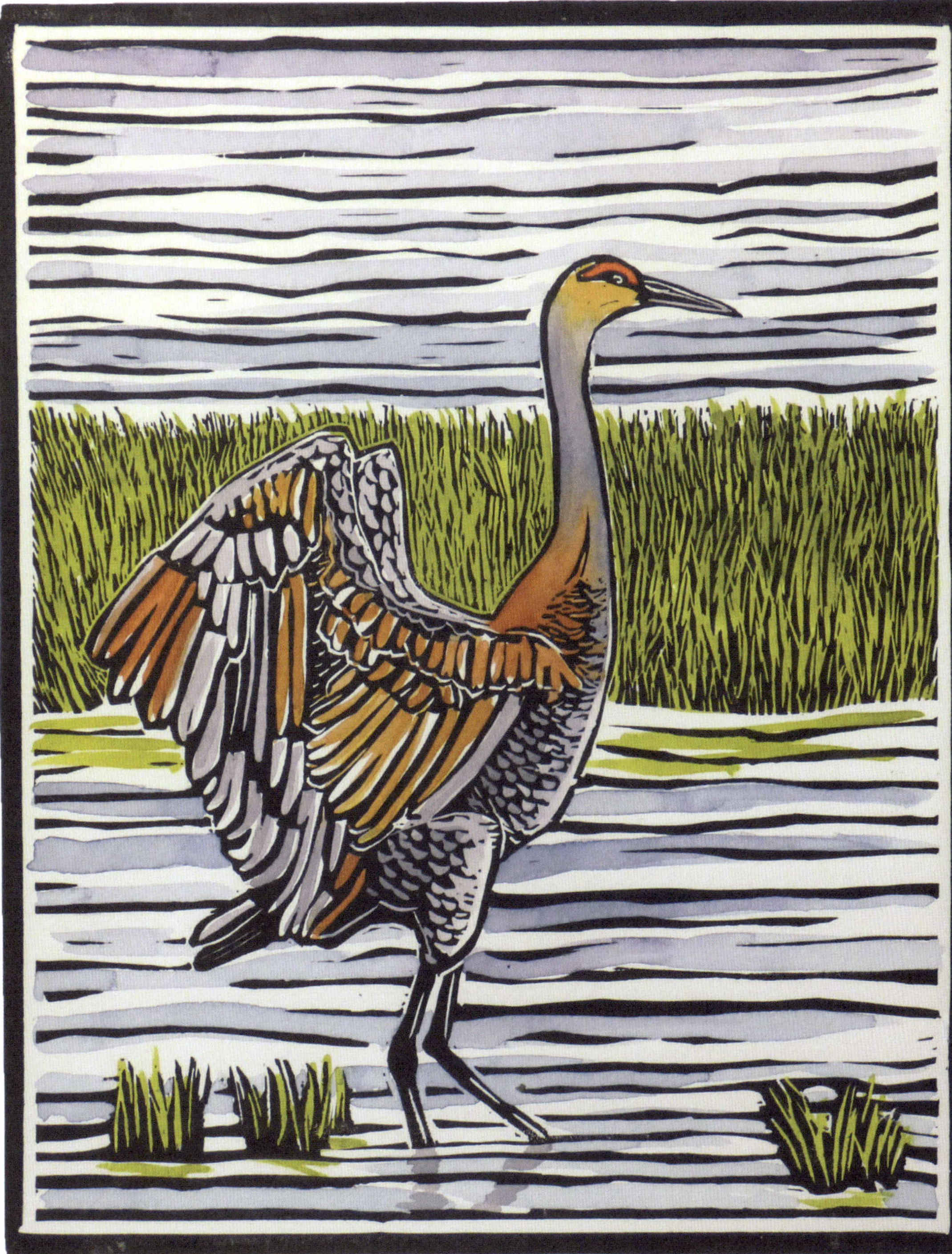

Shoreline & Beach

coast

littoral

seaboard

seaside

oceanfront

esplanade

lido

beach bursage

sand-verbena

dune grass

salal

reed grass

rhododendron

salmonberry

Sitka spruce

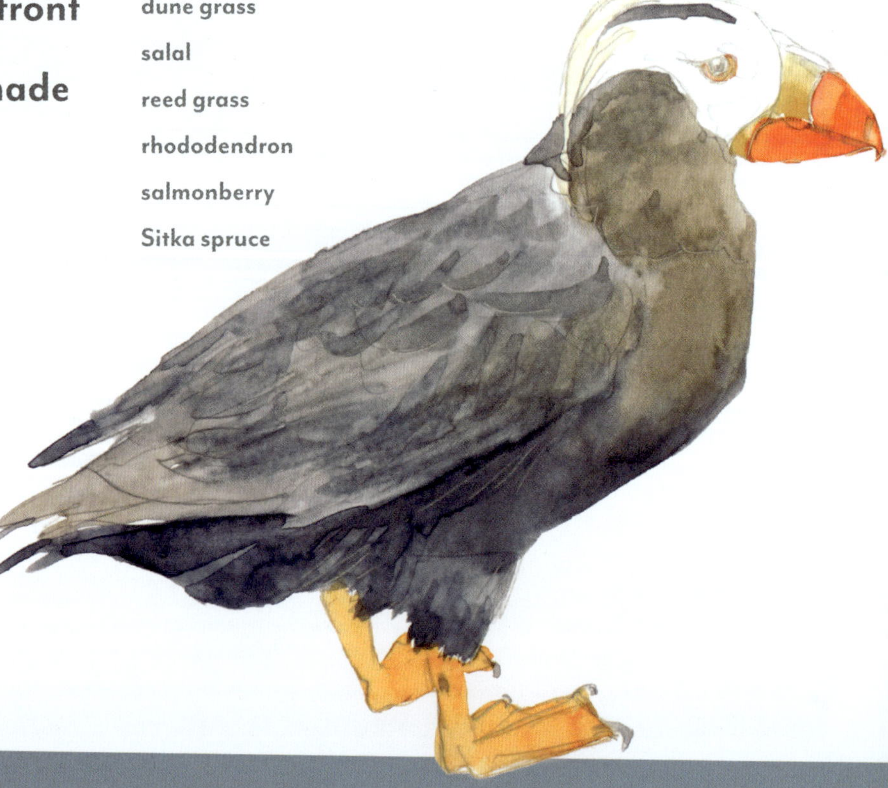

There is a pleasure in the pathless woods,
There is a rapture on the lonely shore,
There is society where none intrudes,
By the deep Sea, and music in its roar:
I love not Man the less, but Nature more …

—**George Gordon,** Lord Byron, *Childe Harold's Pilgrimage*

Beaches conjure up images of children building sandcastles, breakers crashing, and crowds enjoying summer vacations, but there are also quiet days of inclement weather in summer—and often in fall, winter, and spring—when people stay indoors. Those special circumstances can bring the most interesting bird sightings because shorebirds (other than gulls and crows, which benefit from most things human—fish and chips, anyone?) avoid contact with us—we are large, potentially dangerous mammals. Sanderlings run, like wind-up toys, back and forth in flocks across the retreating surf and fly off suddenly when you approach. Caspian terns rest onshore in large groups, interrupting the monochrome of pale beach and white feather with their orange beaks; then they take off singly and fly a hundred yards out to sea, diving precipitously to feed, before returning to shore. Pelicans patrol offshore in long, flying legions and then suddenly drop to catch fish. Onshore they pad along the tideline, top-heavy with their enormous bucket bills. Closer to the dunes, snowy plovers lay their eggs, and you may encounter signs and fences designed to keep them safe. Their populations on the Pacific coast are declining, and they're listed as a threatened species. On a Northwest coastal shore, it's not uncommon to see black oystercatchers picking their way across black basalt shiny with the surf, their pink legs and scarlet bills the only visible difference between the birds and the rock. If you find a viewing place above the rocks, you'll see murres and cormorants flying back and forth along with the gulls, and with a pair of binoculars you may spy auklets and tufted puffins, as I did on Haystack Rock at Cannon Beach in Oregon.

The shore habitat includes rugged coastlines with cliffs, islands, and the smaller remnants of headland capes called sea stacks. These provide ledges and grassy areas atop for nesting birds, as well as rest stops for birds along their coastal migration. Rocky shores are perfect habitat for mussels, anemones, and other intertidal creatures that many seabirds rely on for food. Other birds, including pelicans, cormorants, and terns, harvest their meals directly from the sea by diving for fish.

Oregon has six national wildlife refuges—Oregon Islands, Cape Meares, Three Arch Rocks, Nestucca Bay, Siletz Bay, and Bandon Marsh—that protect shoreline habitat along the coast. More than a million seabirds may nest at them. Fourteen different species nest on Oregon Islands and Three Arch Rocks, including black oystercatchers, rhinoceros auklets, Cassin's auklets, and western gulls; these places are ideal habitat because predatory mammals can't reach them. Near Oregon Islands and Three Arch Rocks, Nestucca Bay and Siletz Bay provide feeding and resting spots for migratory birds. Among Washington's refuges are Dungeness National Wildlife Refuge at Sequim and Padilla Bay National Estuarine Reserve in the Skagit Valley. The coastal refuges extend from Flattery Rocks on the northernmost coast, through Quillayute Needles, Copalis, Grays Harbor, and Willapa on Willapa Bay in southwest Washington. Common murres, tufted puffins, and pigeon guillemots are among the species that thrive there.

In addition to Pacific coastal birds, this chapter includes birds that are found in both coastal and inland waters, such as the great blue heron, long-billed dowitcher, and bald eagle.

Black oystercatcher *(Haematopus bachmani)* · **BLOCK PRINT**

You can find black oystercatchers all along the West Coast, probing rocks and tidal pools for mussels, limpets, and other shellfish, prying them off the rocks with their very capable, long scarlet bills. They rarely eat oysters. I sketched one at very close range at the Seattle Aquarium and also used a photo I had taken at the beach to create a block print to celebrate the diversity and beauty of tide pools.

Oystercatcher

No Arctic tern or sooty shearwater or bar-tailed godwit,
you don't set any Alaska to Antarctica nonstop flight records,
instead poke your way down the shore searching out
mollusks and bivalves with that orange syringe bill,
you're stout for a bird, smudgy, black or white-bellied,
and you wear coral-pink stockings. Like me, you often
come with a friend, as familiar to my Saturdays as
clouds, breakers, wind, rain, sun.
Oystercatcher, when you taxi down the beach and take off
with that "kleep-kleep," you're better than Lindbergh,
Amelia Earhart, or any of that ilk, you've got the moves
of Chaplin, Groucho Marx, a muse to all flights of fancy.

—Jane Graham George

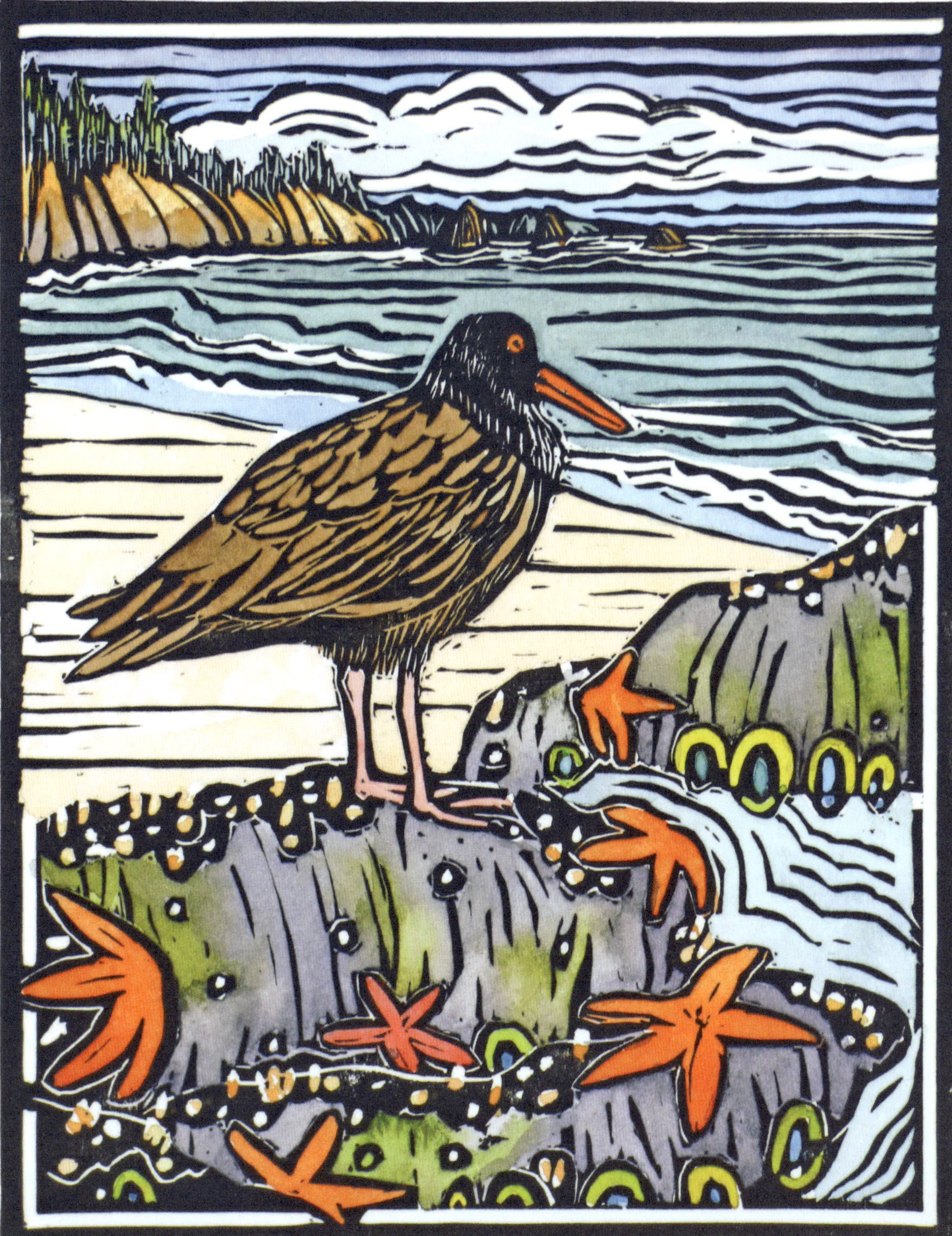

Long-billed dowitcher *(Limnodromus scolopaceus)* • **WATERCOLOR, ETCHING, RELIEF PRINT**
The name *dowitcher* possibly came to North America with European settlers, who may have called the bird "deutscher" or "duitsch" snipe, but more likely its name is just the settlers' approximation of the Mohawk word for snipe, *tawistawis*, which the dowitcher resembles. I sketched the long-billed dowitcher after visiting the Magnuson Park wetlands in northeast Seattle in June. The bird wasn't at all worried about me. I observed it for at least twenty minutes and pointed it out to a young boy who was visiting with his grandmother. Dowitchers feed by probing the mud with their impossibly long bills, using a bobbing motion that has been likened to a sewing machine needle's up-and-down. The birds are common in North America during the winter and during their migration, but they breed in Siberia.

In the watercolor version of the bird, the surrounding reeds and water tell the story of habitat. Etching allowed me to further explore the dowitcher; the elegance of its stiltlike legs and beak invited a linear treatment. Notice the closely spaced hatch marks on the feathers that help show the darker coloration. The plate was printed with a mix of ultramarine blue and soft black inks on a blue-toned paper. The block print medium captures the stark lines of the bird silhouetted in early morning light. It's a simple and direct approach that I like to use with birds that surprise and delight me with rare encounters in the wild.

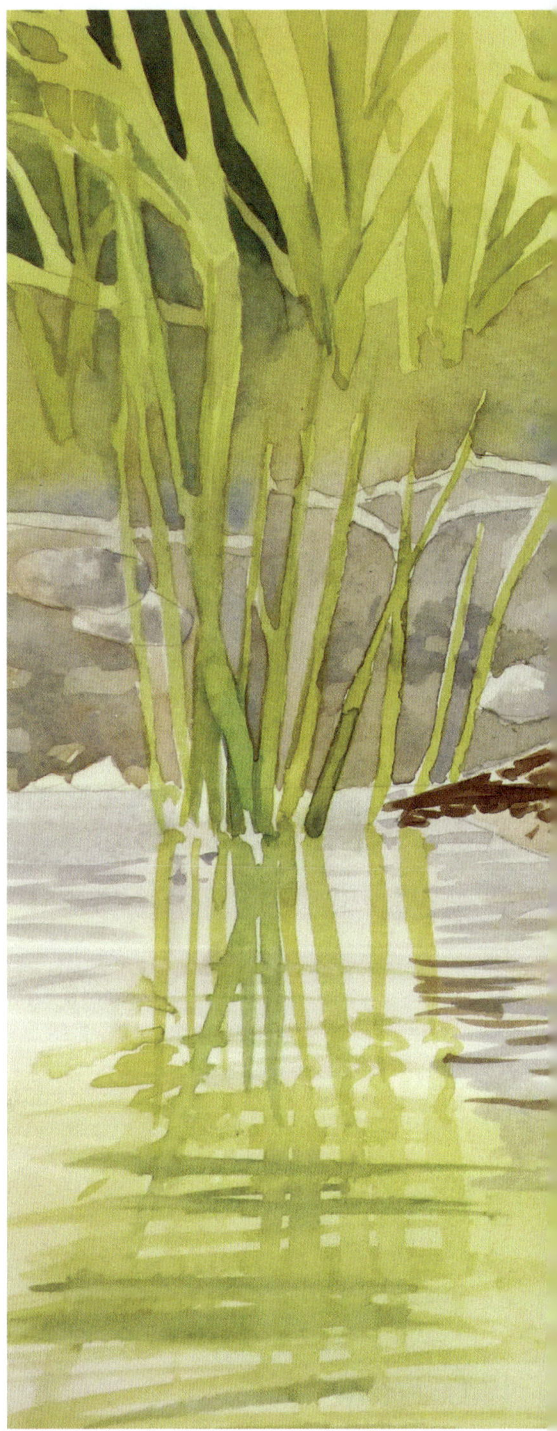

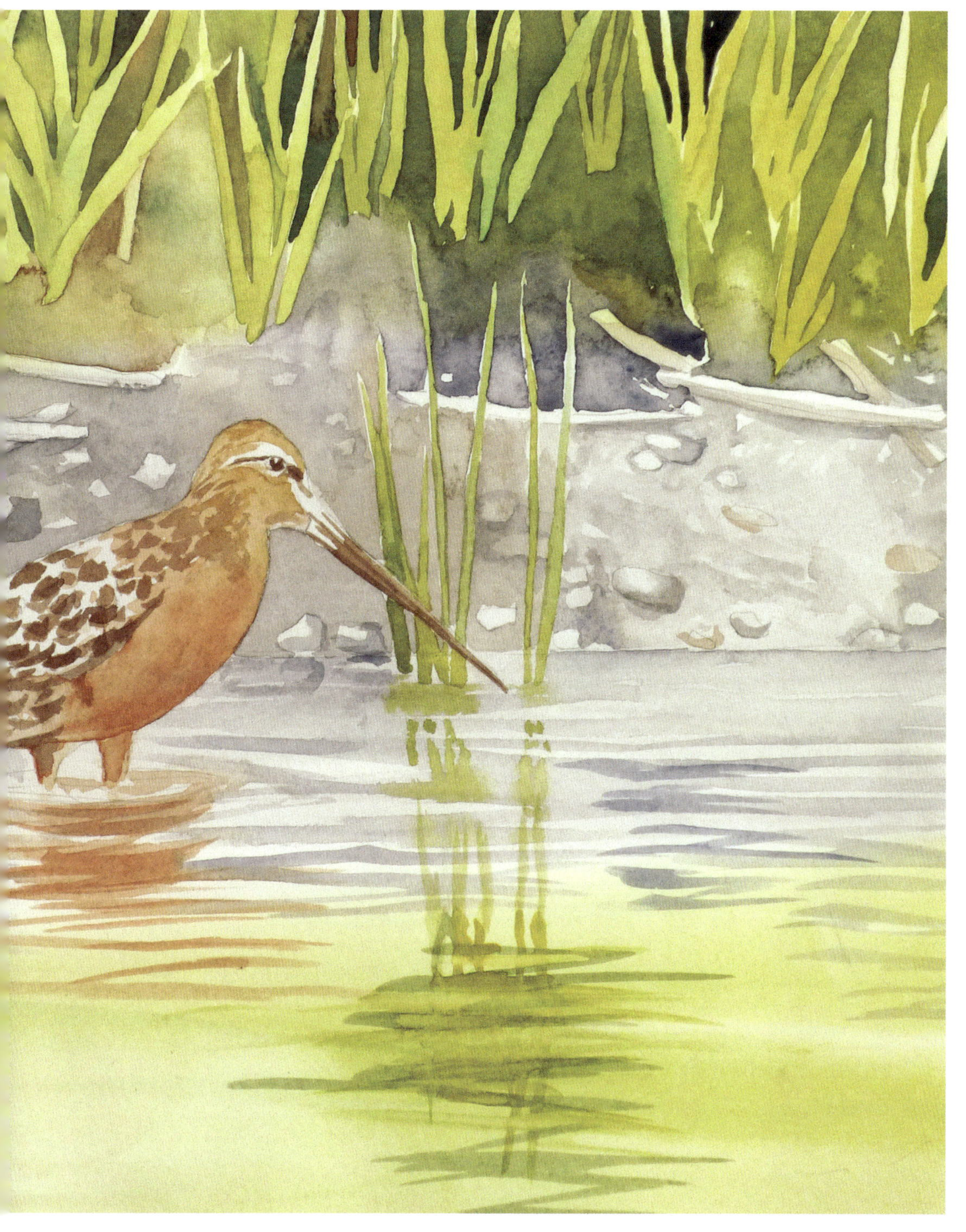

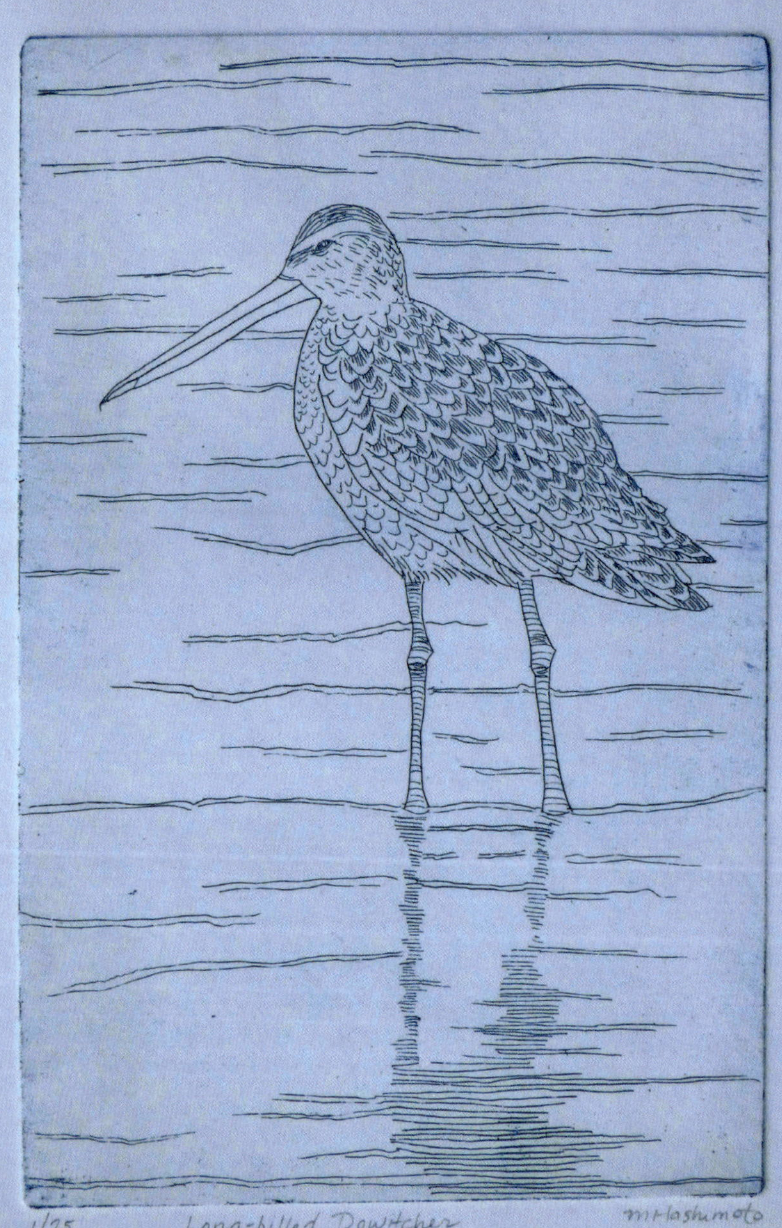
1/25
Long-billed Dowitcher
mHashimoto

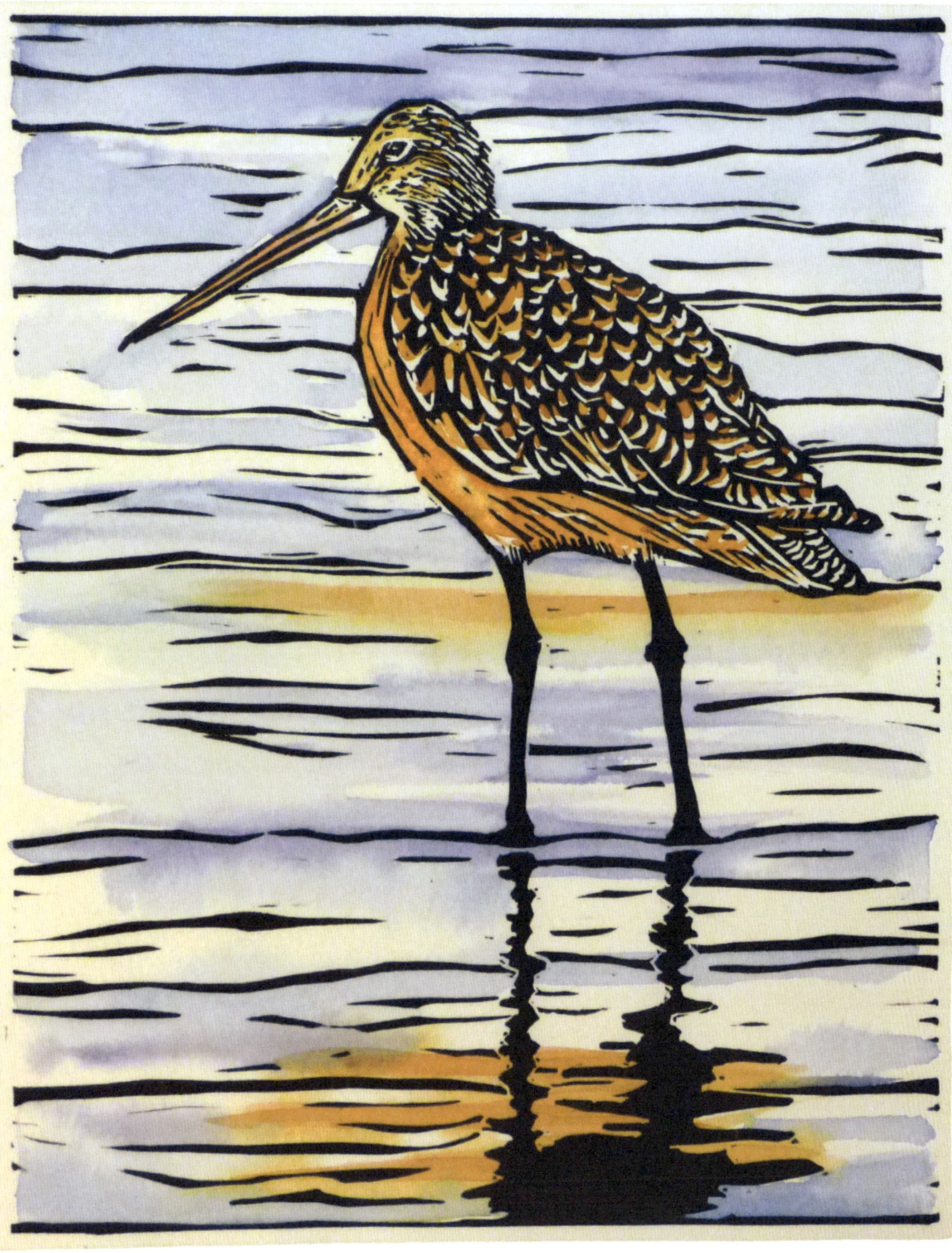

Black-necked stilt *(Himantopus mexicanus)* • **WATERCOLOR SKETCH**

I'd never seen a stilt until this viewing at Lower Klamath Lake's tule marshes, located in northernmost California. Early in the twentieth century, Audubon's William Finley described the Lower Klamath's "tule marshes and club-rushes as the most extensive breeding ground in the West for all kinds of water birds." Stilts live year-round on the California coast but go inland only during breeding season. The bird stood just a few yards from me among the reeds in the shallow marsh—cause to marvel, yet again, at the incredible diversity of the bird world. What to liken this amazing creature to? Fred Astaire in top hat and tails?

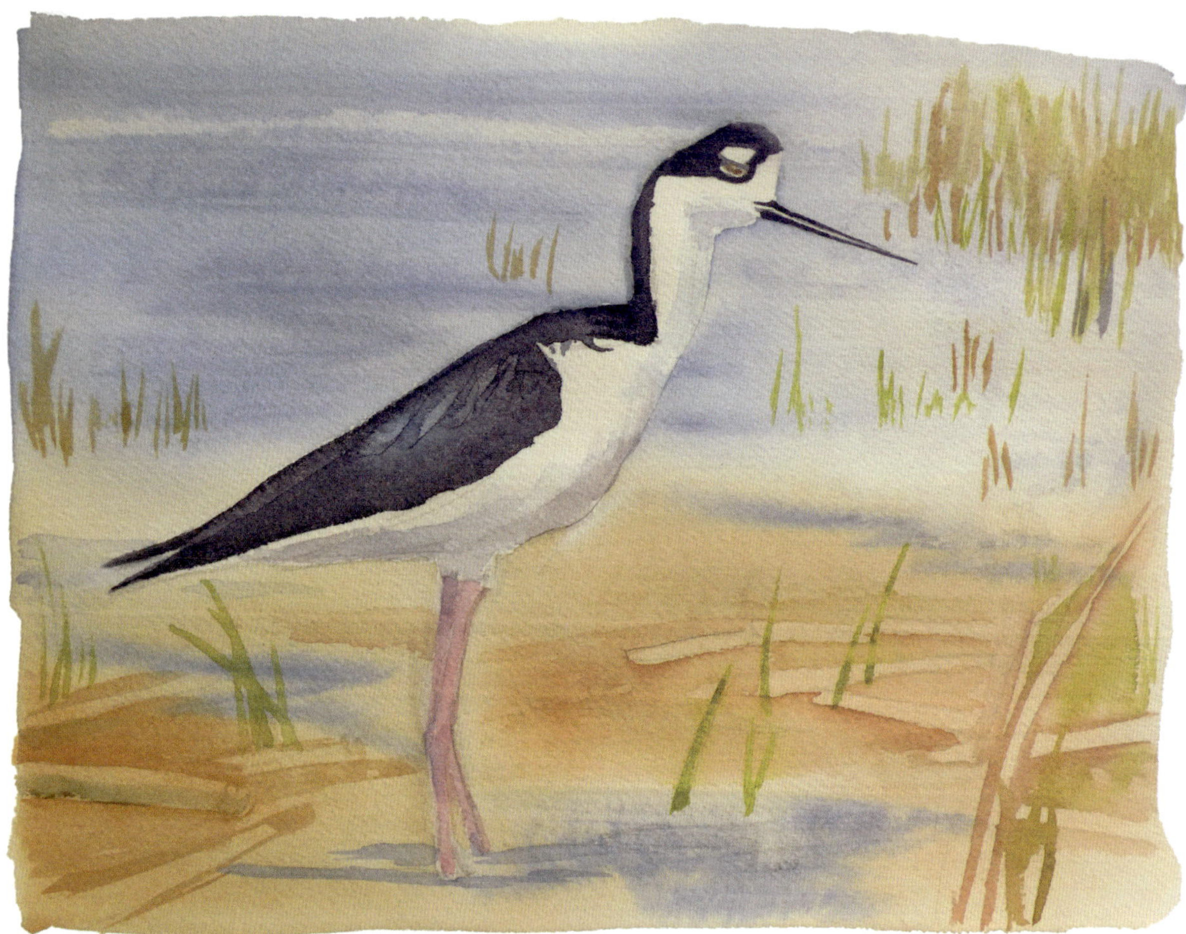

TECHNIQUE
Gestural Drawing with Acrylic Ink & Watercolor

A gestural drawing is done loosely, so a light hand grip on the tool gives the best playful effects—what you're attempting to show is the posture and general characteristics of the subject, not specific details. I began this piece with a light pencil drawing, just to make sure the proportions of the great blue heron (*Ardea herodias*) were somewhat convincing, but didn't add much detail, merely positioning the head, tail, neck, and legs. Then I loaded a chopstick with a rich blue acrylic drawing ink; I dragged it across the ink bottle to prevent any drips and blobs but still kept a fair amount of ink on it. Using the chopstick, I roughly sketched over my light pencil lines, breaking them up at times, drawing the most delicate lines (the feather shapes, leg outlines, and eye) last, after the chopstick had unloaded most of its ink on the broader, coarser lines of the bird's outside contours. Using the blue-hued ink was a bold suggestion of the gray-blue plumage of the bird and best captured its watery world.

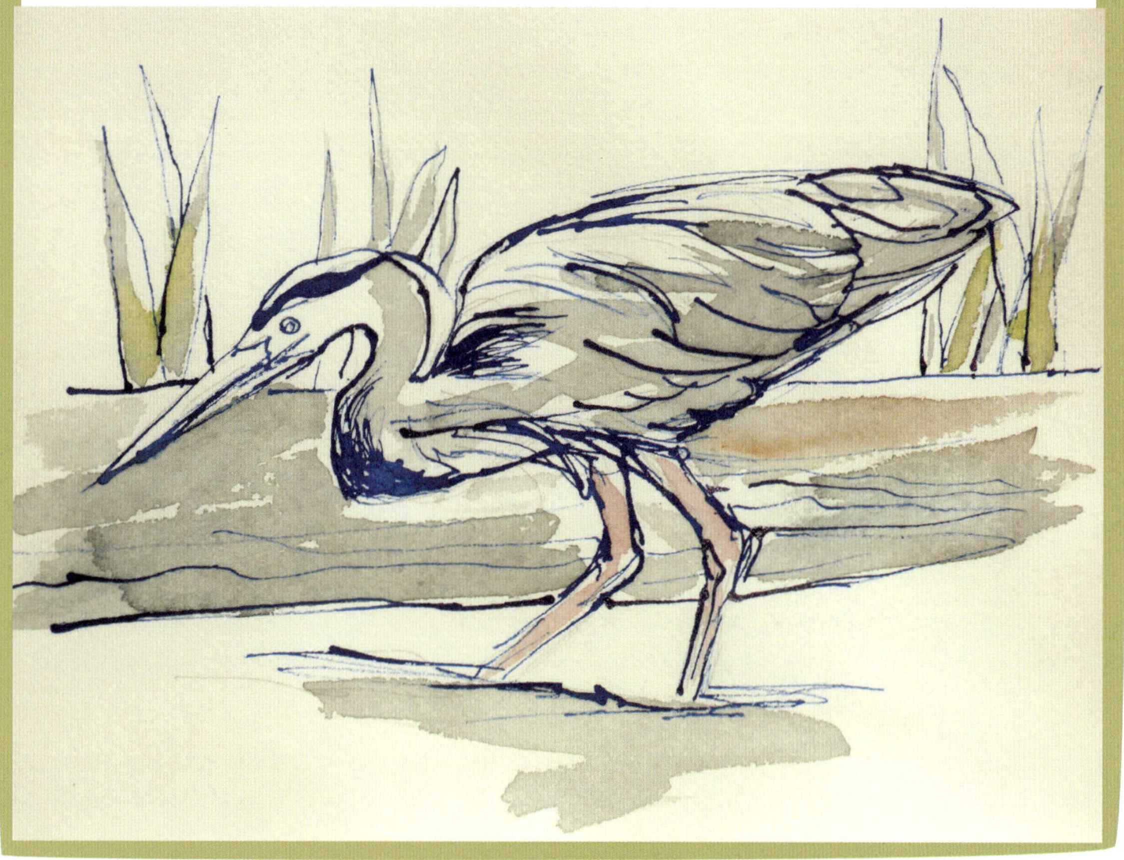

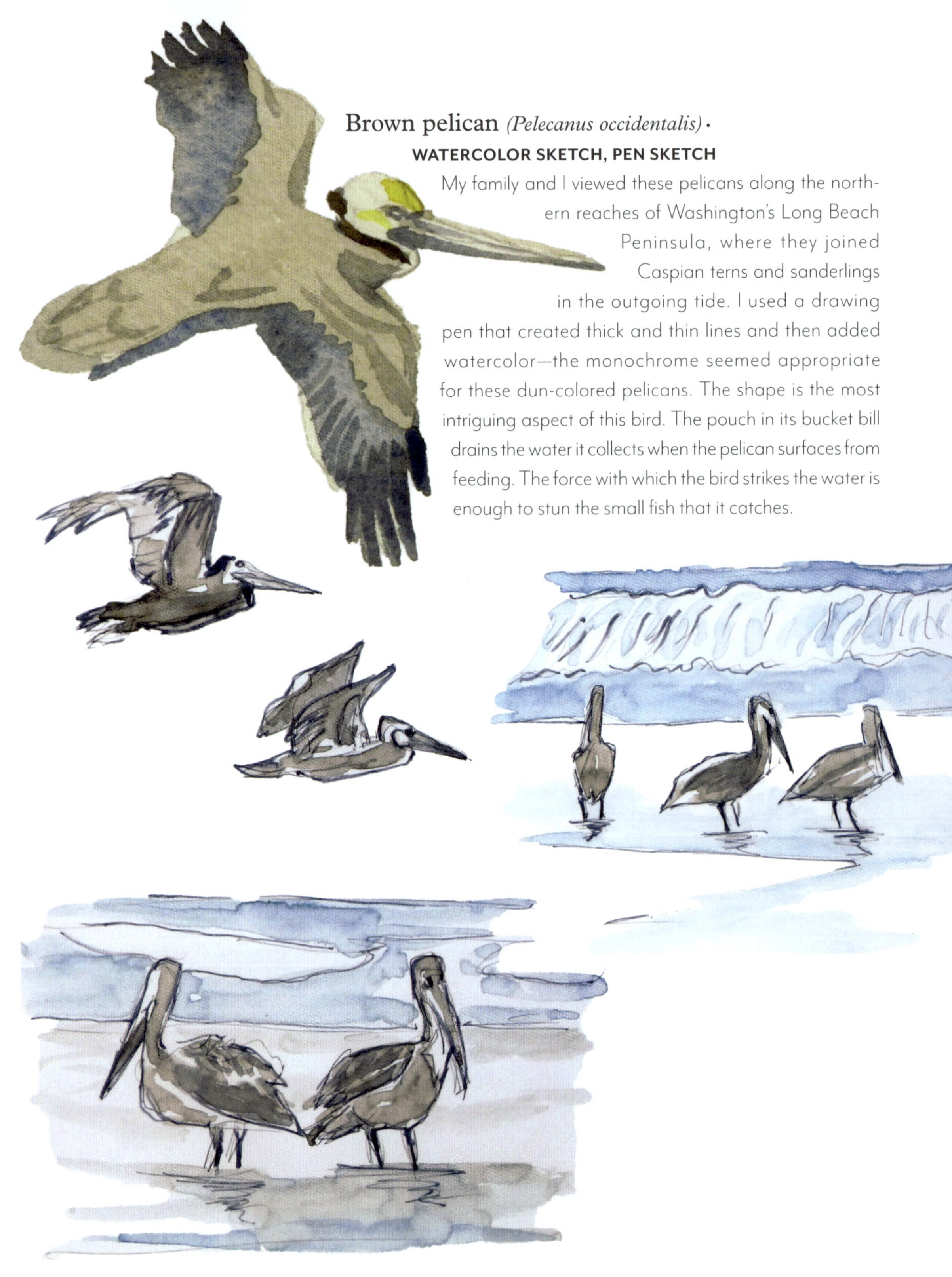

Brown pelican *(Pelecanus occidentalis)* • **WATERCOLOR SKETCH, PEN SKETCH**

My family and I viewed these pelicans along the northern reaches of Washington's Long Beach Peninsula, where they joined Caspian terns and sanderlings in the outgoing tide. I used a drawing pen that created thick and thin lines and then added watercolor—the monochrome seemed appropriate for these dun-colored pelicans. The shape is the most intriguing aspect of this bird. The pouch in its bucket bill drains the water it collects when the pelican surfaces from feeding. The force with which the bird strikes the water is enough to stun the small fish that it catches.

Caspian tern *(Hydroprogne caspia)* •

PEN SKETCH, BLOCK PRINT

Watching the hovering, then diving flights of terns is exciting, with their noisy and unmistakable squawks a raucous accompaniment. David Sibley describes their vocalizations as "harsh, heron-like screams." Their black heads and bright scarlet bills create a dramatic pattern as they fly or gather on beaches. If I were a textile pattern designer, I'd make use of a cotillion of terns, either in flight or on the beach.

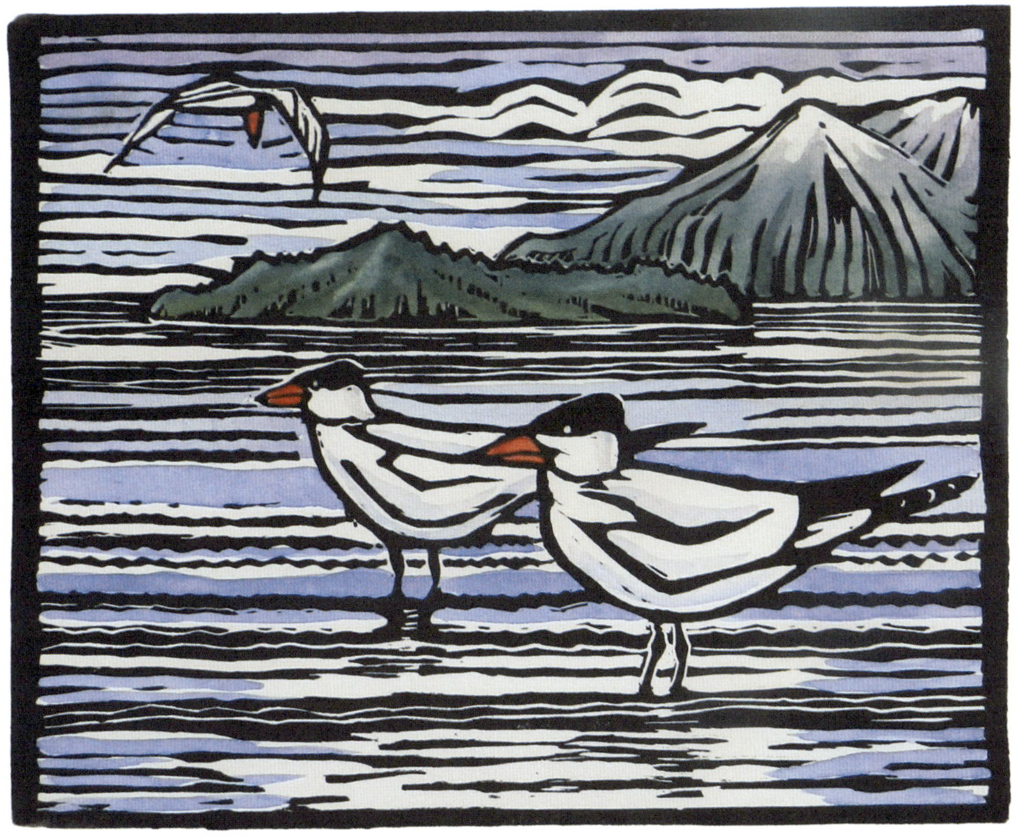

Black turnstone *(Arenaria melanocephala)* · **WATERCOLOR SKETCH**

The turnstone was walking among the rocks at low tide in Lincoln City, Oregon, a surprising sight given the very busy summer beach scene there, and one to be valued all the more—brave bird, carrying on your life in spite of human interruption! As its name suggests, the turnstone uses its bill to overturn rocks and seaweed to find mollusks, barnacles, worms, and crustaceans. I spent a couple of hours that day peering into tide pools and felt very much like a probing bird, discovering new forms of sea life to draw and photograph.

Western sandpiper *(Calidris mauri)* · **EGG TEMPERA**

There are seven species of *Calidris* sandpipers, all of them rather small and hard to identify. I'm not totally sure which of the seven this is, but my guess is the western. For this painting, I set up a still life with a piece of driftwood and some weather-beaten beach pebbles and added the sandpiper by looking at one of my photos from the Oregon coast. The arched enclosure evokes the framing devices used in late medieval and Early Renaissance altarpieces, as well as the small diptychs and triptychs used for private devotions. The altarpieces and smaller works had multiple panels that were hinged and could be opened and closed, depending on the liturgical calendar—for example, the outer wings on a triptych altarpiece could be closed during Lent. The backsides of the panels were often painted in monochrome gray, also called "grisaille." Then, on Easter, the panels were opened to reveal rich full-color paintings. Beautiful triptych examples include Duccio's *Maesta* altarpiece in the cathedral in Siena, Italy; Matthias Grünewald's altarpiece for Isenheim's Monastery of St. Anthony, now displayed in the Unterlinden Museum in Colmar, France; and Hubert and Jan van Eyck's Ghent altarpiece in Belgium.

The other creatures with which we share this world have their rights too, but not speaking our language, they have no voice, no vote; it is our moral duty to take care of them.

—**Roger Tory Peterson,** *All Things Reconsidered: My Birding Adventures*

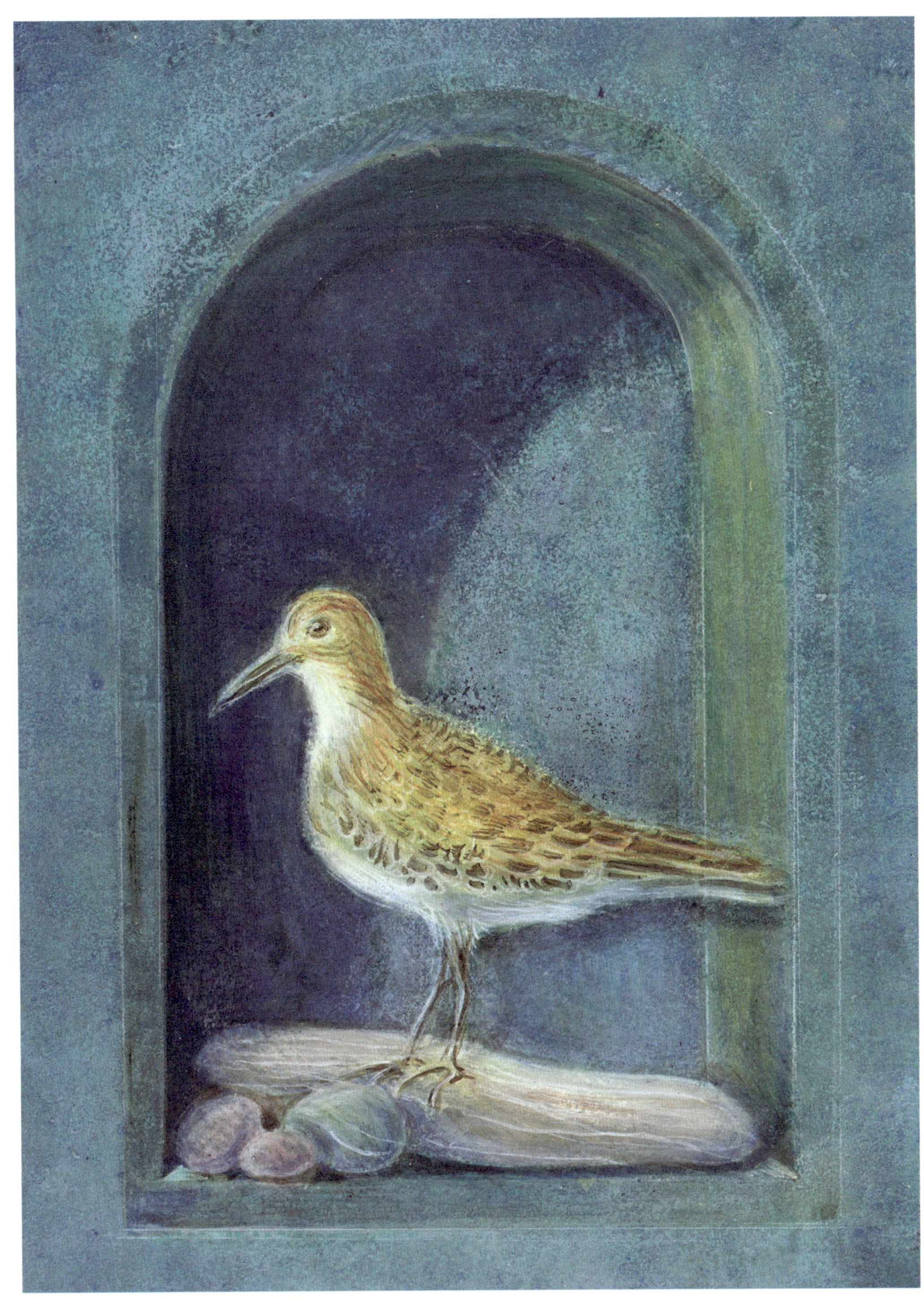

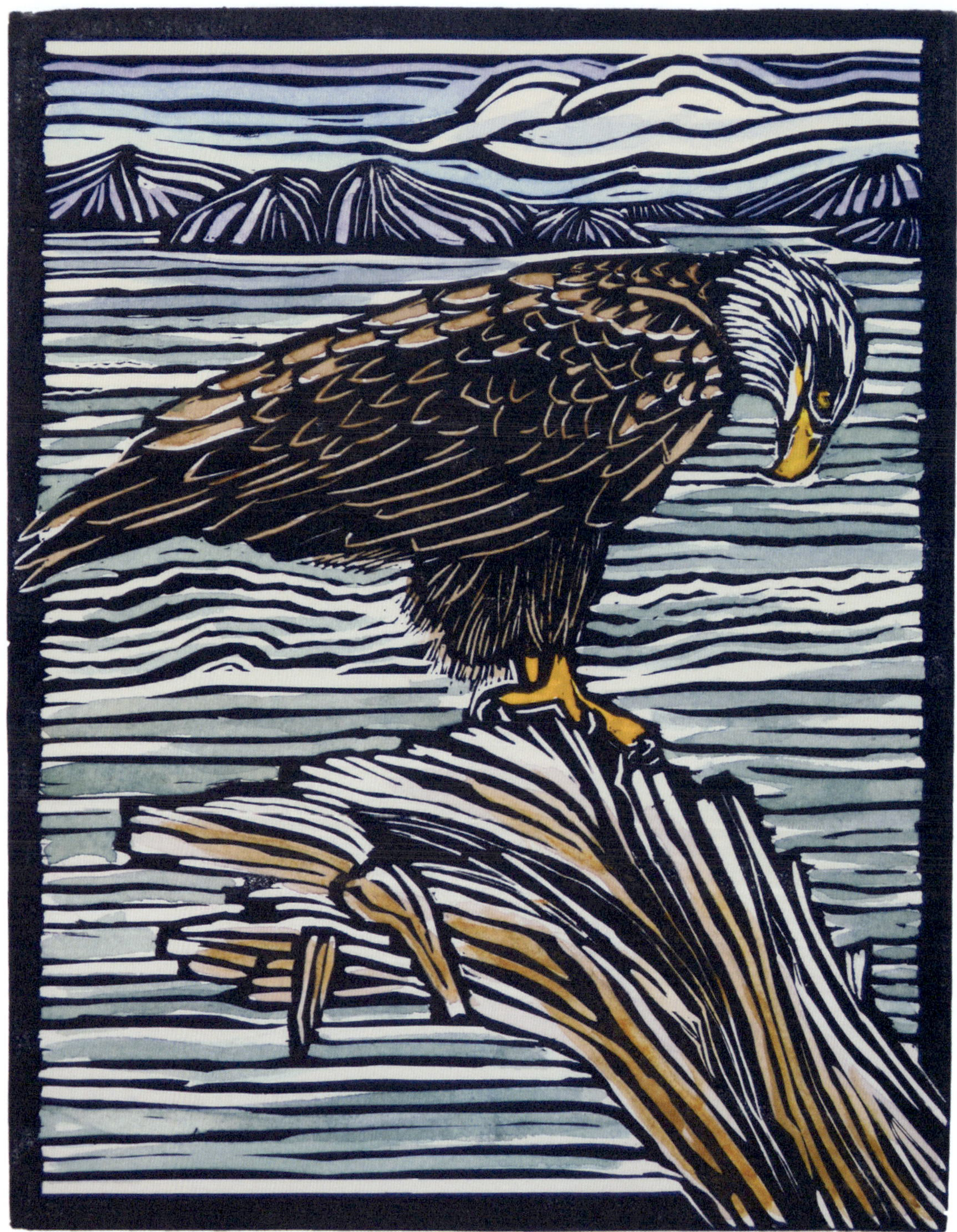

Bald eagle *(Haliaeetus leucocephalus)* • **BLOCK PRINT**

The bald eagle perched in a gigantic downed tree that had washed ashore in a storm at Grays Harbor on the Washington coast. The dramatic setting was an invitation to try a strong, not understated, medium—a perfect subject for a print. Sometimes with a print it's more powerful to have lines working against one another; here, the wood grain on the trunk creates a counterpoint to the wave marks and mountain contours.

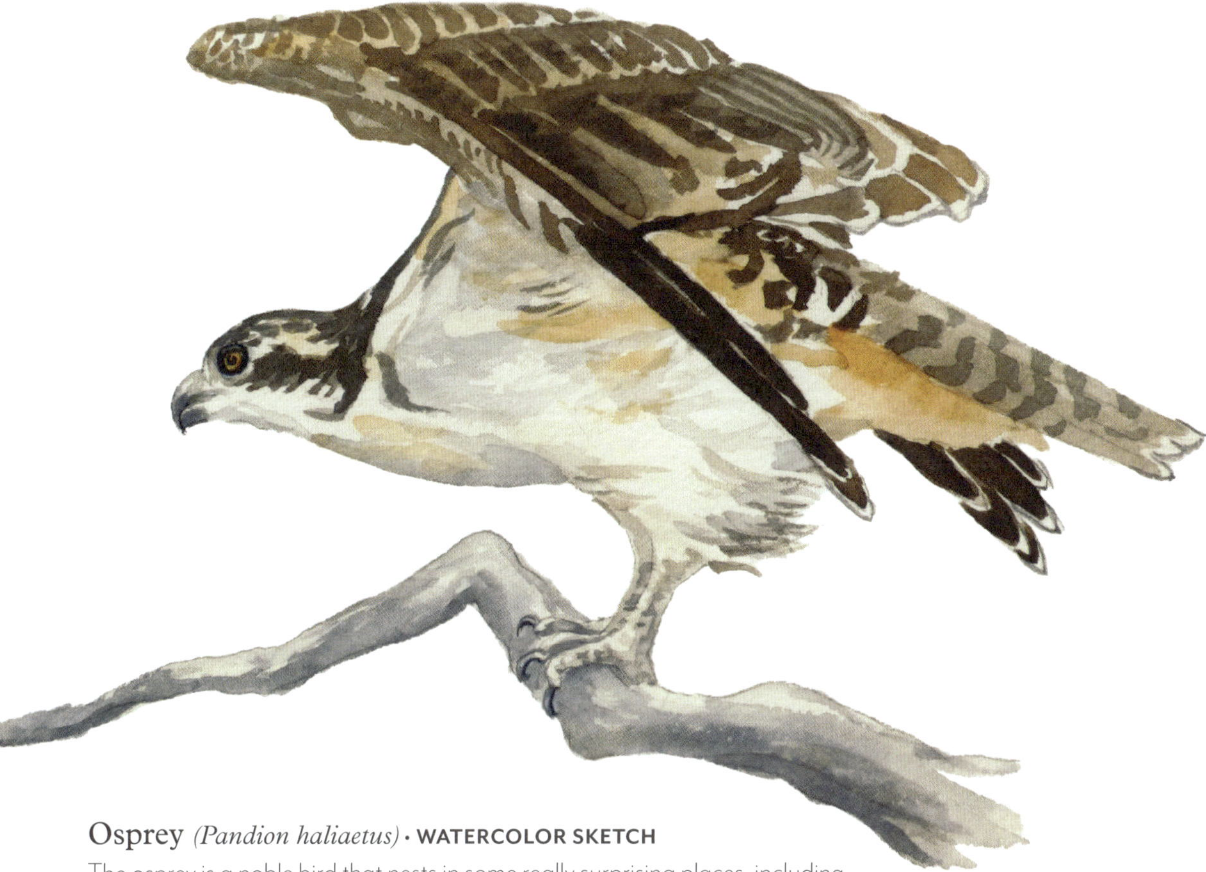

Osprey *(Pandion haliaetus)* • **WATERCOLOR SKETCH**

The osprey is a noble bird that nests in some really surprising places, including the cell phone tower of our local home improvement store. None of us, customers or employees, would have known the birds were there in the tower so high above us, except for the loud screeches that issued from the nest. I found it touching to hear one of the employees describe them as "our ospreys." The osprey in this sketch is the sort a designer might use as a model for an elegant automobile hood ornament; preparing to take off, it implies limitless power and speed.

Sanderling *(Calidris alba)* • **BLOCK PRINT, WATERCOLOR SKETCH**

Watching sanderlings on a California beach with an incoming or outgoing tide is one of the most entertaining pastimes imaginable. They look like mechanical toys as they scurry back and forth along the tideline in unison and then fly off as you approach. In their winter, nonbreeding plumage, they are pale, but in breeding plumage, the head, back, and shoulders are rust-colored. At sunrise and sunset their white bellies absorb the gold, orange, pink, and blue-violet light.

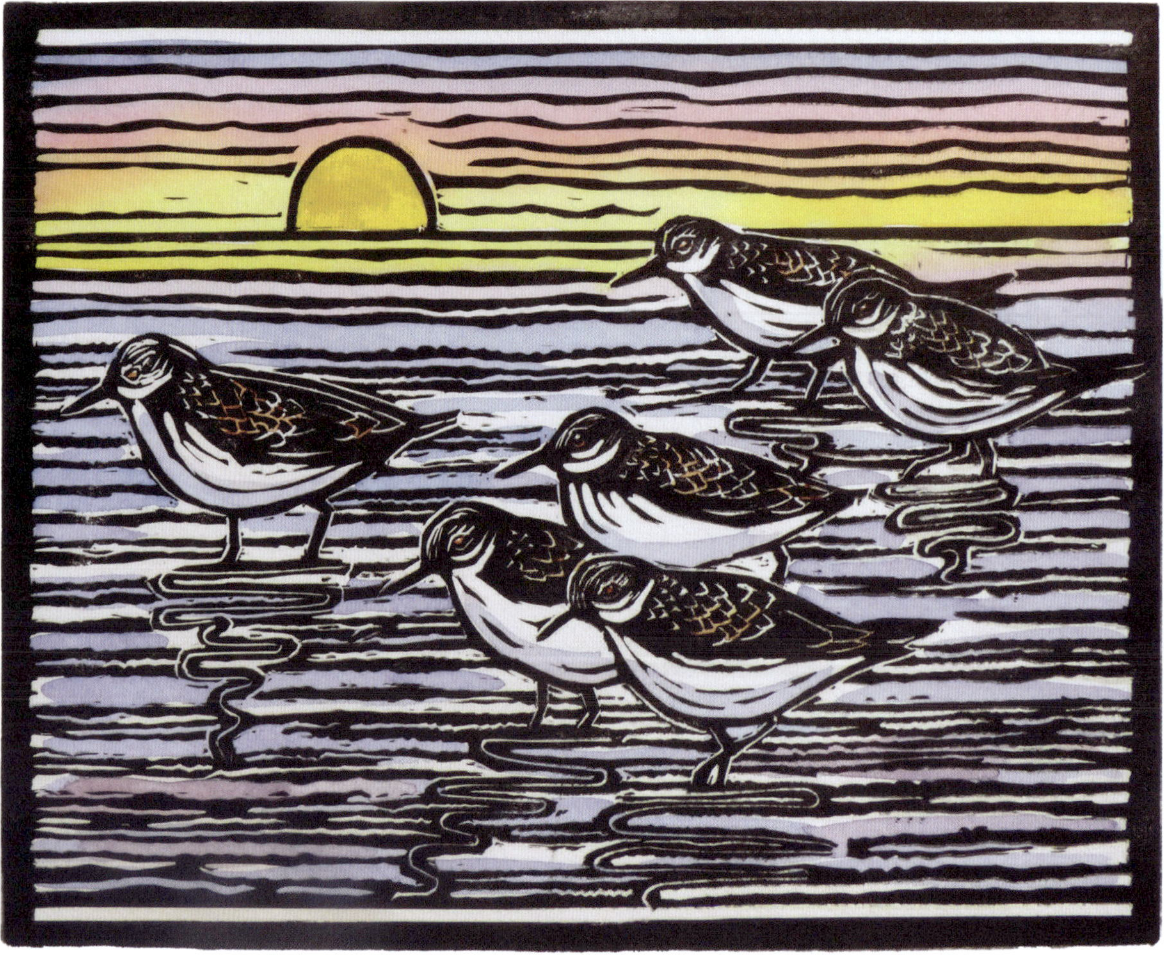

Between feedings [sanderlings] face northward—energetic, feet stamping with readiness—and we remember the advent of spring in our own veins.

—**Lyanda Lynn Haupt,** *The Living Bird*

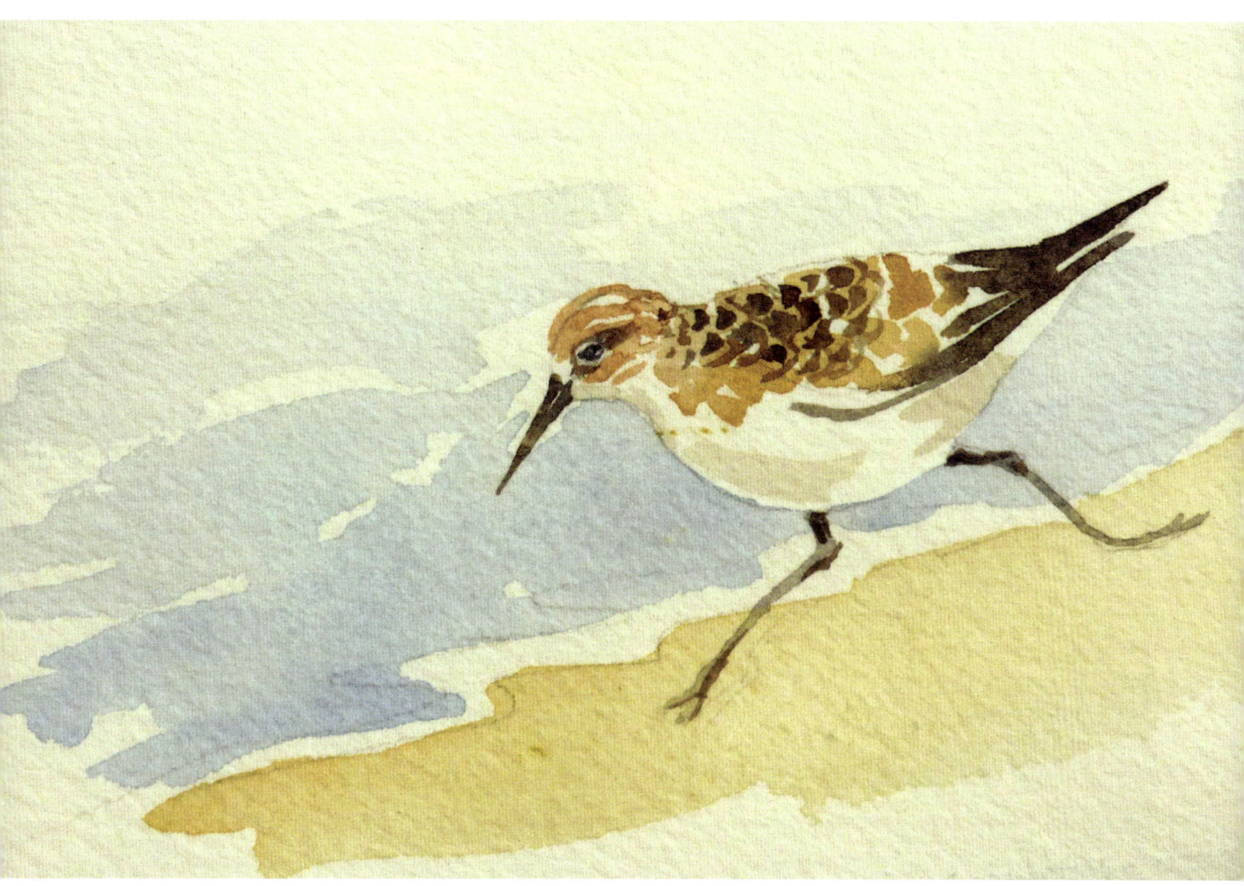

Great blue heron *(Ardea herodias)* • **BLOCK PRINT**

Union Bay Natural Area supports a number of great blue herons, and watching them peer into the depths among the blooming irises was an experience I wanted to remember. Occasionally it seems important to add landscape elements in a print, as I did here with Mount Rainier, which hovered above Union Bay on this fine spring day. I like situating a bird—not just in a generic habitat, but in a specific place that evokes a season and sometimes an historic moment. Recently, more lanes were added to Highway 520 in Seattle, and a high-rise bridge was erected that obscures the lower portion of the view of Mount Rainier from Union Bay. The many prices of progress!

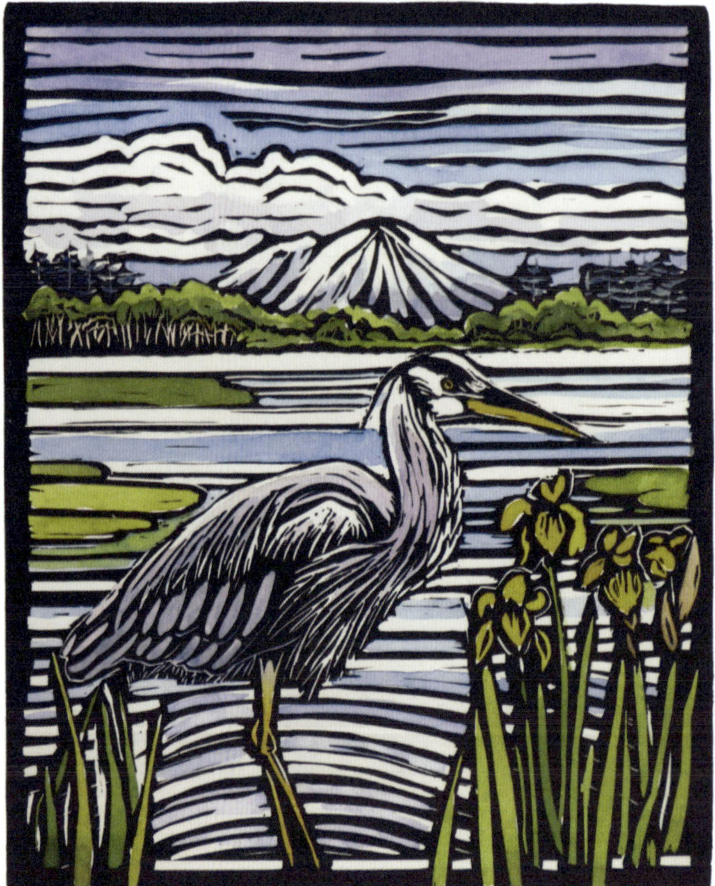

Great egret *(Ardea alba)* • **BLOCK PRINT**

Egrets are very common on California's Monterey Peninsula. At Point Lobos State Natural Reserve, this egret was only a few yards away from us, stalking a creature we couldn't see beneath the blooms and foliage. In the water, the large bird feeds on small fish and amphibians; on land, it seeks insects, reptiles, and small mammals. The egret's white plumage glowed in pure contrast against the flowering California poppies and yarrow of the headland. The intricacy of the flowers was challenging to carve—using a variety of tools, I was able to make different marks to represent parts of them. With a small U-gouge I made scooped-out circles for the yarrow florets, and the smallest V-gouge was just right for the line work required for the umbels' stems. Umbels are multiple small flowers that emerge from a central point on the stem, forming a kind of umbrella shape.

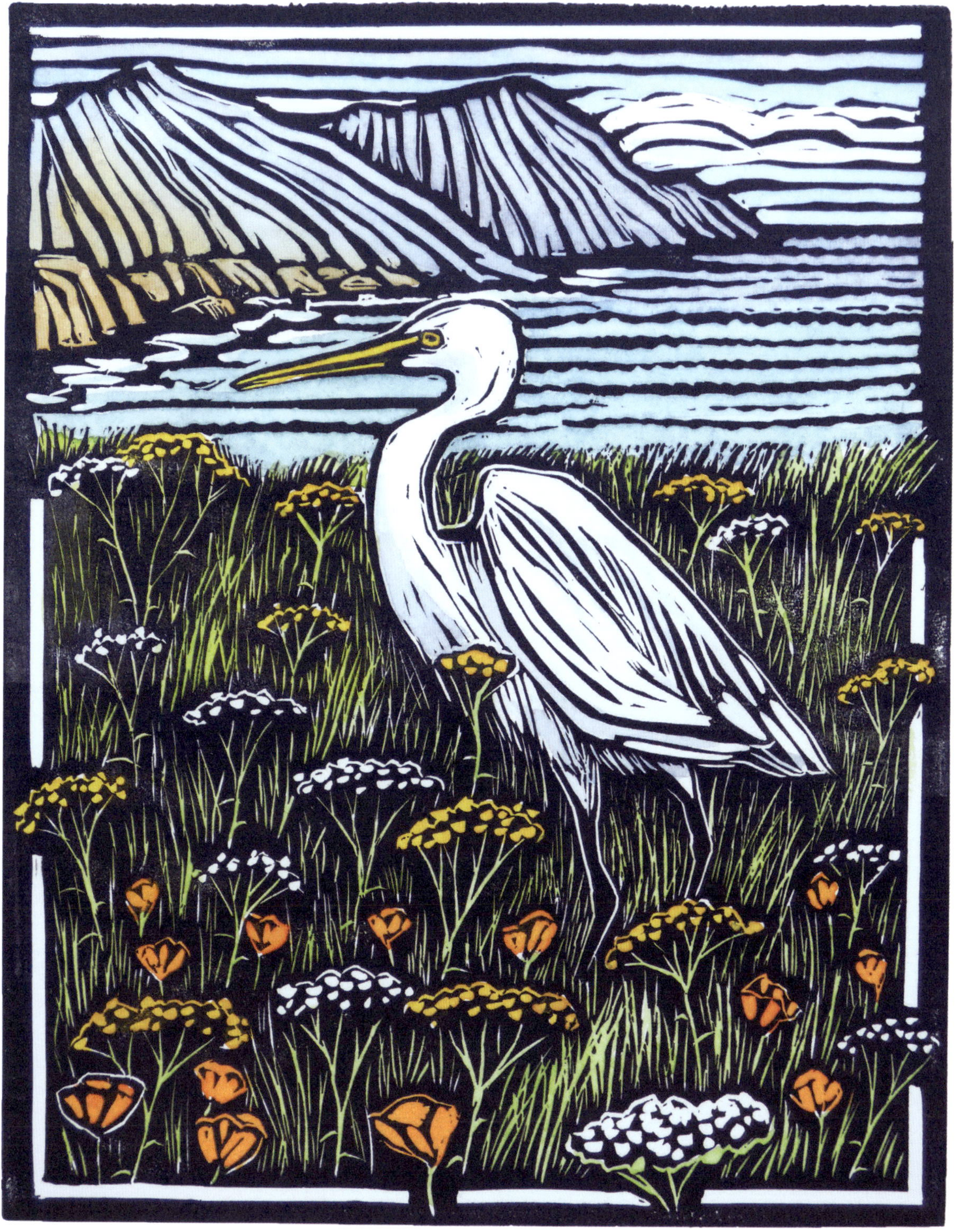

Brandt's cormorant *(Phalacrocorax penicillatus)* • **BLOCK PRINT**
Cormorants look bejeweled in their breeding plumage. My husband and I traveled to the Monterey Peninsula in California to see the wildlife, including cormorants, at Point Lobos State Natural Reserve. The pattern created as the birds rested beside one another on nests with their curved necks and bills was so striking that I couldn't think of a medium better suited to them than the block print, with its high contrast of black and white. The bright amber and turquoise colors reminded me of some of Russian Vasily Kandinsky's early block prints. He was inspired by the largely primary hues used in folk art and combined them with large areas of black, blue, and orange in his gouache paintings and block prints.

TECHNIQUE
Mixing Oil-Based Inks

I took some liberties with the black-crowned night-heron (*Nycticorax nycticorax*) block print—I actually saw it in the late afternoon. Adding the moon to this image required using a dark background, and I decided to try it in both black and indigo. With the indigo, I wanted to make a cultural reference to Japanese prints, which often employ a blue that gradates to darkest indigo. To mix the indigo, I used a combination of soft black and ultramarine blue etching inks. Both of the prints were tinted with watercolor after the oil inks dried, with yellows for the moon and the breast feathers and green for the reeds.

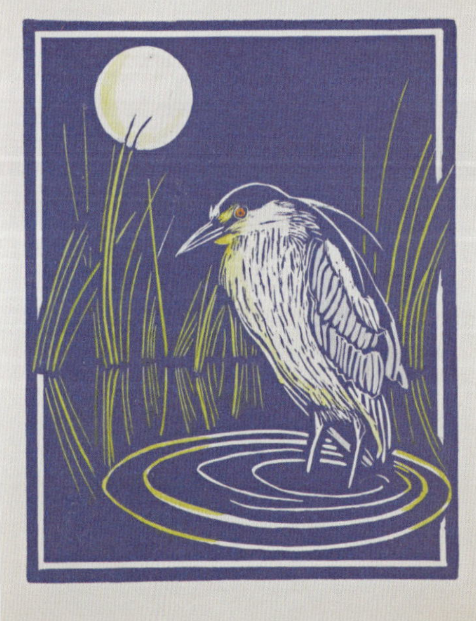

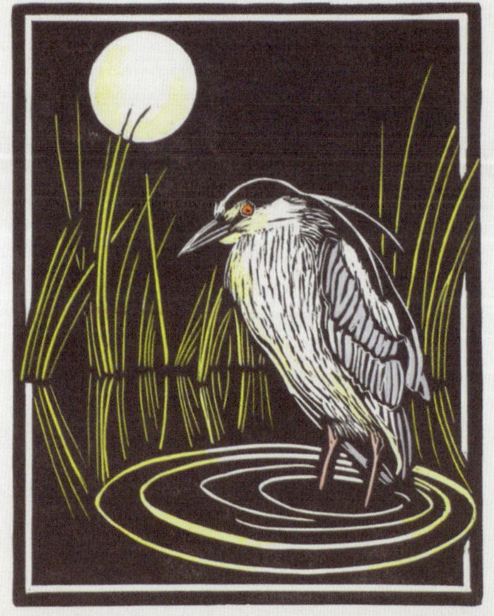

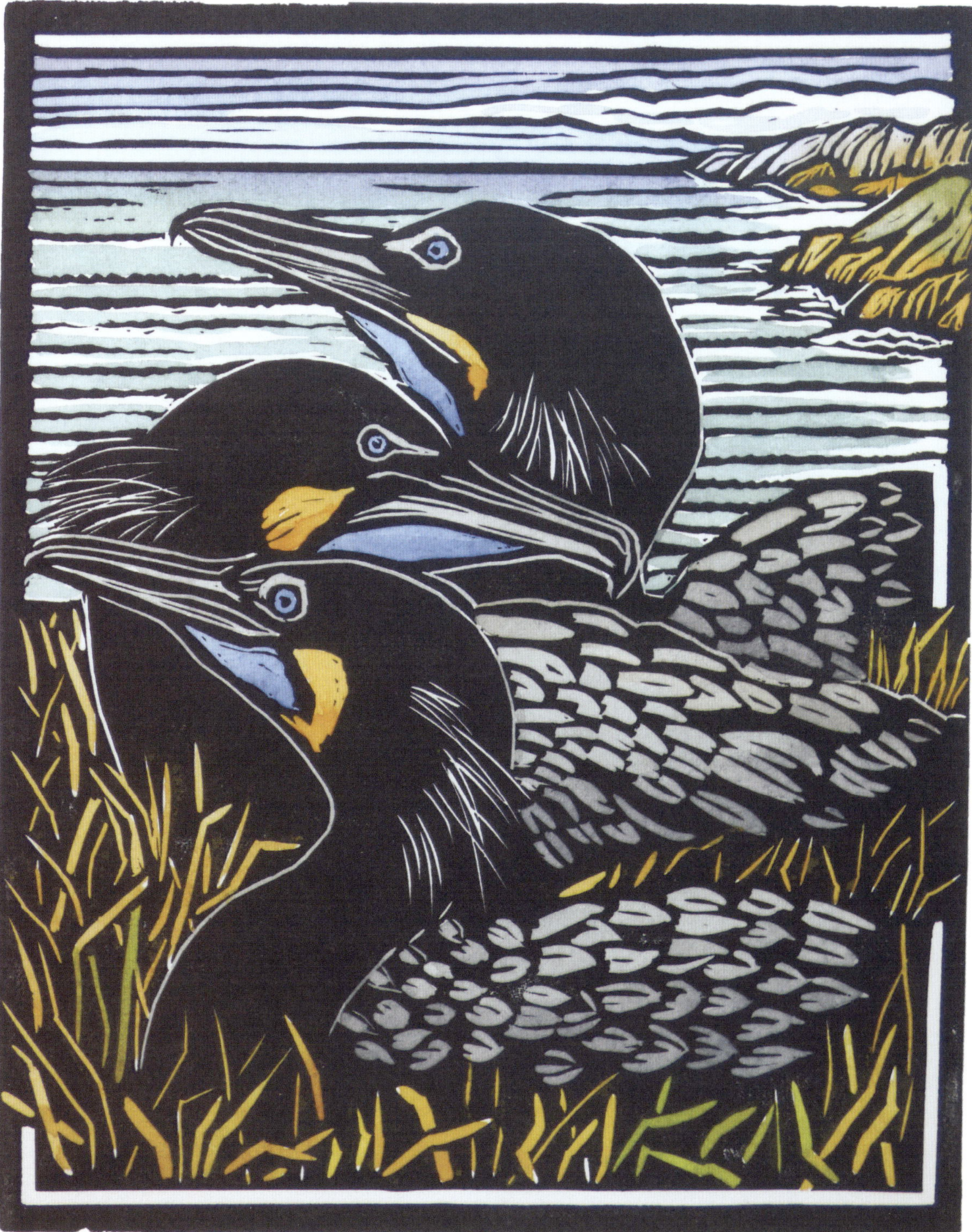

TECHNIQUE
Drawing from Life

One Sunday in June, my husband and I traveled by light rail downtown and visited the Seattle Aquarium along with scores of youngsters, babies in strollers, parents, and grandparents. The aquarium is a great place for children under five—they get right up to the viewing windows and are allowed to reach into the hands-on exhibits and touch anemones and other tidal creatures.

I realized as I stood drawing the tufted puffin (*Fratercula cirrhata*) and long-billed curlew (*Numenius americanus*) that the only way a person over the age of five can react to nature as a child does, with an innocent lack of expectation and genuine excitement, is to approach living creatures as if you've never seen them before, or heard of them, or read about them, or learned their names. One way to do that is to try to draw them. Then you aren't thinking, "puffin, plover, oystercatcher." All you're doing is experiencing the colors, the shapes, and the movements. You're thinking, "big black body with huge orange bill," not "black oystercatcher (*Haematopus bachmani*)." You may also be feeling really surprised at how different these birds are from you; yet you understand, the way a child does, that the birds are also so very much like you, as they stalk around hungrily looking for food.

When I draw from life, I use an HB pencil and a method of sketching with multiple tentative lines, as explained in "Sketching." I try to use my pencil almost like my eyes—mostly taking in the birds and not feeling too connected to the drawings themselves. What I did at the aquarium might be more accurately called modified blind contour drawing, a method commonly used for drawing the human figure in which you very infrequently look at your paper, but almost exclusively at the model, moving your pencil on the paper and astonishing yourself once you finally look at your drawing. It can be amazingly convincing. (In blind contour drawing, you never look at your paper.) Here, I did look at my paper, but not too often. The drawings you do this way are much more powerful than carefully rendered lines.

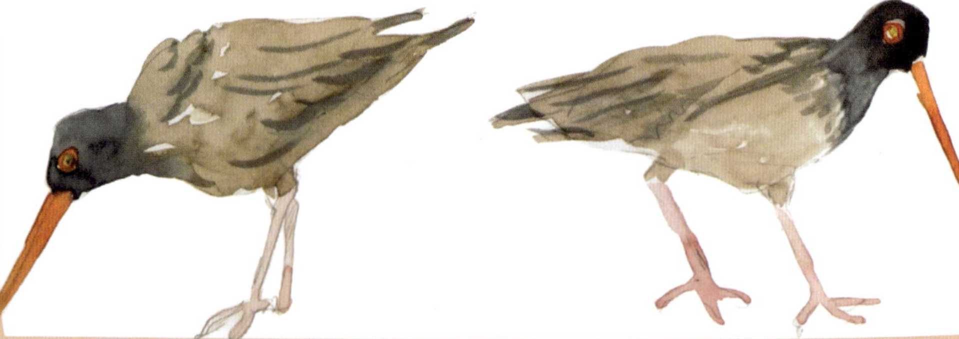

In quick-sketching situations when you're drawing multiple species, it's difficult to get any sense of scale, so the black-bellied plover (*Pluvialis squatarola*) looks bigger than the puffin in my drawings. When you try this, don't worry about that—just getting the basic proportions of each bird right is all you need to focus on.

You'll also find challenges as the birds move. Try to get the basic contours of the body and head first; then add legs and feet later. As long as the birds don't fly away, you may be able to see them move back to their original positions if you wait a few minutes. And if they do fly away, you can always consult a field guide or photos on the internet to finish your work. Remember, it's a sketch, and it doesn't have to be perfect. I waited until I got home from the aquarium to add the watercolor, simply opening up a field guide and working with the colors I saw there.

The puffin at the aquarium was shy about eye contact, and I felt rather bad about all the photographs and drawing. Most animals and birds view direct eye contact as a challenge, an attempt on the part of the viewer to establish dominance. We're so used to connecting with other human beings through eye contact that we forget how it affects other creatures, so it can be best to look at a bird or other creature obliquely, without the threat inherent in direct eye contact. I didn't get a very good drawing of the puffin's profile, which shows some of the more interesting features of the bird—the bill, eyes, and white plume atop the head—so when I got home I looked for copyright-free images on the internet and redrew the profile with the aid of an online photo. This profile may be the least animated of all the sketches since I wasn't working from a living, moving bird.

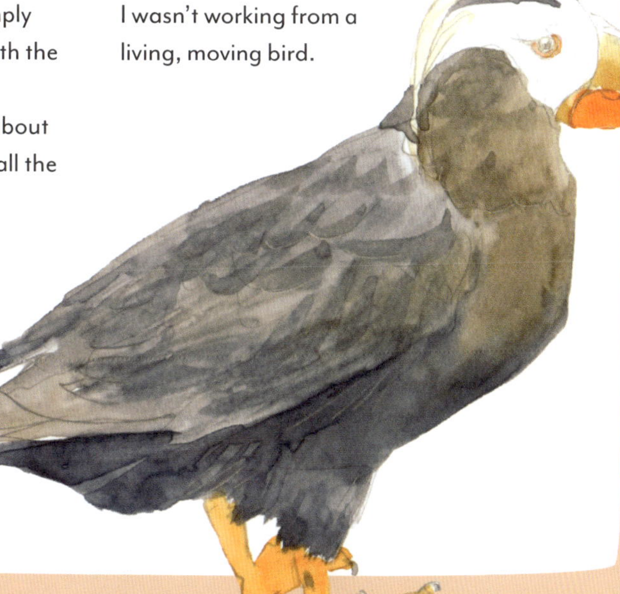

Harlequin duck *(Histrionicus histrionicus)* • **WOODBLOCK PRINT**

The harlequin character in *commedia dell'arte*, an Italian theater genre popular from the 1500s through the 1700s, wore a multicolored suit with diamond patterns outlined in white. I'm drawn to the idea of the harlequin drake, bedecked in theatrical plumage, putting on a stunning show for his partner. It reminds me of ornithologist Richard O. Prum's belief that humans are not the only artists in the natural world; he writes that we need to adopt a "post-human aesthetic philosophy that places us, and our artworlds, in context with other animals." A recent visit to Rosario Beach near Deception Pass in Washington granted me my first ever sighting of a harlequin. Among waterfowl of the West, the drake is equal only to the wood duck for breathtaking color and markings.

The woodblock carving was rather simple and economical, with just two blocks, one for each color: one carved and printed the water and sky, and the other the drake and small islands in the background. (For the more basic rubber blocks, I typically carve only one, ink it in black, and then tint with watercolor. But with some types of woodblock printmaking, you need a separate block for each color you want to print.) This method of printing doesn't require a press because you can use delicate Japanese papers and thinned-out inks; absorption of the ink doesn't demand the extreme pressure required by thicker inks on heavier paper.

Here I used etching inks, which I prefer over relief inks because of the wide range of colors and high quality of the hues. The only drawback to using them is that you need to thin them with burnt plate oil so that they roll out easily. This also gives you a slightly more transparent look. I used a technique called rainbow rolling, in which different inks are rolled onto one brayer in order to achieve the gradation from dark to lighter blue that you see in the water.

On the drake, I used very small rollers for the orange on his head and body in order to prevent the orange from covering areas that were gray and blue. I appreciate that this kind of woodblock printmaking can be done in a home studio. The only drawback is the amount of space you need to roll out the various ink colors. I use plexiglass plates and brought out four of them to keep the inks separate for the printing. I found that my big table was completely covered by the plates and wished I had a bigger studio! There are always drawbacks to working in a home studio, but I prefer it. I never feel as if I'm actually working, since I'm at home and can take breaks for tea, neighborhood walks, and birdwatching in our garden.

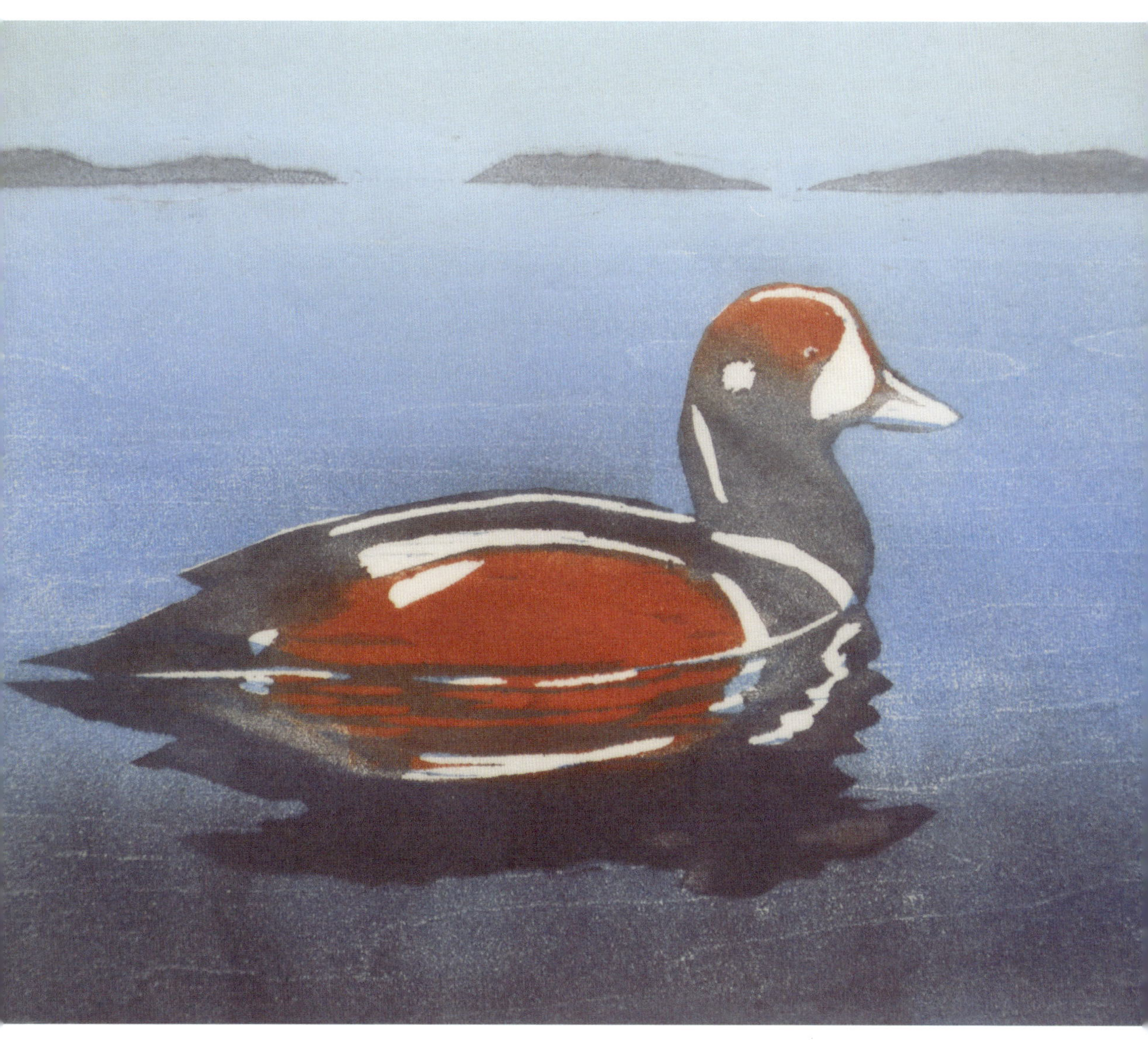

Meadow & Grassland

savanna

grassland

plain

prairie

heath

steppe

meadow

wheatgrass

basin wildrye

Idaho fescue

Indian ricegrass

big bluegrass

blue camas

shooting star

prairie violet

yellow balsamroot

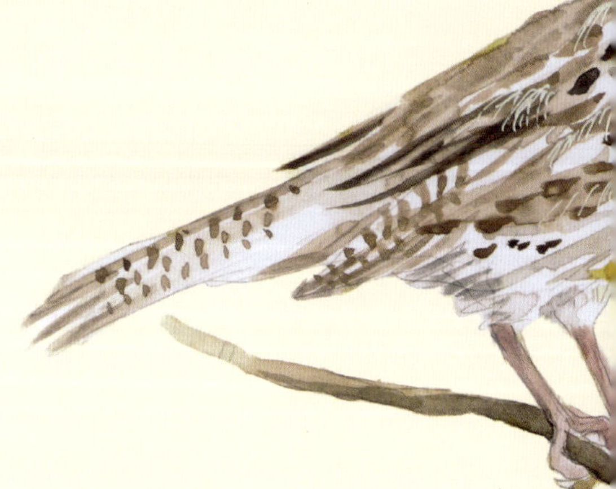

Soul melting scenery that was about me! A place where the mind could think volumes . . .

—George Catlin, *Letters and Notes*

A short-eared owl hunts for voles by day in winter in the meadows of Washington's Skagit Valley while kestrels perch on a fence beside farm fields gone fallow. Treeless expanses heat up during the day, and insects fly out, perfect for birds like swallows that take their food midflight. Killdeer lay their eggs in gravel and dead grasses—it would be a stretch to call these small depressions nests, their only protection the adults' vigilance as they lure away intruders. Grasslands and meadows provide valuable nesting materials as well as camouflage for some species, and the grass seeds are important food for birds like sparrows. Birds of prey, with their amazing long-distance vision, roost on high beside meadows, spotting rodents as they venture from their underground burrows. Scrub-jays make forays from low shrubs, and western bluebirds survey from atop granite boulders. Lewis's woodpeckers make their nests in cavities within the trunks of rare Garry oaks that dot disappearing oak savannas.

Grasslands are one of the most threatened ecosystems in the United States. In the past, periodic fires restored them by burning encroaching forest. Some of those fires were natural occurrences, and others were manmade: Native Americans set deliberate and controlled fires to manage these areas because they relied on the oaks for food, and the meadows made good deer and elk hunting sites. In modern times, grazing practices can perform some of the same functions. Cows and other range animals trample and eat young shoots and seedlings of unwanted trees and shrubs, and even fertilize the ground with their manure, but the intensity of some ranching methods disturbs valuable bird habitat. Some birds require longer grasses, others very short, so federal and nonprofit wildland managers are seeking to create a mosaic of grassland types, working with public and private lands.

Even surrounding Washington State's Puget Sound, where most people would expect heavy timber and forests all the way to the edge of the water, there are prairies and meadows. South of Olympia are the Tacoma prairies; from Interstate 5 at Fort Lewis, you suddenly notice mature oak trees growing everywhere, and wide open spaces continue all the way down to the Columbia River just north of Portland, Oregon. In the nineteenth century, William Tolmie, a medical officer of the Hudson's Bay Company, wrote admiringly: "The shade of a lofty pine [is] beautifully interspersed and surrounded with oaks . . . through the gaps in the arch we see the broad plain extending southward to the Nisqually." Arthur Kruckeberg described this area as a "gravelly outwash plain," created by the residue from gravel-laden glacial meltwater when the last continental ice sheet covered Washington.

In addition to these plains, there are countless meadows in the Pacific Northwest that are more unstable habitats—the aftermath of logging, or pasturelands, or agricultural fields, both growing and fallow. The ubiquitous Douglas firs will eventually overtake many of these habitats, but in the meantime birds make use of them.

Killdeer *(Charadrius vociferus)* • **BLOCK PRINT**

Killdeer are found in open meadows and are common in city parks with wide areas of grass—the birds nest in the ball fields in the park near our house. The subject of this block print was observed along a golf course cart path in southern Oregon, with low mountains in the distance. The bird was fanning its tail to look menacing, and we probably wouldn't have even noticed the eggs, so well camouflaged were they, had the bird not been putting on such a display. Sometimes distracting behaviors can be counterproductive!

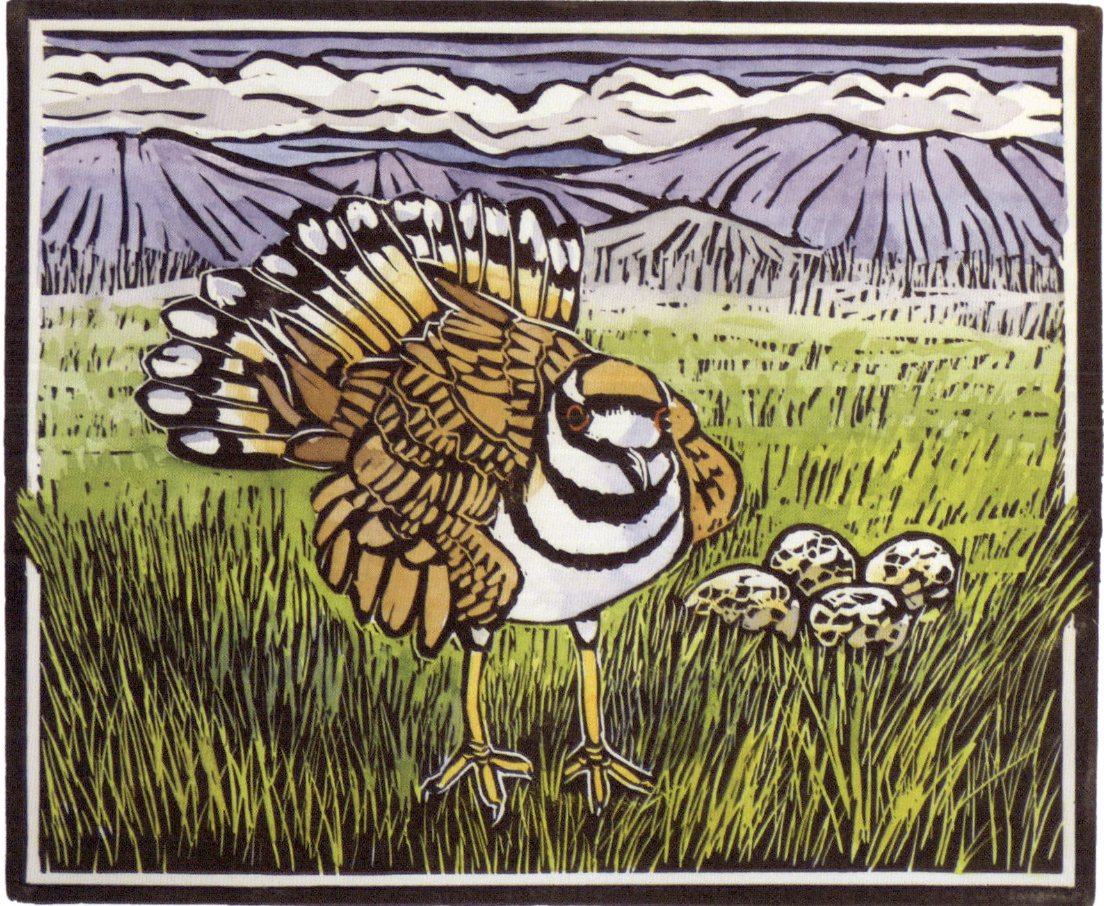

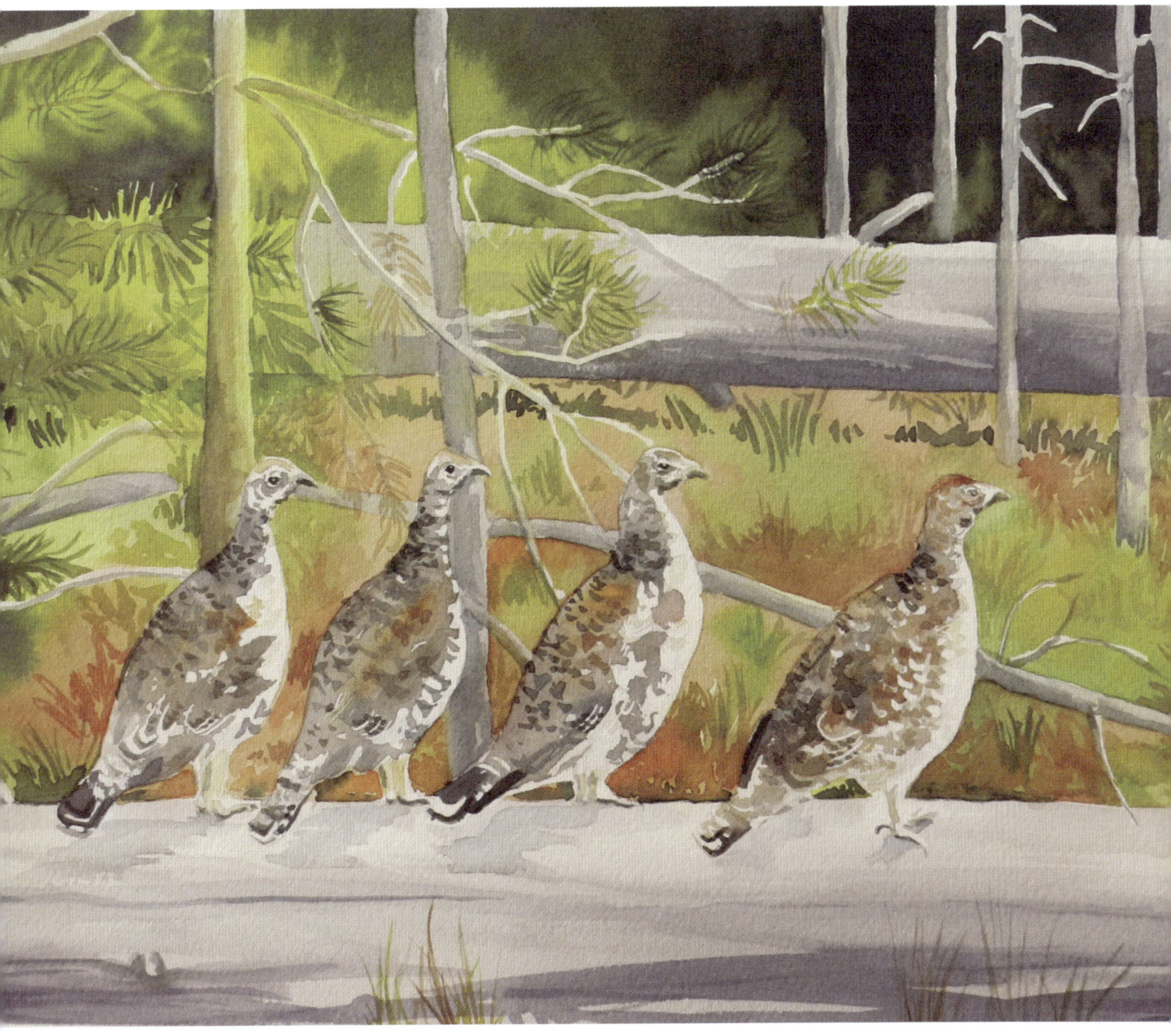

Ruffed grouse *(Bonasa umbellus)* • **WATERCOLOR**

This remarkable chorus line paused on a downed log above Mammoth Terraces in Yellowstone National Park. The landscape where the grouse live year-round is an open-canopy lodgepole pine and aspen forest adjacent to meadows, where the birds feed on clover, strawberries, and insects. When feeding out in the open, they're vulnerable to raptors, so the birds are well camouflaged, disappearing equally in a forest of small pines or on a sagebrush flat with ochres, grays, and golds. I chose warm neutral hues as the overall palette for this watercolor, a very subtle array of colors that the grouse evolved to blend into its surroundings.

Short-eared owl *(Asio flammeus)* • **WOODBLOCK PRINT, BLOCK PRINT**

The winter fields of the Skagit Valley in Washington support a number of short-eared owls. Fortunately for artists, photographers, and birdwatchers, those owls hunt by day. You can see them roosting in small trees as well as in flight. I took dozens of photos on one winter trip to the valley and interpreted them in watercolor sketches (see "The Beauty of Birds" in the Introduction) in my journal after I returned home.

I created the block print after seeing the owls' ear tufts erect. The tufts really have nothing to do with their ears, which are just behind the facial disc, around the level of their eyes. There are three hypotheses about the purpose of the "ear" feathers in eared and horned owls. One is that they frighten other predators by making the owl look like a mammal predator—for example, a lynx. But there aren't any of those predators in many of the owl's habitats. The second hypothesis is that the tufts give the owls a distinctive silhouette so that other members of their species can recognize them. Owls, however, generally identify one another by vocalizations. The final possibility is that the ear tufts serve as camouflage when the owls perceive approaching danger—the tufts help them look more like broken branches. This is the most likely explanation and perhaps why the block print worked: the jagged edges of the winter tree looked quite a bit like the owl markings, as did the ear feathers. It amazes me how many times I've discovered a botanical or ornithological truth by making art. I've seen the owl tufts erect only a couple of times, and both times, I was approaching, possibly alarming the owl. Even the camera's zoom was a little too close for the owl's comfort. Though field guides show these owls with tufts, it's more likely you'll see them as I usually do, with their ear feathers lowered or barely visible.

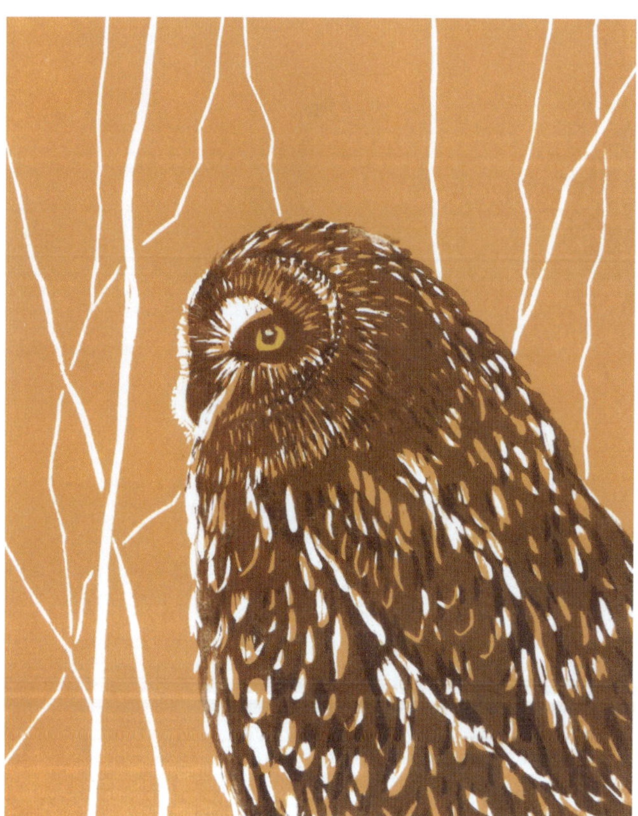

To create the woodblock print, which is made with oil-based inks, I carved three blocks. The first block was printed in a gold/sienna mixture; only the whites were carved out. The second block also carved out the whites and left in relief the medium-hued feathers on the owl. The third block carved out everything except the darkest feathers. When printing with oil, it's not necessary to let the inks dry; I printed each of the blocks within minutes of one another.

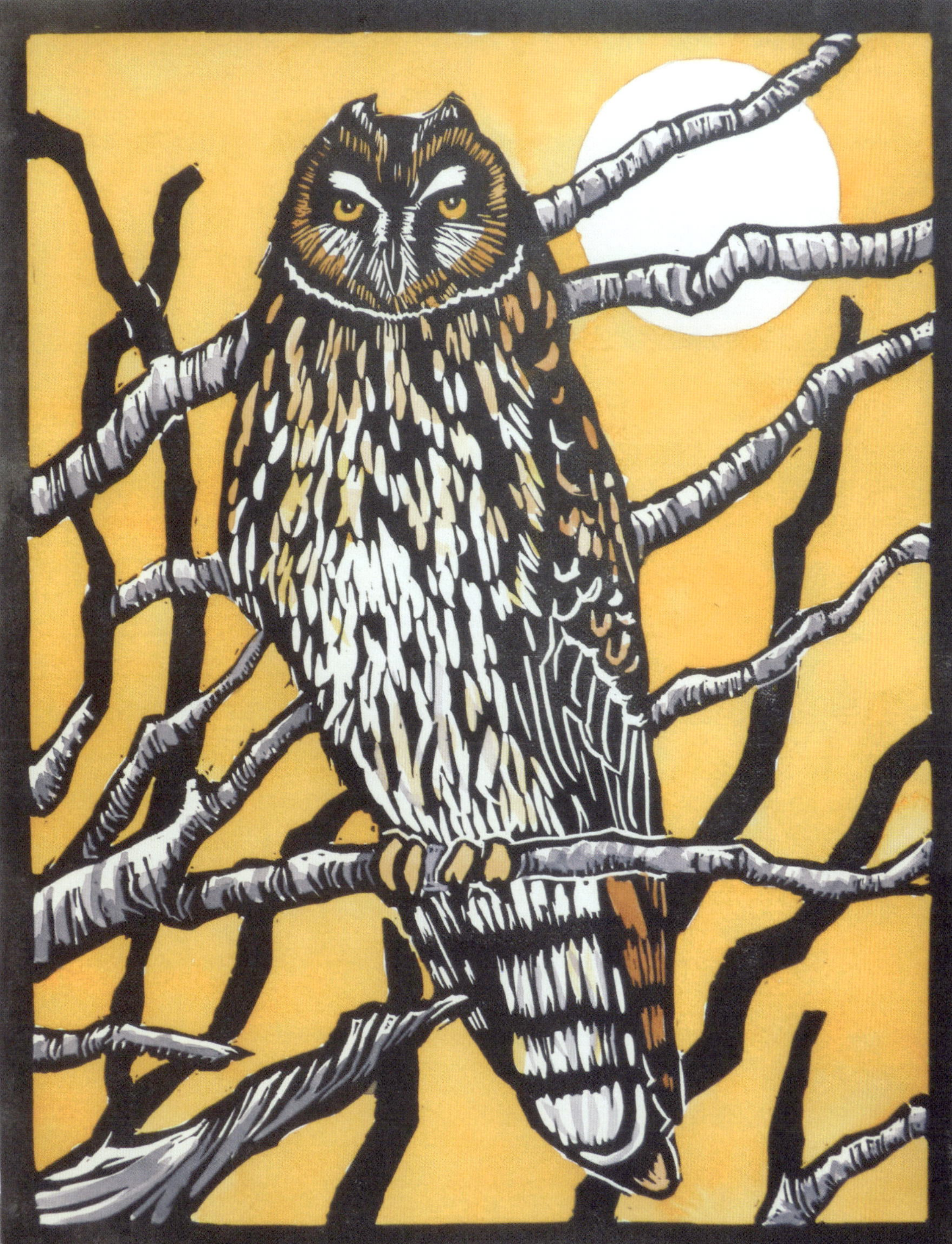

Feathers PENCIL SKETCH, WATERCOLOR

And in the meantime, I must stop writing, because I've to draw a peacock's breast-feather, and paint as much of it as I can without having heaven to dip my brush in.

—**John Ruskin,** *Fors Clavigera*

Feathers are among the most elaborate and efficient appendages to the vertebrate body, much more intricate than mammal fur or fish scales. They perform so many functions, allowing for flight, insulation, waterproofing, camouflage, and sexual ornamentation.

A feather has several parts, beginning with the base of the stem, which is known as the quill, or calamus. Emerging from the quill a short distance from the base are the vanes, or web, comprised of interconnecting barbs that have small hooks, called barbicels, that interlock with each other, keeping the feathers in top condition. A bird uses its beak to preen, which allows it to reestablish the all-important meshing of vanes. If you've ever picked up a slightly damaged feather, you've discovered that you can pull the vanes through your fingers and neaten the feather, which is just what birds do. Farther along on the stem, the quill is called the shaft, or rachis.

There are a number of types of feathers. Down feathers are soft and fluffy and may lack the shaft altogether. They are close to the bird's body and help to keep it warm. Next come semiplume feathers, which serve to further insulate the bird as well as give shape to its body so that contour feathers—the ones most

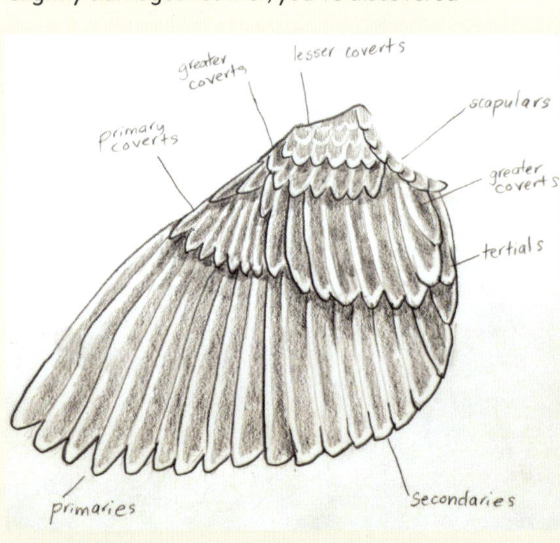

WING FEATHERS

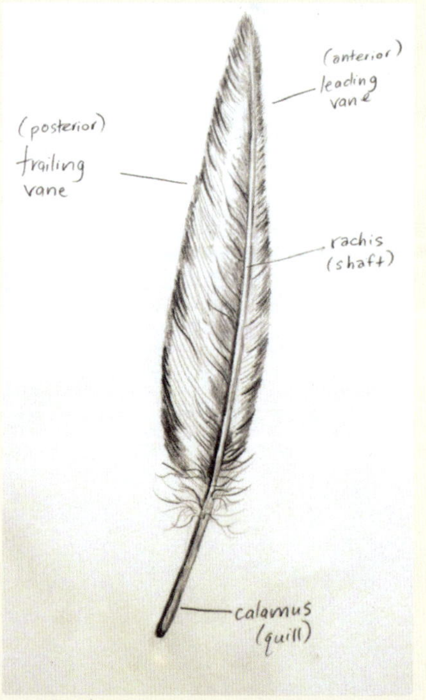

PARTS OF A FEATHER

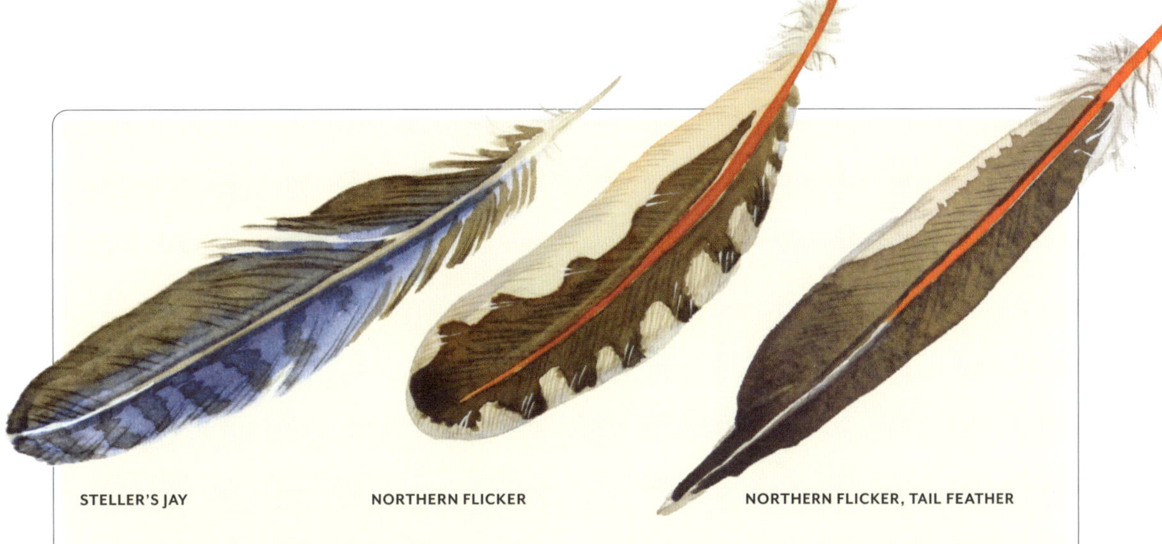

STELLER'S JAY NORTHERN FLICKER NORTHERN FLICKER, TAIL FEATHER

of us recognize—have a solid base on which to lie. Contour feathers are complete with shaft and vanes and include the flight feathers.

There are two types of flight feathers: the primaries, attached to the bird's skeleton in a place that would correspond to the human hand, and secondaries, corresponding to the human forearm. There are also flight feathers on the tail. A smaller set of feathers, called coverts, cover the area akin to our shoulders and also sit at the base of the tail feathers and underside.

Feather color is one of the most interesting aspects of birds to me as an artist. Thor Hanson's book *Feathers* explains: " . . . sexual selection and female choice have played a powerful role in the evolution of showy displays . . . Over time, feathers responded with two main strategies: pigment-based colors and structural colors." Pigment-based colors are created either in the cells of the birds or through diet. Think of flamingos—if they're deprived of their diet of beta-carotene-rich crustaceans, they turn white. The way that we (and birds) perceive color is based on absorption: when light strikes a feather of a certain hue, all the other colors are absorbed and only the specific hue is reflected back to our eyes. If all the colors are reflected we see white, and if all are absorbed we see black.

Structural colors are quite different; they're iridescent and appear in the dazzling ruby sheen of a hummingbird throat or the incomparable sparkling blue of a jay's wing and tail. The structural colors we see rely not on absorption, but on the scattering of light. You'll understand this if you've ever noticed that a hummingbird's throat doesn't sparkle in all angles of light—the bird has to be positioned in order that the light hits its feathers just so. For structural colors, Hanson writes: "the whole spectrum is reflected back from the feather surface by nanoscale features built into the keratin." (Keratin is the protein that is the main component of the feather cell.) Compare the watercolor of the northern flicker feather to the Steller's jay feather. I used an orange and a sienna paint for the rich rust hues of the flicker feather shaft. I chose cobalt blue paint for the Steller's jay but then brushed on a thin wash of iridescent electric blue. The iridescent paint includes tiny mica particles with a small amount of titanium white to give them body; the mica particles sparkle and scatter light in the same way the cells in the Steller's feather do.

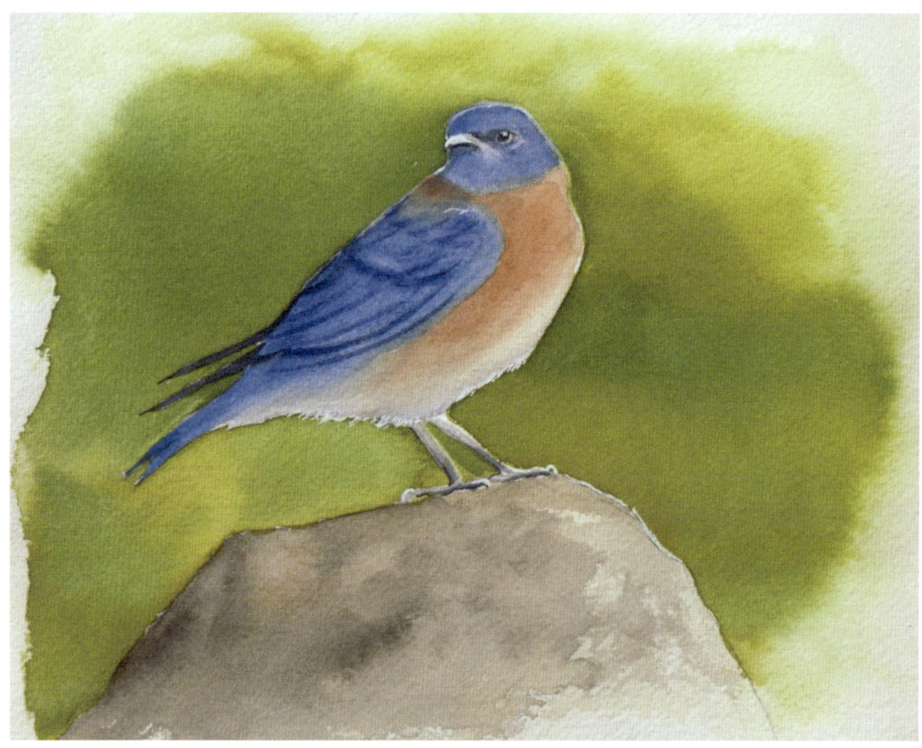

Western bluebird *(Sialia mexicana)* • **WATERCOLOR SKETCH**

Western bluebirds are uncommon west of the Cascades. I've been lucky enough to see bluebirds on the Upper Missouri in Montana and in south central Oregon, just outside Klamath Falls, as well as in Yellowstone National Park. Bluebird enthusiasts have placed nest boxes along bluebird migration paths in the West as well as in other parts of the country, so the birds are very easy to find in those areas. This bluebird was perched on a granite boulder beside a meadow in southeast Oregon. I had to mix several blues to achieve the right intense blue: cobalt blue, one of the purest primary blues; phthalo blue red shade, a blue with a hint of red; and verditer blue, which has a tiny bit of titanium white in it—the combination making for a very saturated color.

American kestrel *(Falco sparverius)* • **BLOCK PRINT**

Kestrels are small falcons that hunt for rodents, birds, and insects and are commonly seen along the edges of meadows and farm fields. They're found year-round throughout the continental United States. In summer, their range extends to Canada and Alaska; in winter, they can also be found in Mexico. When they're breeding, the male does all the hunting and brings the food back to the nest. Both the male and female have dramatic colorful markings, which I attempted to distinguish in my carving and tinting of this block print. The female is on the left and is more russet-colored. The male is pictured on the right and is distinguished by his blue-gray wing and black-spotted breast.

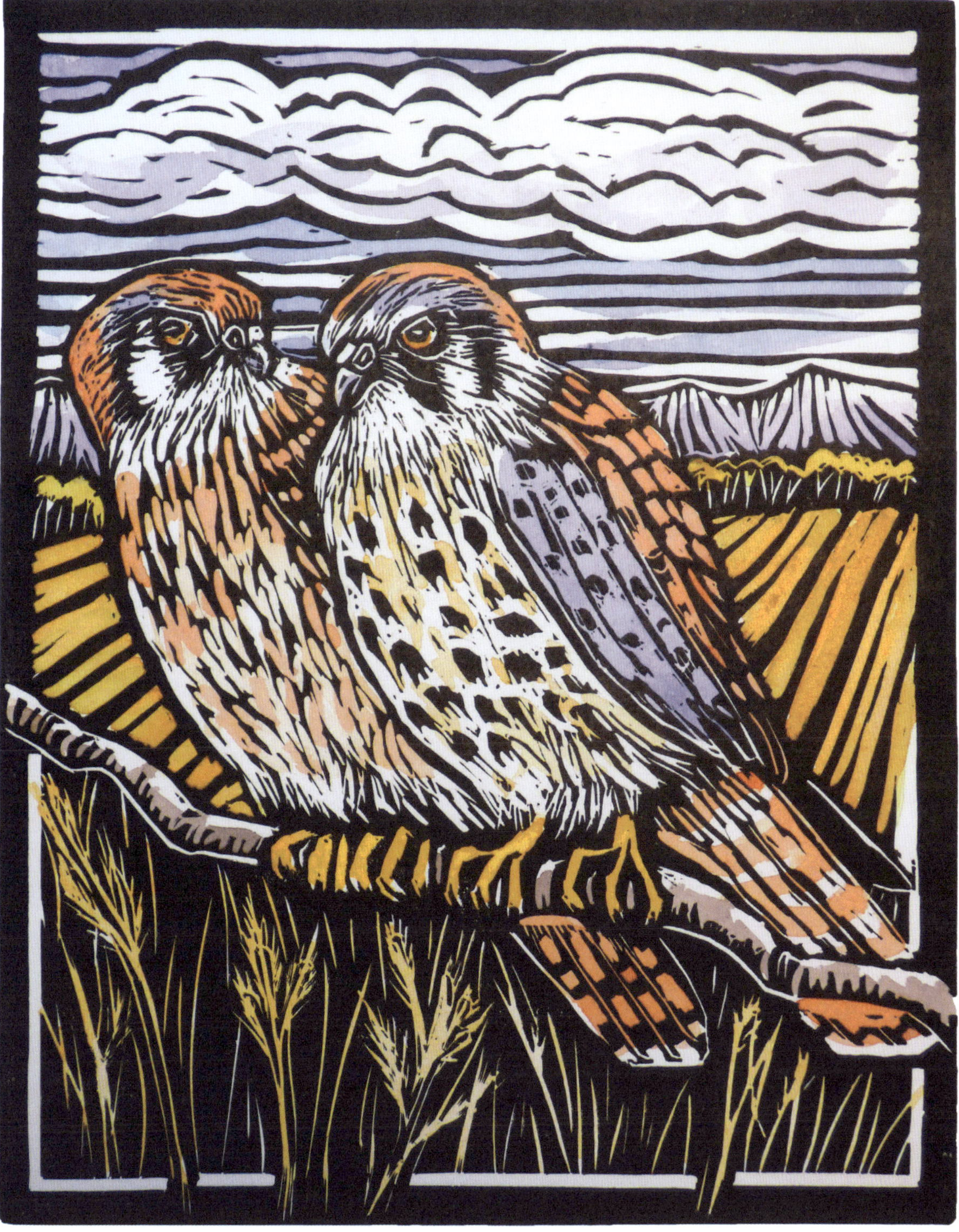

Wings WATERCOLOR

I borrowed a magpie wing from Seattle Audubon, which shares specimens with the Burke Museum of Natural History and Culture at the University of Washington. Audubon often acquires birds and bird parts from people who find them after birds have been hit by cars, killed by window strikes or feline predation, or died of natural causes. The federal Migratory Bird Treaty Act of 1918 makes it illegal for anyone to own these with the exception of organizations and institutions that have a waiver for educational purposes.

Of course, all wings keep birds aloft, but different wing types help different species in their specific environments. The four basic wing types are categorized by aspect ratio, which refers to the ratio of a wing's length to its width. The length divided by the width yields the ratio, either a low or a high number.

Low-aspect-ratio elliptical wings: These short, stubby wings are common to game birds and passerine (songbird) species, which live in brushy, shrubby environments and need a lot of maneuverability.

High-aspect-ratio wings: These long, slim wings are suited to birds, such as the albatross, that make gliding flights of great length. These birds are very clumsy on takeoff, and quick movements are all but impossible, but once aloft, they have remarkable lift.

High-speed wings: Very long, angled, and narrow with a boomerang shape, these wings suit birds, such as falcons, terns, and sandpipers, that need to make dramatic rapid dives. Peregrine falcons have been measured at speeds up to 200 miles per hour.

Slotted high-lift wings: Also known as soaring wings, these are equipped with long, fingerlike feathers that can separate from one another in flight and allow for reduced air pressure

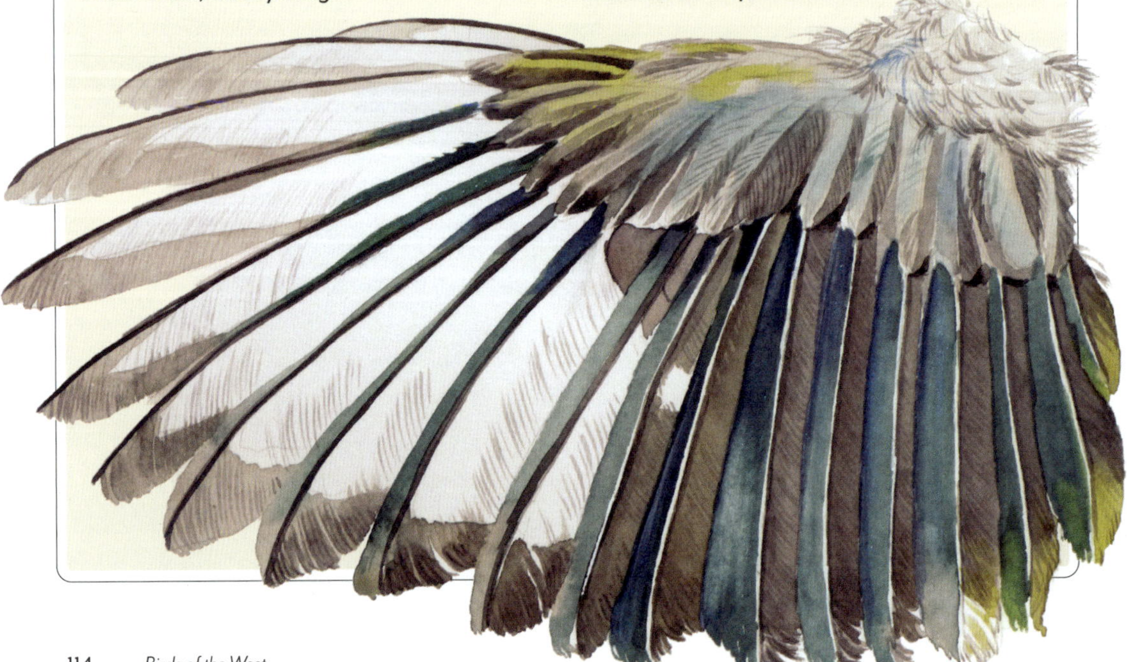

and lessened wind resistance. Such wings are found on eagles, many hawks, and some owls. You'll recognize this wing type if you've ever looked up and seen one of the larger hawks or an eagle soaring above you—you can see the individual feathers at the tips of the wings (see the red-tailed hawk in "Desert & Sagebrush Steppe").

Tree swallow *(Tachycineta bicolor)* · **BLOCK PRINT**

Tree swallows are occasionally found in grasslands. I saw this pair in a ponderosa pine in south central Oregon, in between wild flights of twisting, turning maneuvers about fifty feet above a nearby meadow. It's likely their nest was close by, since tree swallows build nests in tree cavities, often making use of holes excavated by woodpeckers. The rust-colored ponderosa pine contrasted sharply with the birds' azure-tinted plumage; studying a color wheel (see the Introduction), you'd see that these hues are near complements of each other, which creates an energetic color dynamic.

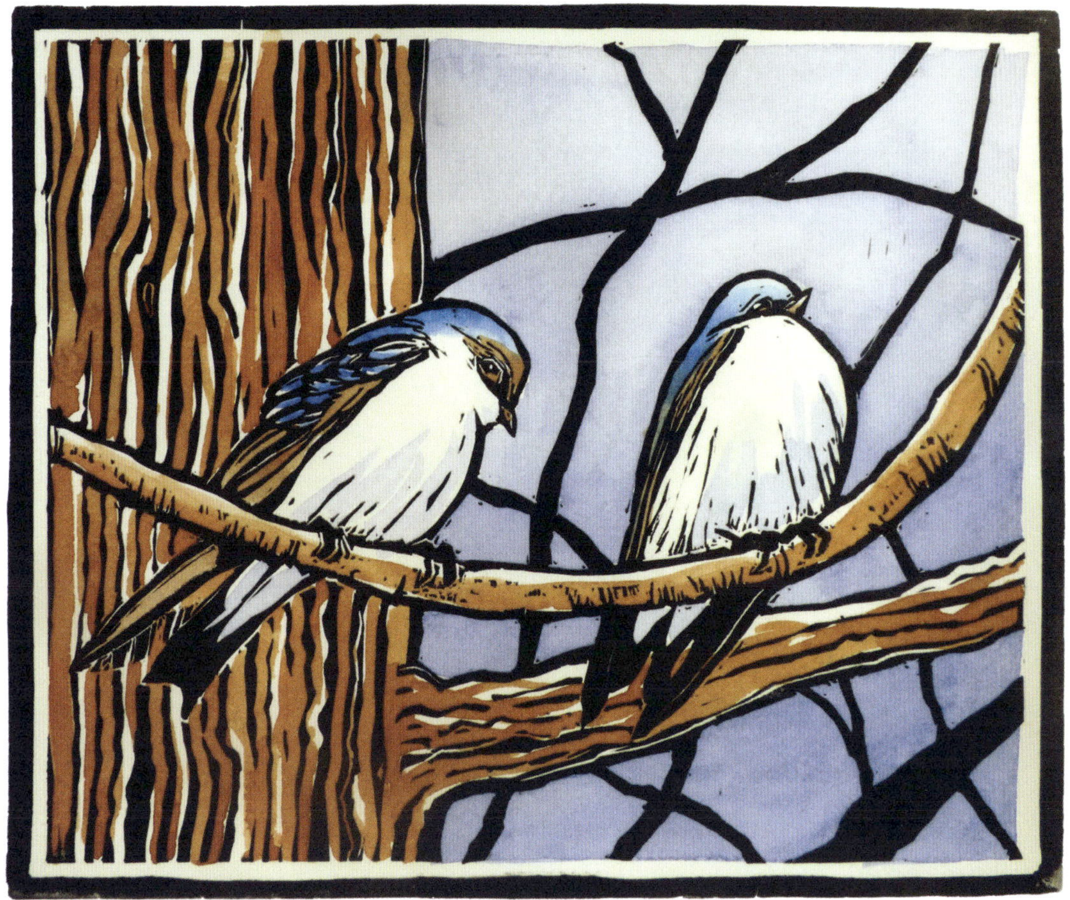

TECHNIQUE

Using Brush Pens

The bridled titmouse (*Baeolophus wollweberi*) lives in oak woodlands and grassy savannas in the dry country of Arizona and western Mexico, where it feeds on insects, insect eggs, and larvae. To create this sketch on toned paper, I used several brush pens, which are much like other felt-tip pens except that the tips are softer, yielding both thick and thin lines, depending on how you angle the pen and the amount of pressure you apply. I also used a bit of permanent white gouache paint and let the gray paper serve as the tone for the tree trunks and gray on the bird. I used dark brush pens for the bridle and crest and a white pen for the light-struck edges of trees, the crest, the white face markings, and the small feathers that protrude from the perimeter of the body. The brush pens keep sketching methods loose and playful and are easy to take out in the field since you don't need water to use them.

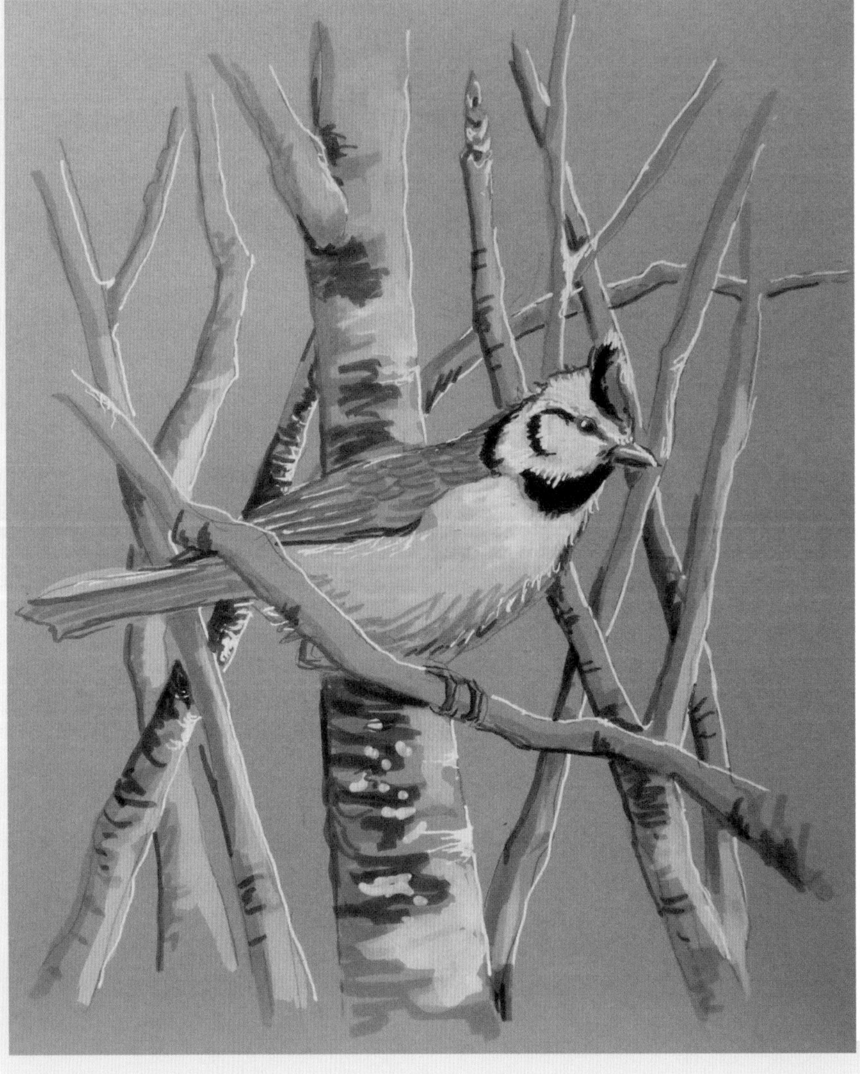

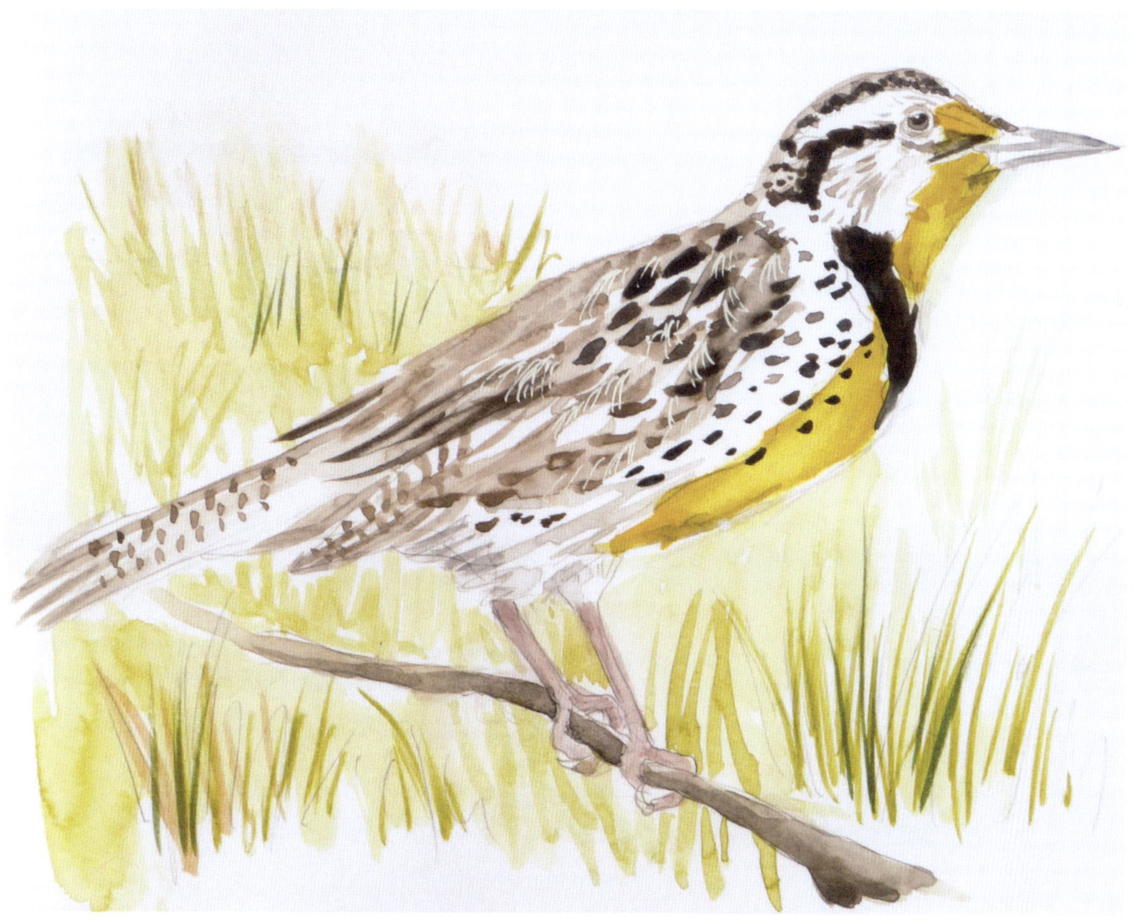

Western meadowlark *(Sturnella neglecta)* · **WATERCOLOR SKETCH**

The western meadowlark inhabits grasslands and farm fields. It builds its grass nests in existing or scraped depressions in the ground. Unfortunately, mowing fields often destroys the birds' nests. Their song is a series of notes that accelerate toward the end of the phrase and has a beautiful flutelike timbre. Listening to meadowlarks reminds me of a popular piece of music by Ralph Vaughan Williams, "The Lark Ascending," in which a solo violin follows the ascending line of a lark's song, accompanied by an orchestra. There were two meadowlarks performing a duet on boulders about fifty yards distant from each other when I walked along the trail at the Horse Lake Reserve near Wenatchee, Washington, one April morning. They flew off when I approached, leaving me in disappointed silence.

To the Scrub Jay on My Office Mate's Desk

As if you know what you're doing
you flick through the window
and here you are, brighter blue
than I've ever seen you in sun,
at ease and cocking your head
as if born for the company
of Kent's papers and cups.
I'll be late for class, stout-bill,
but I have to know why you flew in
to this fluorescent cave
from the air of a fine spring day,
and what's on your mind
as you hop past the stapler—

—and how I can keep you
from the half-open door
just a wing-lift away.
Don't do it, bird.
I can just see you
lost in the halls, slapping
the ceiling tiles, glancing
off dim painted walls,
careening into my class
with your croaking panic
and dodging the startled faces,
flapping and clawing, grazing
the blackboard, finally thrashing
your chalk-smeared feathers
against the window, crazy
for the blue afternoon . . .
That might arouse their interest.

But you have better sense.
With a flex of your legs,
a brush of air on my cheek,
you leave as you came. You're
out where you should be.
I'm left with the half-open door.

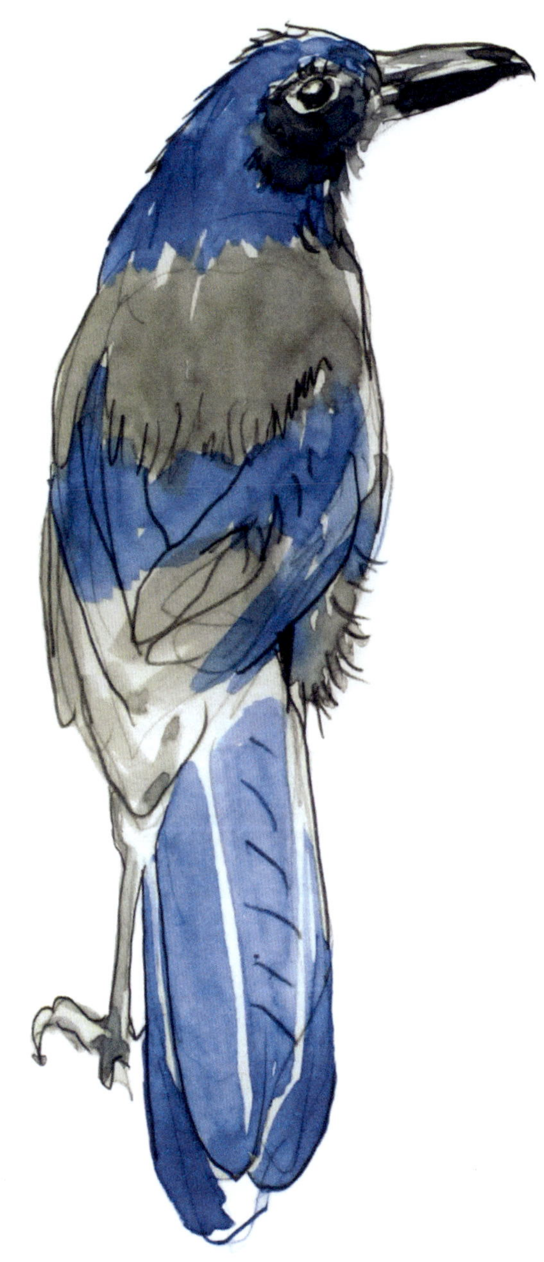

—**John Daniel,** *Of Earth: New and Selected Poems*

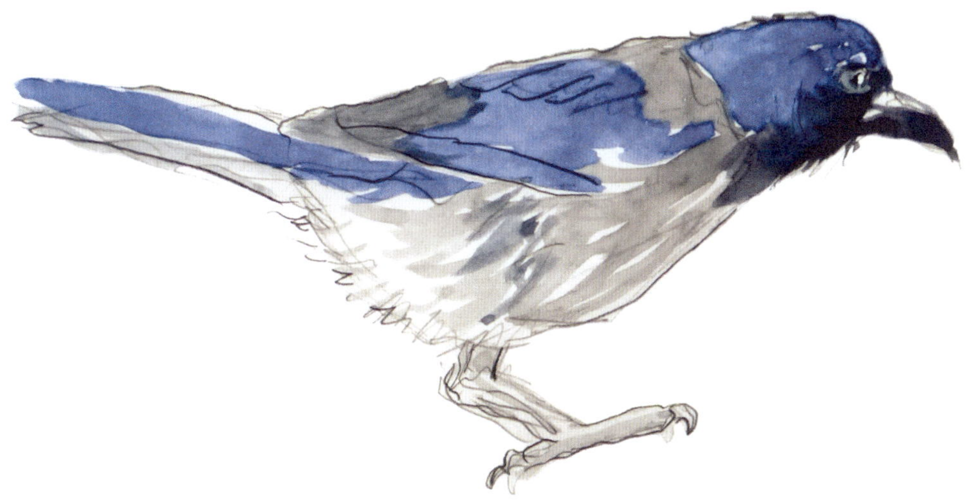

Western scrub-jay *(Aphelocoma californica)* · **WATERCOLOR SKETCH**

I observed these scrub-jays in central Oregon in a wet meadow near the Deschutes River. Their curiosity was obvious in their head movements as they cocked their heads from left to right. I thought the sketch medium captured some of that inquisitive personality. Scrub-jays are members of the corvid group, which includes ravens, crows, magpies, nutcrackers, and all of the jays; they're an especially intelligent, vocal, and social family of birds. After drawing in pencil, painting a bright blue mix of cobalt and phthalo blue red shade watercolors, along with a few areas of dark grays and blacks, helped to animate the sketches.

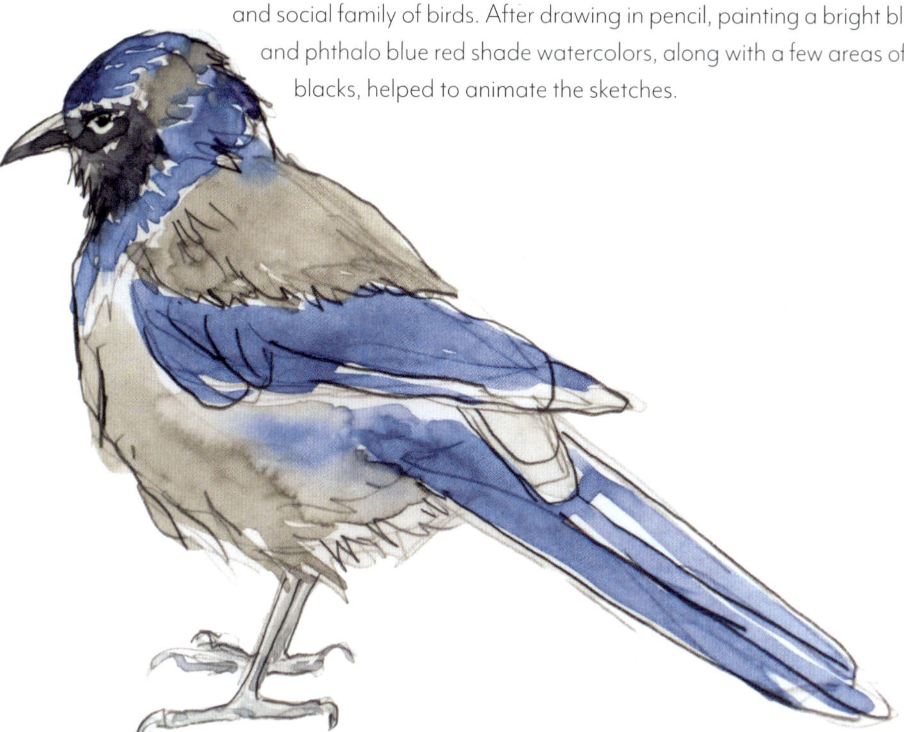

Lewis's woodpecker *(Melanerpes lewis)* • **BLOCK PRINT**

Lewis's woodpeckers can be found in the oak savannas that grow on the eastern side of the Cascade Range and in a few places in western Washington. The oaks live on steep south- and west-facing slopes and grow in shrubby formations of multiple trunks; occasionally, in flatter bowls, you'll see a mature specimen, the classic oak shape with a robust trunk and rounded crown filled out with many large branches. The larger and the older oak trees lose limbs, and the scars that are exposed make very good cavity nesting for both Lewis's and acorn woodpeckers. More than half the bird species found in oak groves are cavity nesters, and Lewis's woodpeckers depend on acorns for their survival in winter.

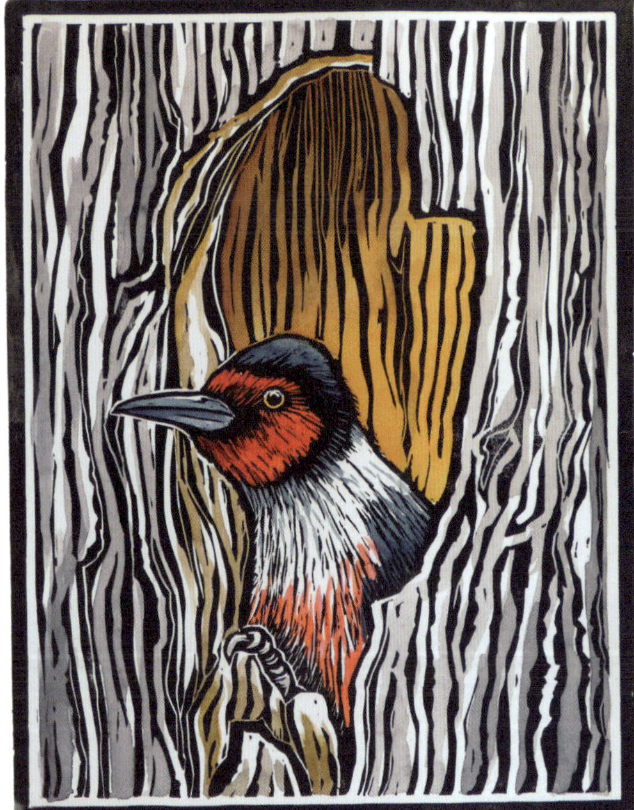

For this block print, I worked with two photos of the woodpecker that my friend Glenn, who lives in eastern British Columbia, shared with me: one showed the entire bird on the trunk of an oak, and the other showed it peering out from the tree's cavity. Although I liked the pose of the bird on the trunk, I thought its head peeking out from the hole was more lively and interesting.

Acorn woodpecker *(Melanerpes formicivorus)* • **WATERCOLOR**

Acorn woodpeckers roost and nest communally; there may be as many as fifteen birds in a colony. All of the birds tend the young, even ones that aren't parents. The woodpeckers store acorns in the holes they drill in tree trunks and branches. These trees are called granaries, can hold up to 50,000 nuts, and have been observed in use for up to fifty years. The acorn woodpecker's range extends from the Oregon Cascades south through California's Sierra Nevada and into the Huachuca Mountains of Arizona. In winter they migrate to Mexico's Sierra Madre.

The acorn woodpecker's markings are often described as "clownlike" in field guides, and the intense contrast and color would certainly make for a good block print. But I decided to try the birds first in watercolor, situating them in a leafing oak tree. I wanted to place the birds in a tree that was important to them, a choice I often make when painting a more fully realized watercolor as opposed to a quick sketch.

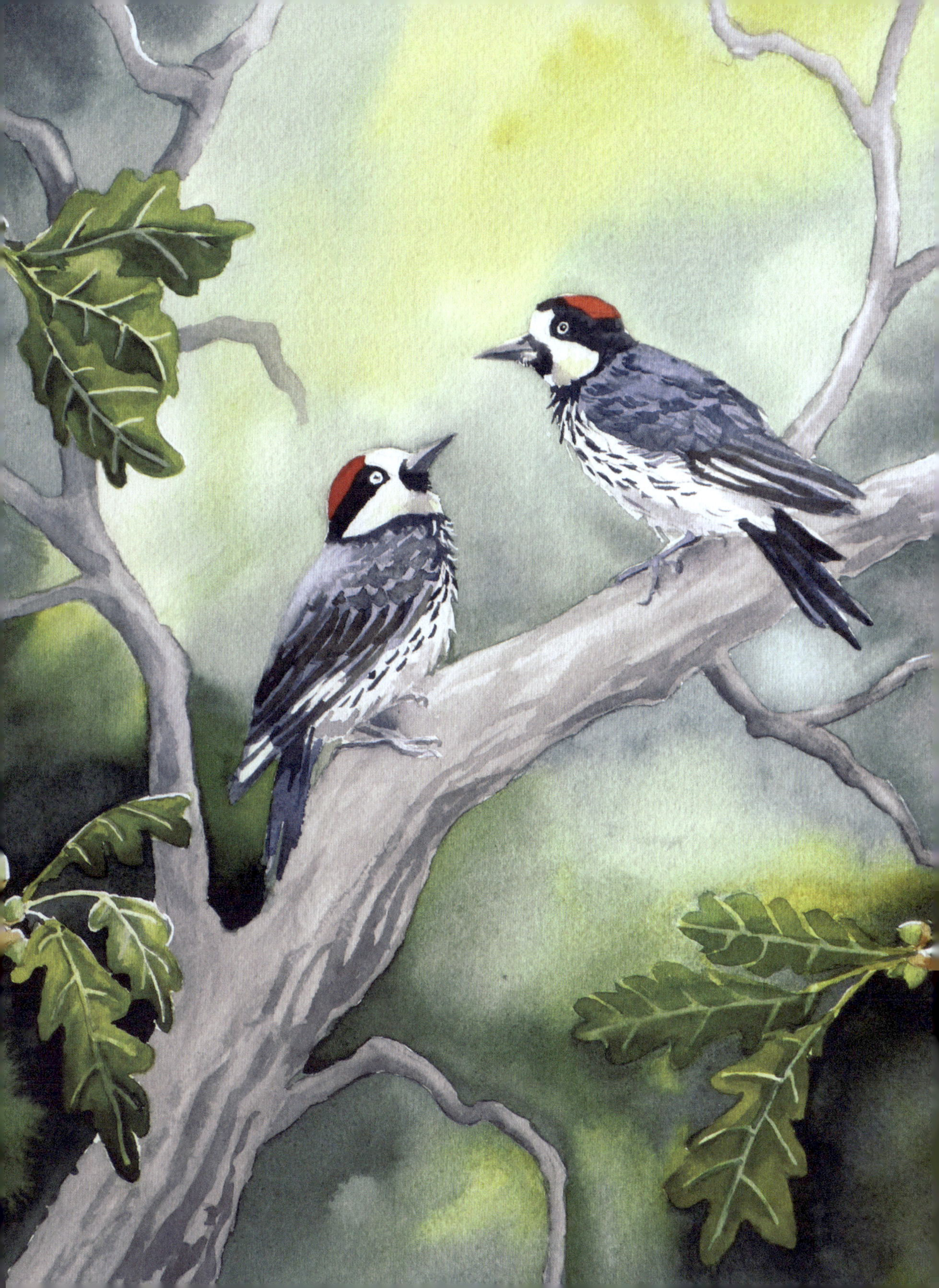

TECHNIQUE

Saving Whites on a Watercolor with Masking Fluid

The song sparrow (*Melospiza melodia*) was perched on some very tall grasses in the open meadow of Union Bay Natural Area, alternately feeding and singing. Back in my studio, when I drew this encounter, I saved the whites of the feathers, as well as the ring around the eye, by applying masking fluid after I'd sketched the bird in pencil. Masking fluid is also known as frisket; it's fluid when applied but dries like rubber cement, allowing you to protect areas that you don't want to paint when working in watercolor. Wherever you want precise areas of white or light hues, it's the easiest way to preserve them. In acrylics and oils you often begin with dark and medium values and finish with your light values by painting with white and light-hued colors. It's the opposite in watercolor, so you really have to do some planning when working on a painting with a lot of white

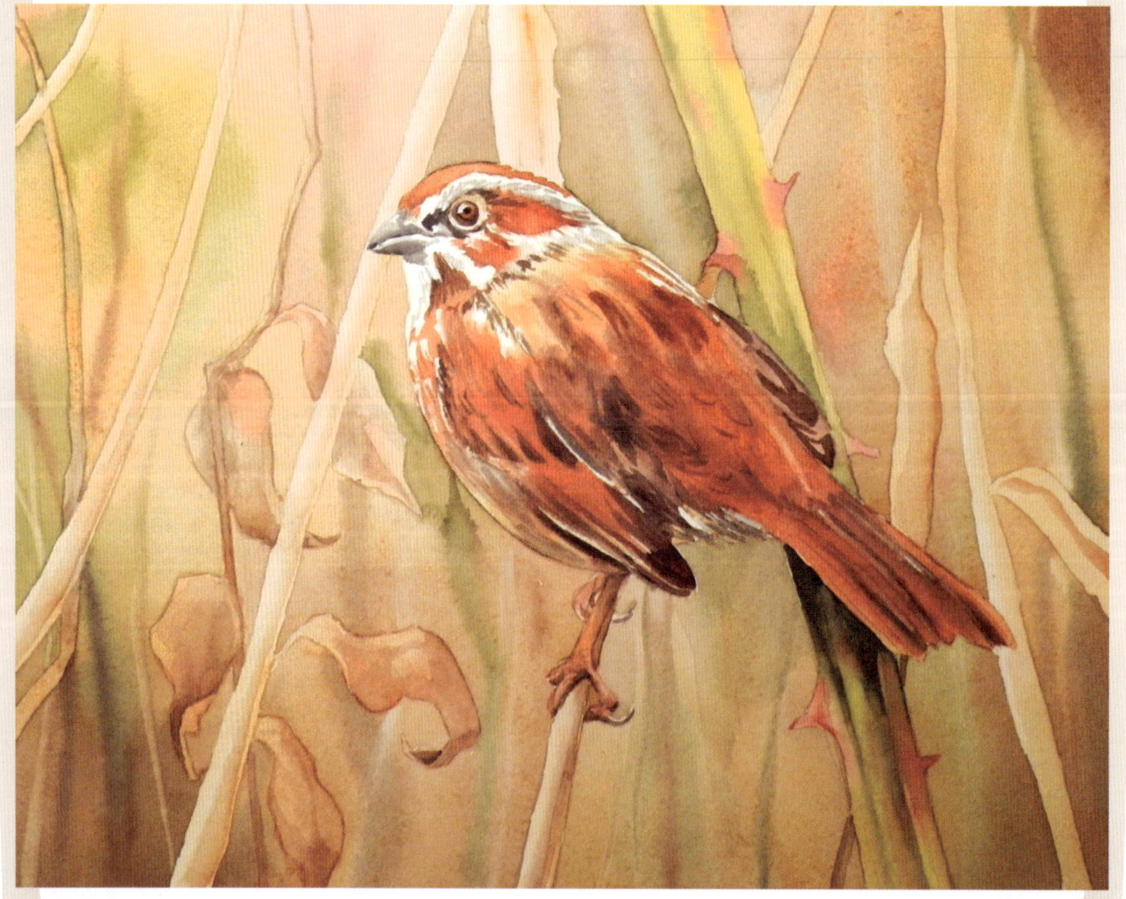

and light areas. Using masking fluid is part of that planning process. It's definitely a studio technique; I never use it outdoors.

Once you've applied the masking fluid, leave it in place; next paint the lightest colors and gradually build up to the darkest darks. Once the watercolor wash is dry, the masking fluid is removed by rubbing with either a clean eraser or a tool called a rubber cement pick-up—a very small plastic square that acts like a sticky magnet. At that point the white of the paper is exposed. You can also use masking fluid to preserve a light-colored grass. First you paint that light color; then apply masking fluid to the areas that you want to remain light, and next paint the darker hues.

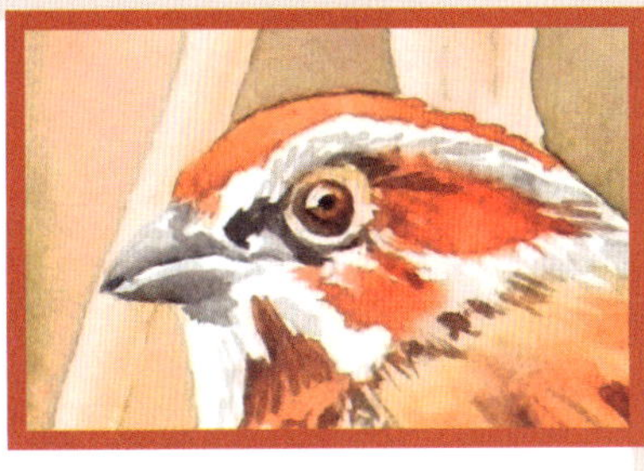

I once had a sparrow alight upon my shoulder for a moment, while I was hoeing in a village garden, and I felt that I was more distinguished by that circumstance than I should have been by any epaulet I could have worn.

—**Henry David Thoreau,** *Walden*

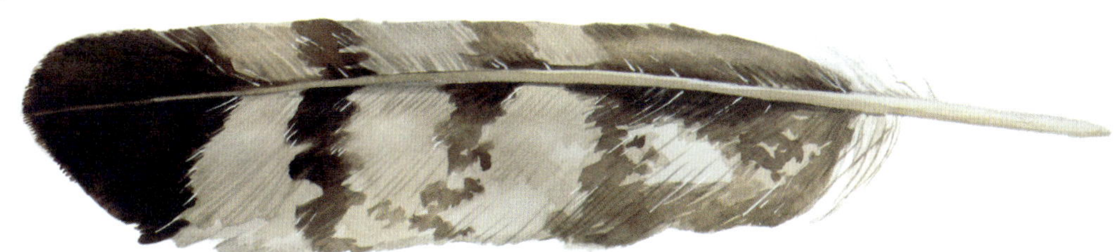

. . . feathers are a symbol of power, of aspiration and the ability to transcend (or escape from) material reality.

—**John Berger,** "Mathias Grünewald"

Desert & Sagebrush Steppe

badland

wilderness

barren

dune

lava bed

heath

artemisia

sagebrush

juniper

ponderosa pine

bitterbrush

rabbitbrush

buckwheat

desert parsley

wild onion

greasewood

saltbush

prickly pear

hedgehog cactus

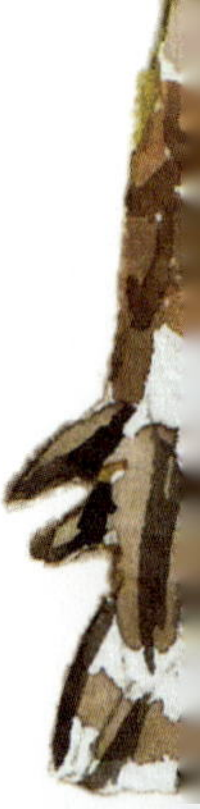

What draws us into the desert is the search for something intimate in the remote.

—Edward Abbey, *A Voice Crying in the Wilderness*

Above the desert, a golden eagle soars, riding the updrafts of dry mountain slopes. Dun-colored sage thrashers and curve-billed thrashers all but disappear into the surrounding brush and dust. A roadrunner raises his head feathers and tail as he speeds along, summoning memories of the cartoon hero—no amount of cunning and firepower will vanquish him!

Most of my desert bird sightings have been in western sagebrush country, which includes the sagebrush steppe and the Great Basin sagebrush desert in Nevada, northeastern California, eastern Oregon and Washington, southern Idaho, southwestern Montana, much of Utah, western Wyoming, and the foothills and valleys of northwestern Colorado.

There are several types of sagebrush steppe, including the lithosol (meaning "rock soil") zone, found primarily atop basalt, a dark volcanic rock. Then there are sandy or dune areas, talus areas, and meadow zones, where drainage in low depressions creates meadows that are wet year-round. These serve as oases for resident wildlife. Finally, there is the saline zone, where calcium carbonates released from rocks create very alkaline soil. Only a few plants are happy here—among them, hop sage, winter fat, and greasewood. Within the larger geographic perimeter of the very widespread sagebrush steppe community there are variations. In the north, in Washington, Oregon, and Idaho, you'll find Douglas fir and ponderosa pine along with *Artemisia tridentate*, the tall sagebrush. Farther south, in the foothills and higher elevations, oaks and junipers and pinyon pines grow. As the steppe stretches southward into the Mojave Desert, plant life becomes more sparse, and saltbush is dominant. In desert country, many animals, including birds, rely on camouflage. To find them, look in the early-morning hours and evening; at other times of day they're not visible, as they lie low to avoid the heat.

The landscape, at first glance, might seem sparse. Ronald J. Taylor, in his book *Sagebrush Country*, describes it perfectly: "To many people sagebrush country is a wasteland, a dusty world of sand and tumbleweeds separating the scattered towns of the West that represent civilization . . . Yet, real beauty exists here for those who seek it, beauty expressed in colorful spring and fall flowers and more subtly in the wondrous adaptations that enable plants and animals to withstand the extremes so typical of the sagebrush steppe."

I've also created art about a few birds of the Sonoran Desert ecosystem, which is found in California, Arizona, and northwestern Mexico. Plant life there includes more than 300 species of cactus, including organ pipe and saguaro, and other succulents such as yucca and agave. There is little or no frost in the Sonoran Desert, but on the upper end of the scale, it has some of the highest temperatures in North America.

In my work on desert birds, I've tried to celebrate the understated beauty of the sage and cactus dwellers and their environs, as well as the majesty of the birds of prey.

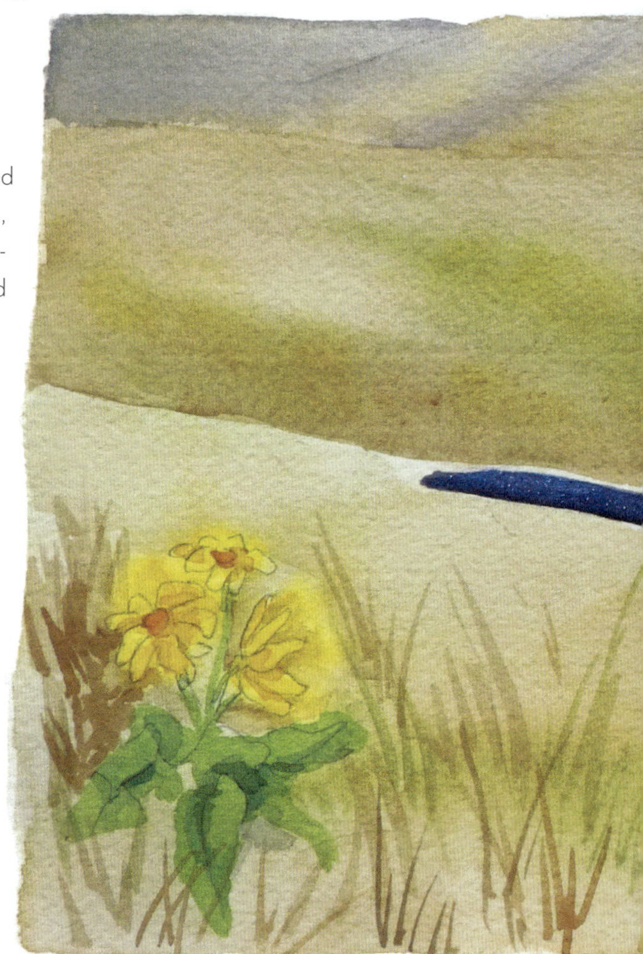

White-crowned sparrow *(Zonotri chia leucophrys)* · **PEN SKETCH**

An extremely wide-ranging bird, the white-crowned sparrow lives year-round in the Northwest, though many populations winter in the southwestern deserts. The birds feed on the ground and often make their nests there, too, as well as in low shrubs and trees. The textural quality of the dramatic markings made this bird an excellent subject for a pen sketch, which I began with various hues of brown. I completed the sketch using white pens for the white markings. A bird with a more widespread color, either uniform or gradated, would be a less obvious choice for pen work and would instead lend itself more readily to watercolor.

Black-billed magpie *(Pica hudsonia)* • WATERCOLOR SKETCH

Although you won't see the magpie on the western side of the Cascades, it lives throughout the West elsewhere. As you drive through the Columbia Basin Reclamation agricultural region in central Washington, you'll see magpies surveying the land on barbed wire fences everywhere. High above orchard country in Wenatchee, I watched this magpie strutting between sagebrush and arrowleaf balsamroot in gorgeous bloom in late April at Sage Hills, part of the Chelan-Douglas Land Trust preserve. Magpies feed mainly on the ground; like many corvids, they raid other birds' nests and don't scorn carrion or human picnics. I love the iridescence on their feathers, and here you see my attempt to express it using watercolors overlaid with iridescent and interference pigments, which belong to a group called luminescent colors, a group that also includes pearlescent paints. The colors don't always reproduce well, but when you see these painted areas in the original art, they sparkle because of the addition of titanium-coated mica particles to the basic watercolor hues in each of the paint types above. For an explanation of the physics of feather iridescence, see "Feathers" in "Meadow & Grassland."

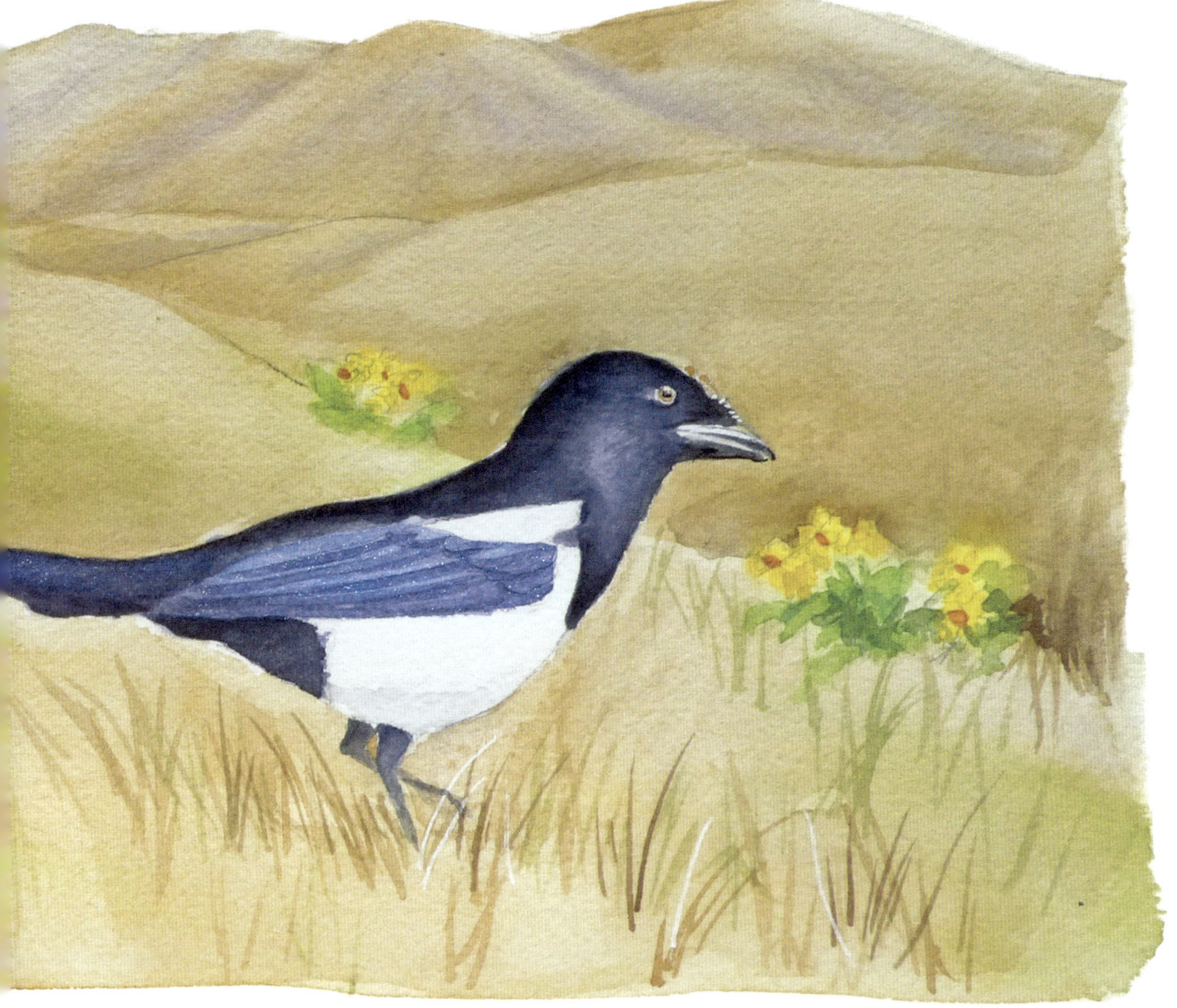

Cactus wren *(Campylorhynchus brunneicapillus)* • **WATERCOLOR**

At eight inches tall, the cactus wren is the largest in the wren family and doesn't cock its tail as others do. The female builds her nest in prickly pear, cholla, or yucca plants. You'll often see the wren perched atop a cactus in the desert Southwest, as I sketched it here.

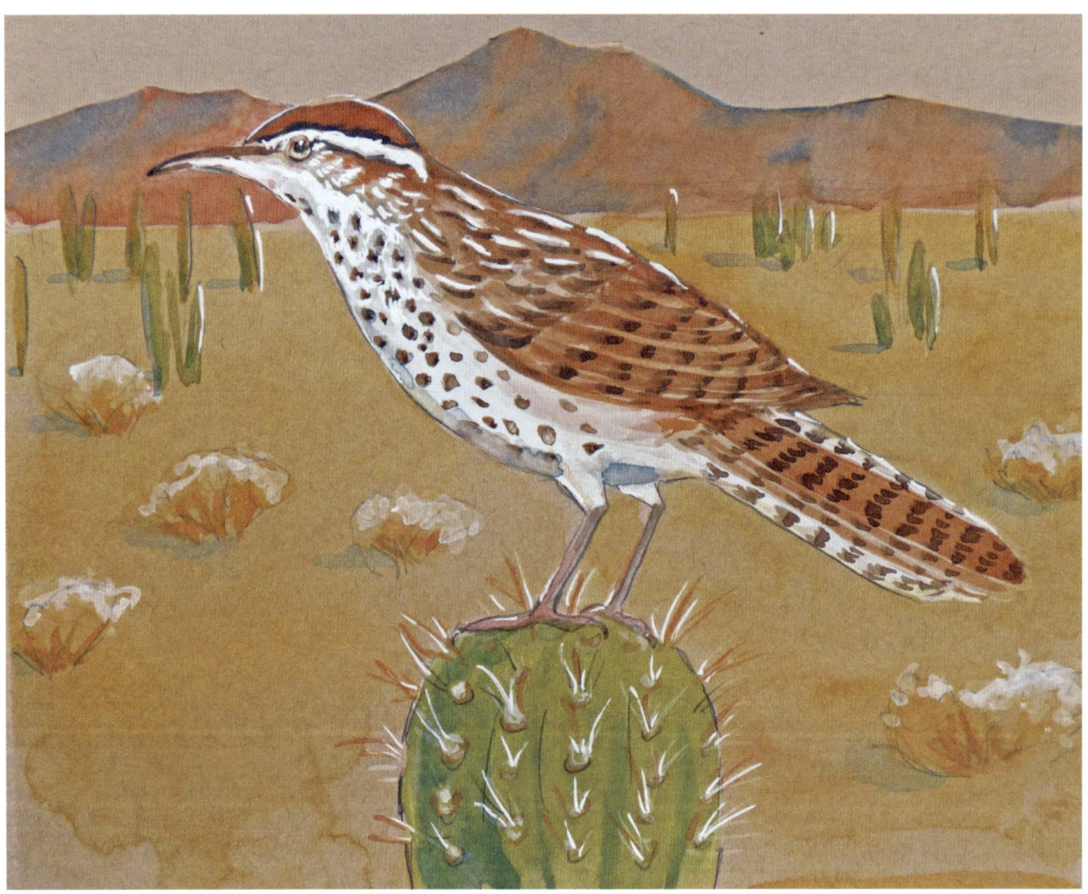

Chukar *(Alectoris chukar)* • **BLOCK PRINT**

The chukar is larger than the California quail (page 134)—up to fourteen inches long, as opposed to the quail's eleven inches. It's a species belonging to the partridge family and was introduced as a game bird to the American West from southern Eurasia in the 1930s. It's now widespread in southern Canada and the Great Basin. This bird was foraging in the snow in eastern Washington, and its colors harmonized with the golden grasses emerging here and there. I've included only this one introduced species in the book; the chukar has not posed much of a threat to other birds and seems here to stay, plus the pattern and its colors are irresistible to me.

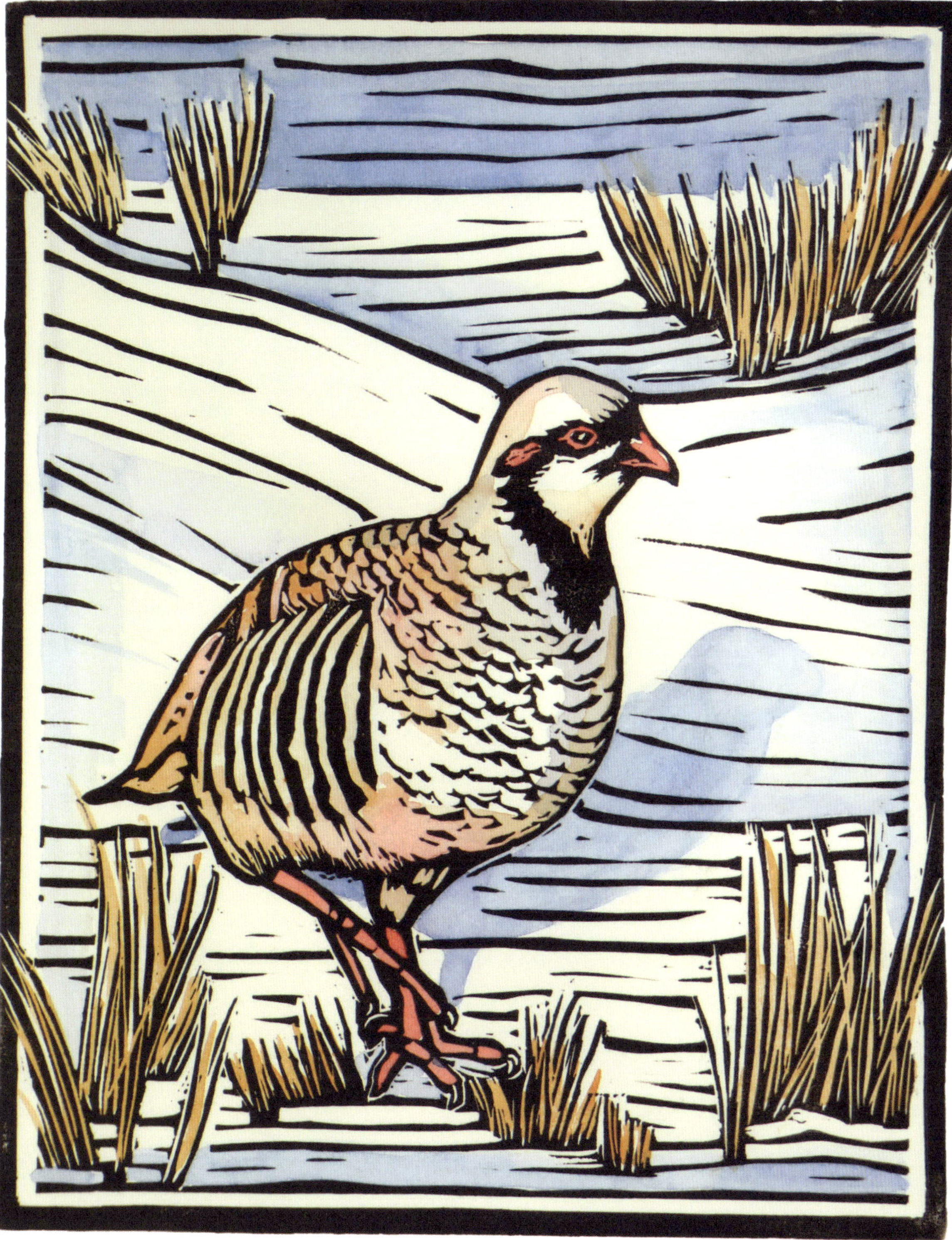

Stars

two black stars fall
through a deep daylight sky:
golden eagles
gripping talon to talon
tumbling in the hard blue

wings out like parachutes
flapping like rags
as the birds turn
upside down
right side up

heads down
they pull apart
before crashing
soar out over fir
pine trees

is it love
or murder
they fall for?

bronze brown feathers cool
in the summer evening
dust and smoke
blast out of the valley
wind scouring
the sage brush
blond grasses

the birds sail up
dots in the sky

—Ilona Popper

Poet's note: *It is rare for golden eagles to clasp talons and cartwheel, circling down or even hitting the ground.*

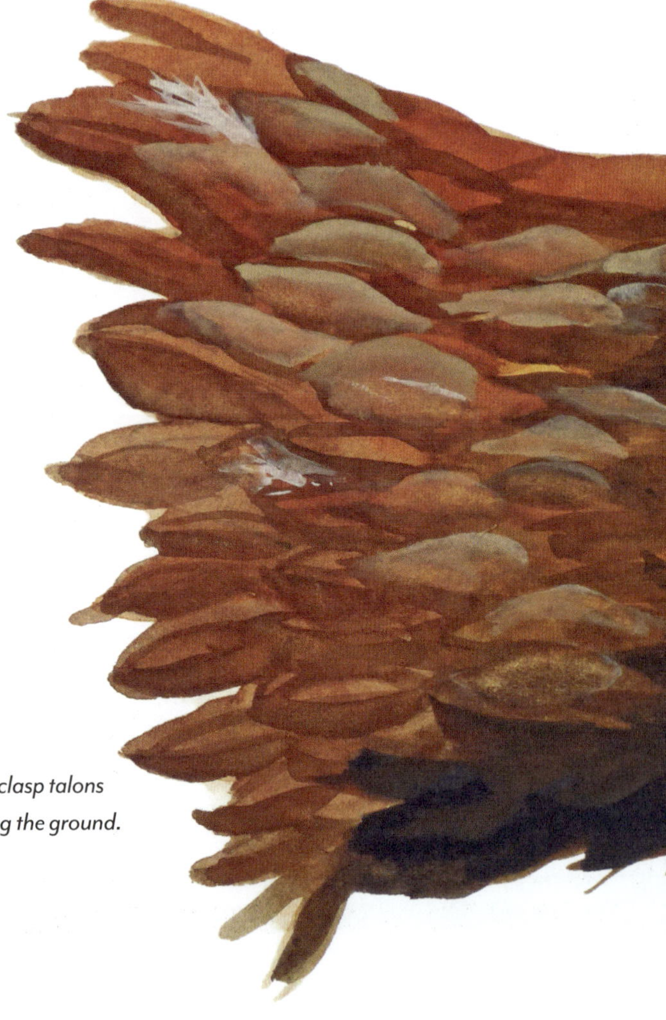

TECHNIQUE

Watercolor, White Gouache, Gum Arabic on Illustration Board

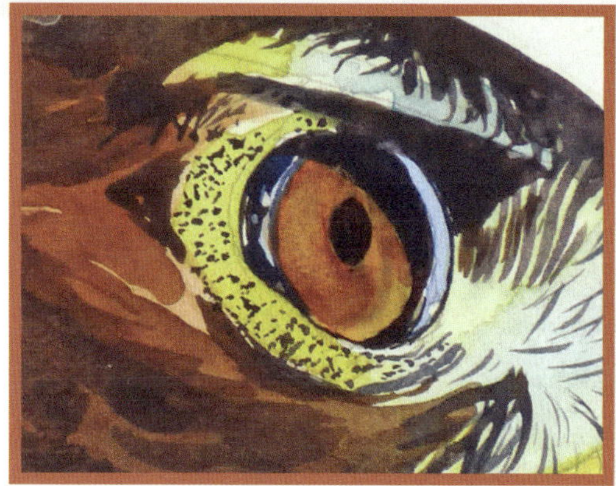

Because of their size and grandeur, eagles have been used throughout history as emblems of empire, notably by the Romans, the Austro-Hungarians, the Napoleonic French, and of course the United States of America.

The golden eagle (*Aquila chrysaetos*) pictured here is a portrait head that I sketched on heavyweight illustration board, which is a hot press watercolor paper bonded to a thick poster board. The slick surface has no texture, so there is no resistance when you apply fine brushstrokes. For the eagle, I used both watercolor and gouache, which makes the process more like painting in acrylics or oils. You can start with darker watercolors and then mix some watercolor paint with white gouache (once you add white to any watercolor, it technically becomes gouache) and apply lighter feathers on top, as I did on the neck feathers of the eagle. On the eye, I attempted a technique favored by Audubon—a thin glaze of gum Arabic (a sap collected from acacia trees and used as a binder in watercolors, as a glue, and in the food industry) to make it appear glossy. I painted the eye area entirely in watercolor (there is no gouache on this part of the portrait), let it dry completely, and then added the gum Arabic.

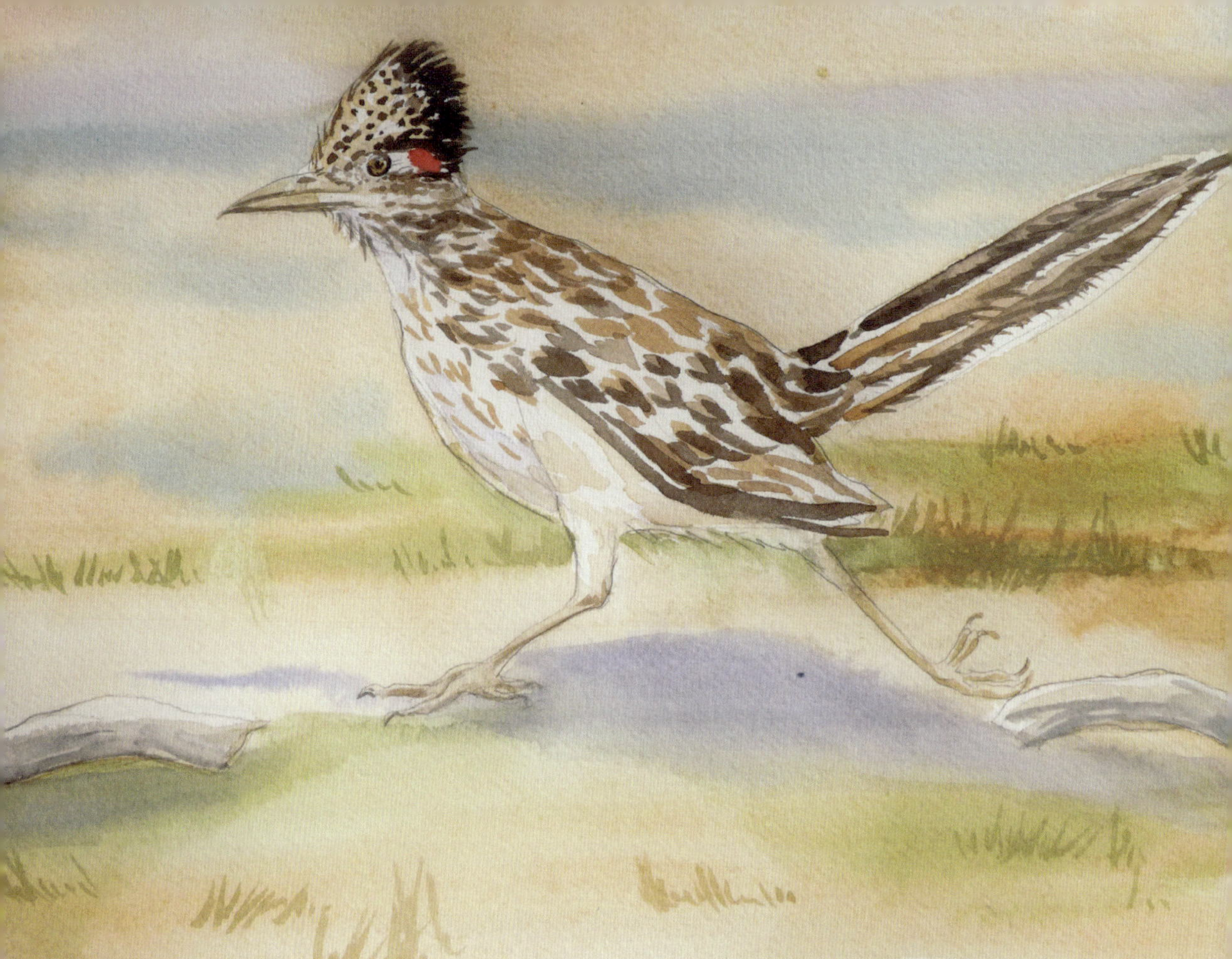

Greater roadrunner *(Geococcyx californianus)* • **WATERCOLOR SKETCH**
The roadrunner, a member of the cuckoo family, is common to scrub desert and mesquite groves in the Sonoran Desert. I sketched the bird in pencil and then added watercolor loosely on the head and body. I try not to be too careful when I'm casually exploring a bird through a sketch. I take the most care with the eyes and beak, so that's usually my last step on a bird portrait—the fussy work always comes last! I completed the bird before adding the background colors; with a wet-into-wet technique, I was able to suggest desert hues without getting too specific.

Burrowing owl *(Athene cunicularia)* • **WATERCOLOR SKETCH**
The burrowing owl is a very small owl—somewhere between the size of a robin and a crow—that nests in abandoned prairie dog burrows. To create this watercolor sketch, I began with a drawing and then taped off a rectangle around the owl. I surrounded the bird outline with water, laid a pale gold-green all around the bird, and then proceeded with the owl portrait. I almost always finish the portrait first and develop the surrounding background or landscape later, not knowing which colors I'll choose until I complete the bird. Burrowing owls prefer wide-open spaces and find ample food sources near prairie dog towns.

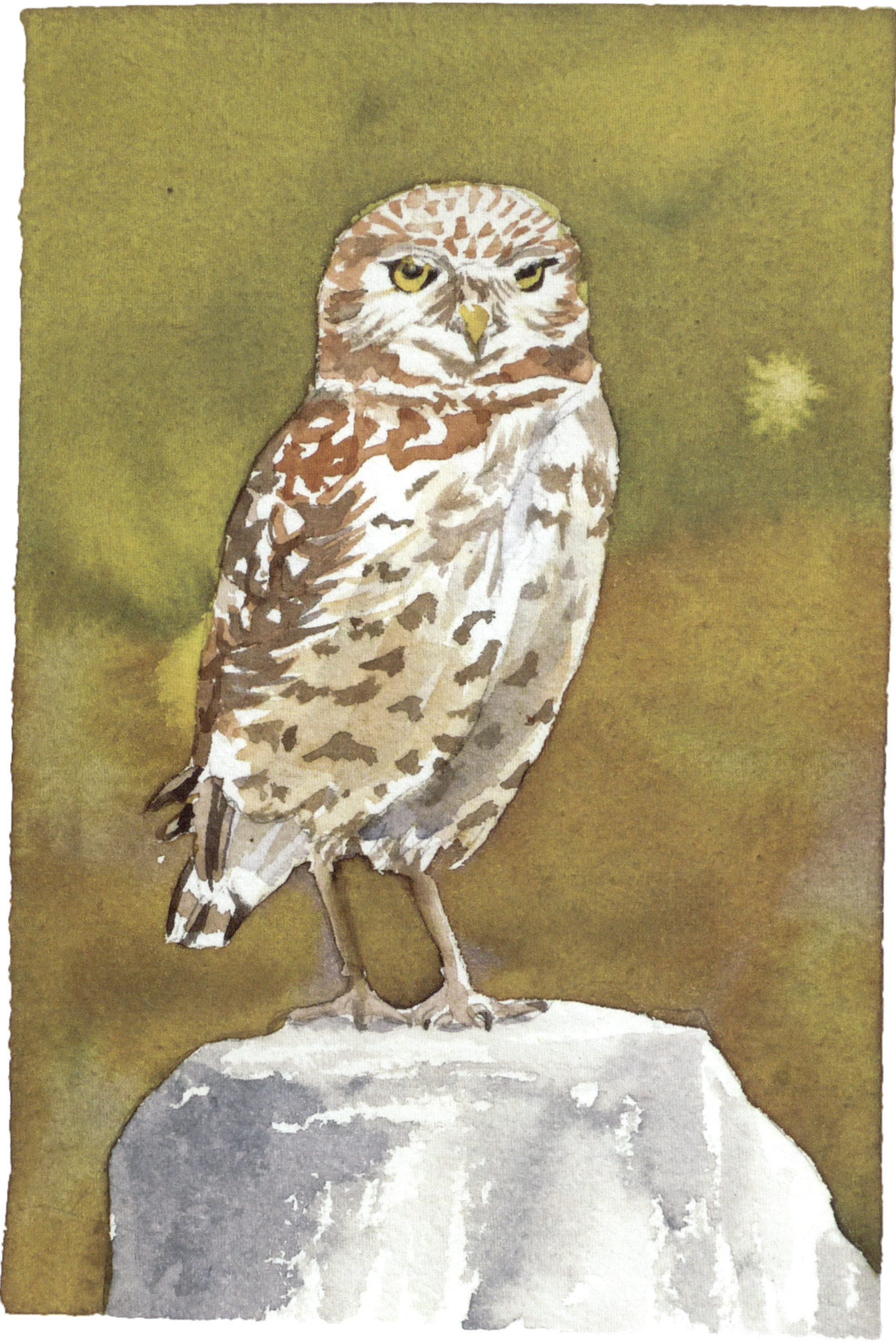

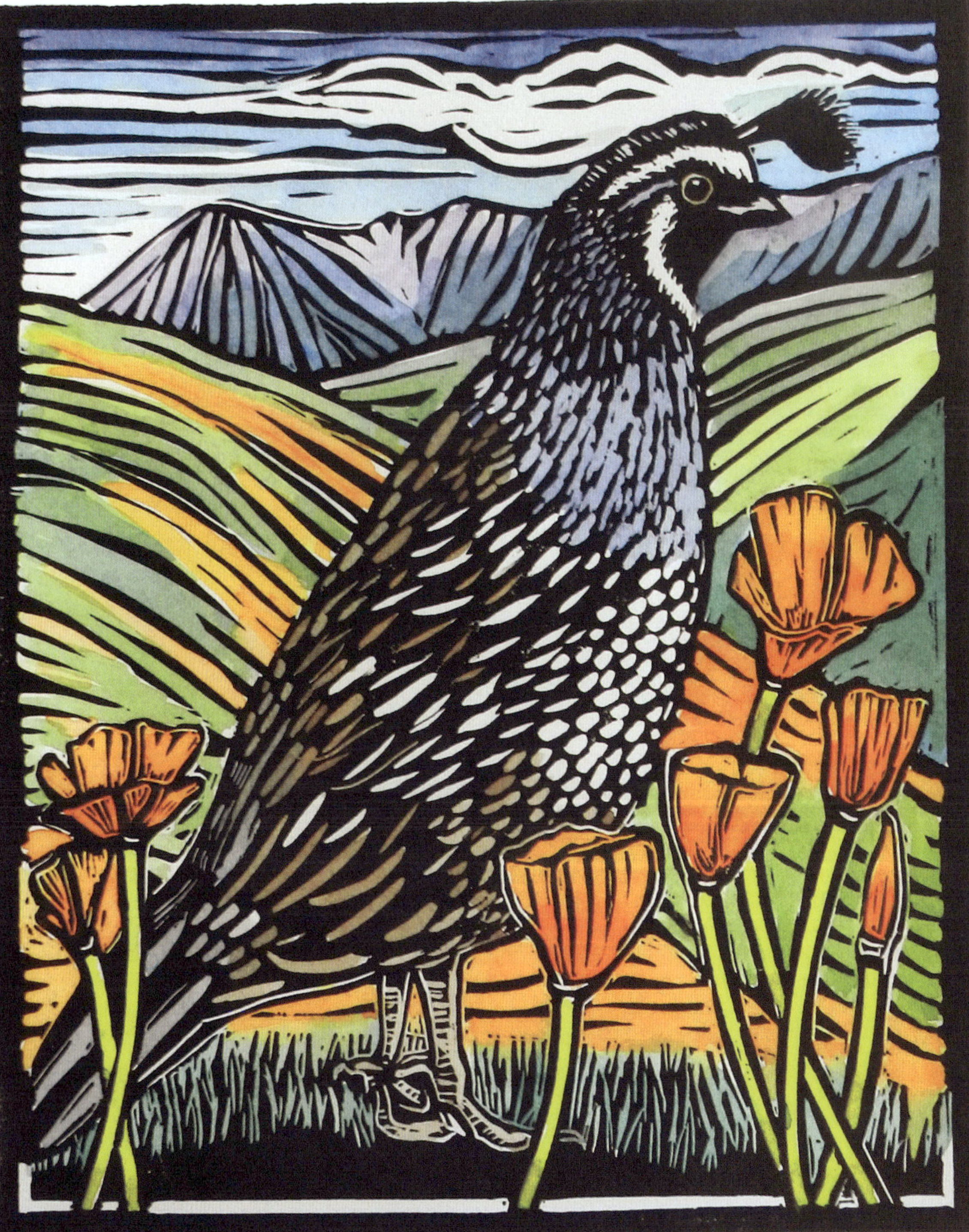

California quail *(Callipepla californica)* • **BLOCK PRINT**

These quails live throughout the West; you can find them from California all the way to eastern British Columbia. Some live in the drier areas of the park near my house, where there's a lot of underbrush for them to hide in.

Once in a while an artist freely interprets, and this block print is an example of that. When I conceived of this print I thought it would be perfect to combine the quail with the California poppies that put on such a show in springtime on the dry hillsides of Northern California. I felt I could take these liberties because of the bird's very wide range. The combination of the paisley-shaped markings on the breast with the bright colors of the poppies made for a dramatic print.

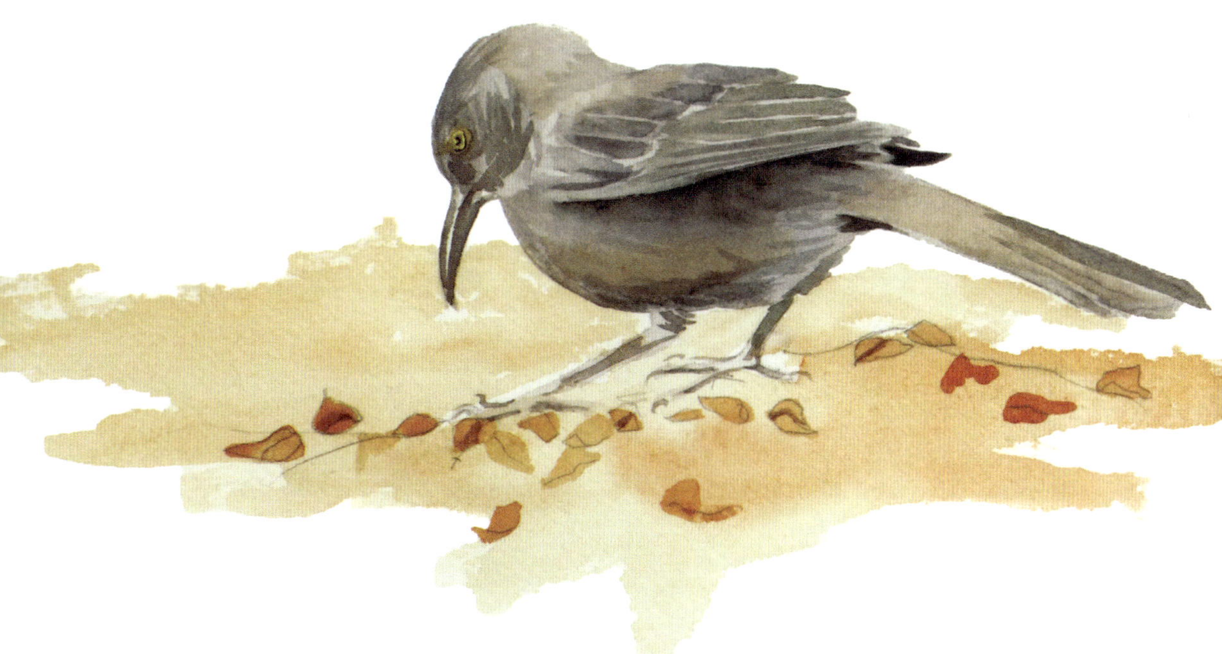

Curve-billed thrasher *(Toxostoma curvirostre)* • **WATERCOLOR SKETCH**

"Thresher" and "thrasher" were names used for the thrush in the Thames Valley and Chilterns area of England, and the name came to North America with the settlers. It was probably chosen because of the birds' beautiful songs; like thrushes, and like the mockingbirds to which they're related, thrashers warble and trill. Curve-billed thrashers are widespread in Arizona, New Mexico, and Texas and range south to Mexico.

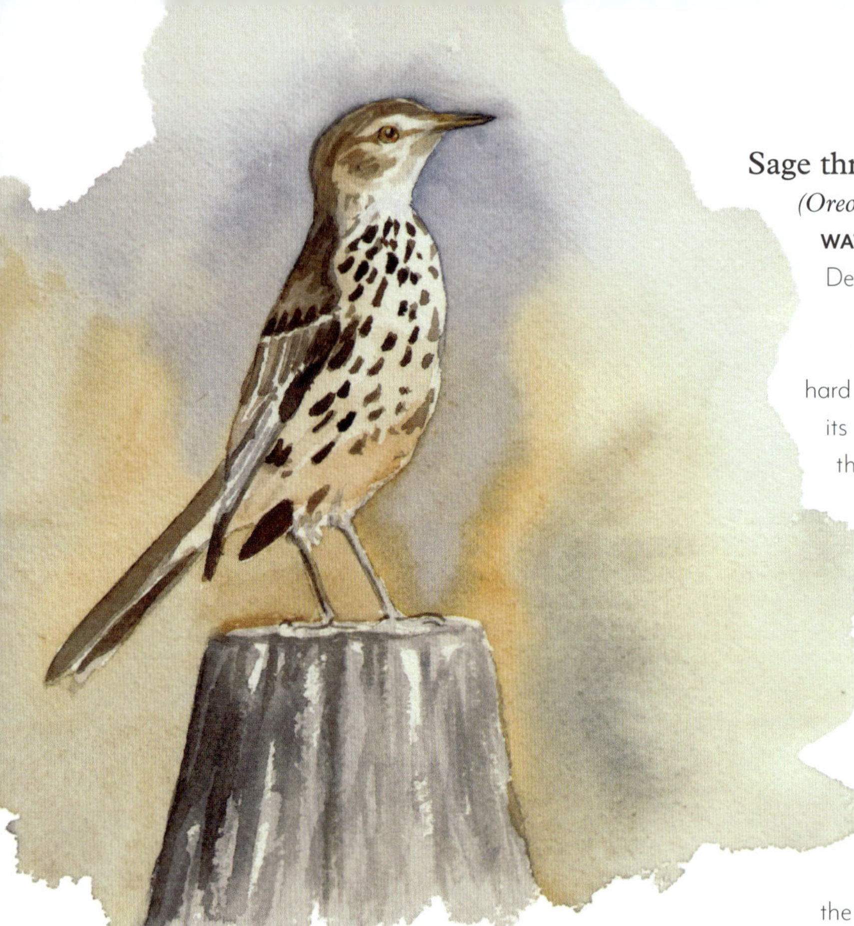

Sage thrasher

(Oreoscoptes montanus) • **WATERCOLOR SKETCH**

Decked out as humbly as sage thrashers are in grays and browns, it would be very hard to spot one without catching its movements first, or hearing the sound of its beak sifting through the dry gravel and scattered leaves. Sage thrashers breed throughout the Great Basin, from Washington all the way to California, but winter in the desert Southwest and Mexico. I chose to sketch both sage and curve-billed thrashers in watercolor because of the subtlety of their colors and the absence of dramatic markings. Those two factors can make for a sensitive watercolor.

Red-tailed hawk *(Buteo jamaicensis)* • **WATERCOLOR**

On a fine spring day in eastern Washington, my husband and I went in search of a waterfall on Nature Conservancy land at the Moses Coulee Preserve, not far from the more famous Grand Coulee. Spring flowers were blooming, and the rust-colored lichens on the basalt cliffs seemed especially bright against the blue sky. It took us a long time to find the trail, well off the road, with only a small marker designating it. Perhaps the best moment of the day was spotting this red-tailed hawk soaring above us. After drawing its outline in pencil, I used masking fluid on the hawk shape so that I could paint a deep blue sky without having to worry about fussing around the bird's wings. Sometimes it's a lot easier to get a smooth wash that way. Then I painted several different colors for the basalt cliffs and sagebrush, all of them on wet paper. Once those colors dried, I began to build up the basalt columns with darker washes and a little more line work. I filled in the hawk toward the end of the painting, appreciating the beautiful harmony between its plumage and the sienna cliffs.

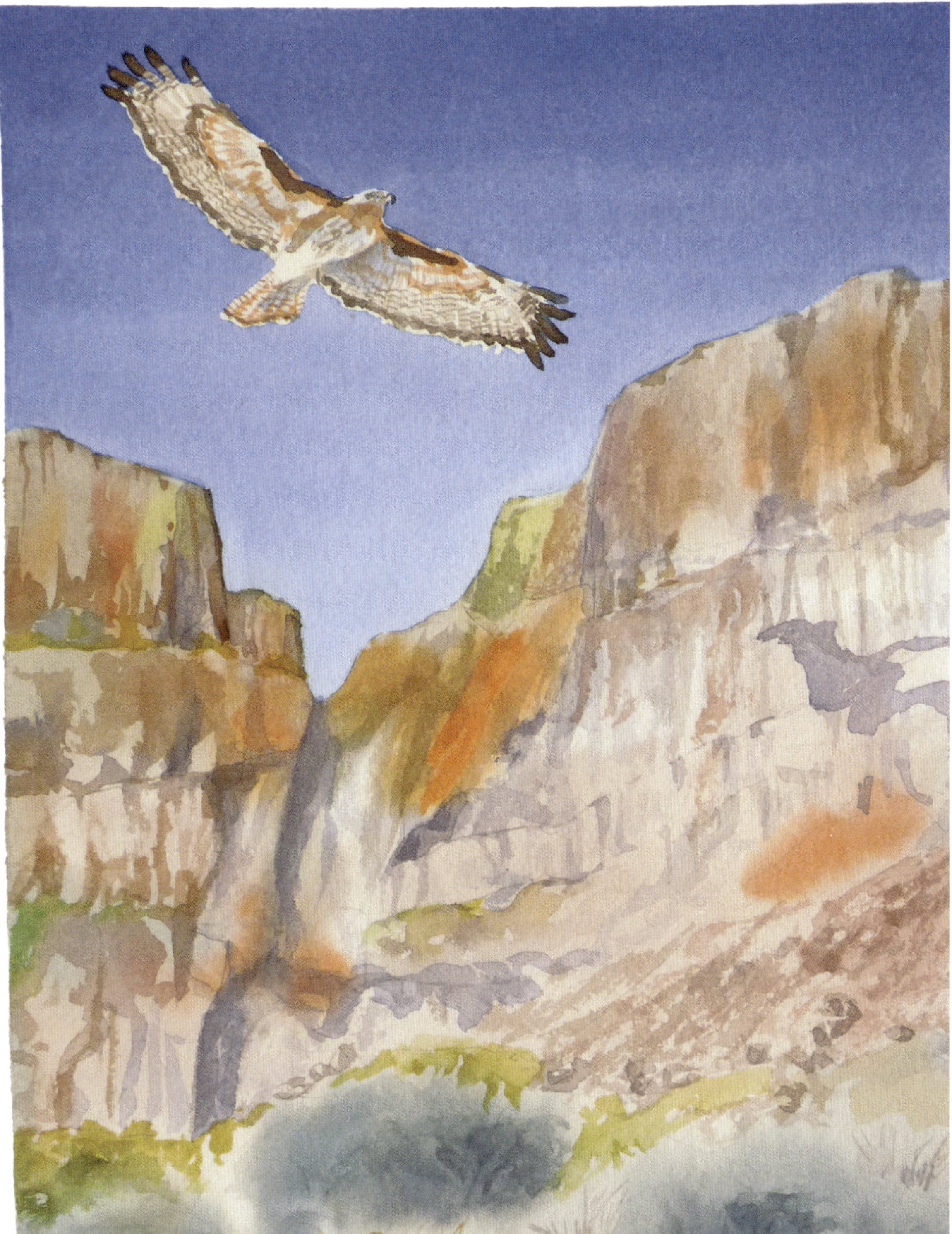

Forest & Woodland

thicket

bosk

coppice

timberland

grove

stand

bigleaf maple

black cottonwood

cascara

cherry

Indian plum

madrone

Oregon ash

quaking aspen

red alder

Pacific dogwood

vine maple

willow

Sitka spruce

western red cedar

western hemlock

Douglas fir

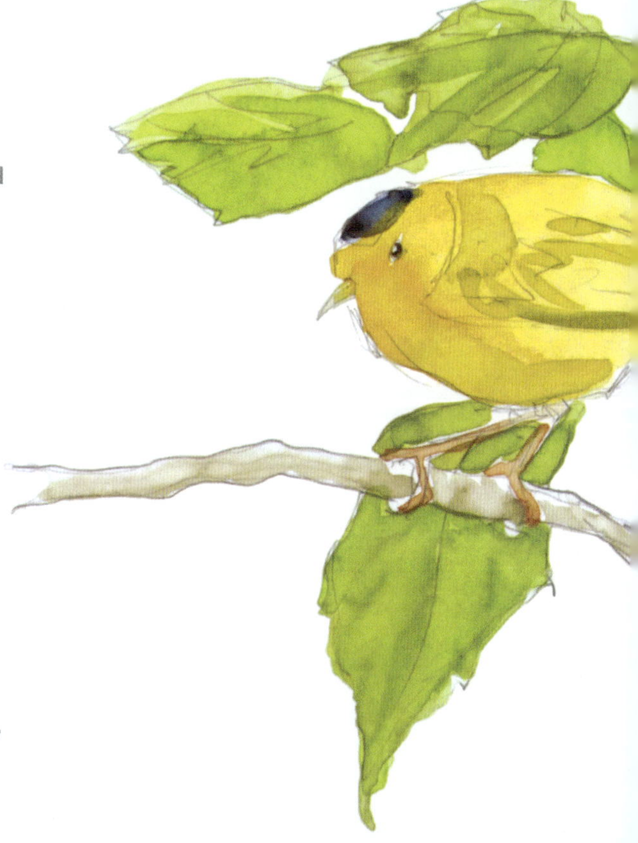

But when . . . wandering in the sublime forests, surrounded by views more gorgeous than even Claude ever imagined, I enjoy a delight which none but those who have experienced it can understand . . .

—**Charles Darwin,** from a May 1832 letter to W. D. Fox

Many hikes in the Cascades begin in lower-elevation forests, so there's a lot of time and hard work involved in switchbacking up to the alpine meadows and grand vistas. Hearing the tap of woodpeckers—and sometimes getting lucky and actually seeing one—helps to keep the forest exciting. Forests all over the West are full of such avian surprises, from a three-toed woodpecker in Yellowstone's Slough Creek area going about its business undisturbed by human presence, to a pileated woodpecker—looking like a Jurassic Park escapee—climbing up a rotting cottonwood in the woods along the Burke-Gilman Trail in Seattle. Along the Burke-Gilman, volunteers are slowly restoring native trees and, especially, the understory plants, removing blackberries and other invasive species, encouraging the return of many of the "avoiders" that Marzluff identifies and I note in the "Backyard & City" chapter. Sometimes forest birds don't want to be seen; among the understory plants, dark branches, and dense foliage of conifers and hardwoods, they're well disguised. But sometimes a crowd of whistleblower jays, crows, or robins will betray the hidden birds—I once heard a mob of about thirty robins shrieking at a great horned owl in a Northwest coastal Sitka spruce forest. Other birds, such as the ruby-crowned kinglet, normally almost invisible as it flits in the upper boughs of conifers, may seek food out in the open in a city park after a heavy snowfall, finding sustenance in rose hips that glow as red as the tiny bird's crest.

Woodland habitats include hardwood (deciduous) forests, mixed hardwood and softwood (coniferous) forests, and nearly exclusively coniferous forests. The coniferous forests, which cover large parts of the West, are ideal for many birds. Pine nuts can be cached to provide meals all year long for some species. Many birds of the coniferous forests have specially adapted bills for prying open the cones. They're also quite agile, so they can climb and maneuver in densely cloaked trees. But within each of these forest types, birds rely on a variety of vegetation layers—ground, understory, midstory, and canopy. Like the types of backyard habitats that are best for birds, messy forests with a lot of snags, logs, and other debris on the ground are generally best for a number of different species. Parklike forests with tall trees and little understory or ground plants have fewer birds. Warblers, for example, require thick understory vegetation for nesting cover.

There are renewed threats to Pacific Northwest forests, not only from industries such as logging—which removes both large timber and understory plants and pollutes watercourses through the road-building required for timber extraction—but from climate change; warmer winters create conditions that breed forest pests, such as the pine beetle, and diseases, which have destroyed many forests. Fire management practices may help to reduce the threat of forest fires, with controlled burning instead of the hands-off approach that caused such devastating fires in the past, but as recent years have demonstrated, there are many forests in need of serious thinning. Beyond those factors, human population growth and the expansion of recreation and residential development significantly reduce the amount of forest habitat for wild creatures.

Cedar waxwing *(Bombycilla cedrorum)* • **BLOCK PRINT**

Many people count the waxwings among their favorite birds—they're striking with their many beautifully blended colors, and their crests are dramatic and uncommon among western species. The cedar waxwing is smaller than the Bohemian by an inch; it's also less gray and has a yellow belly. Occasionally, a Bohemian will travel with a flock of cedars. The waxwing's high-pitched *see-see-see* vocalizations are unmistakable. You'll often find one atop a cedar, but also in alders and, out on the Pacific coast, in Sitka spruce and shore pines.

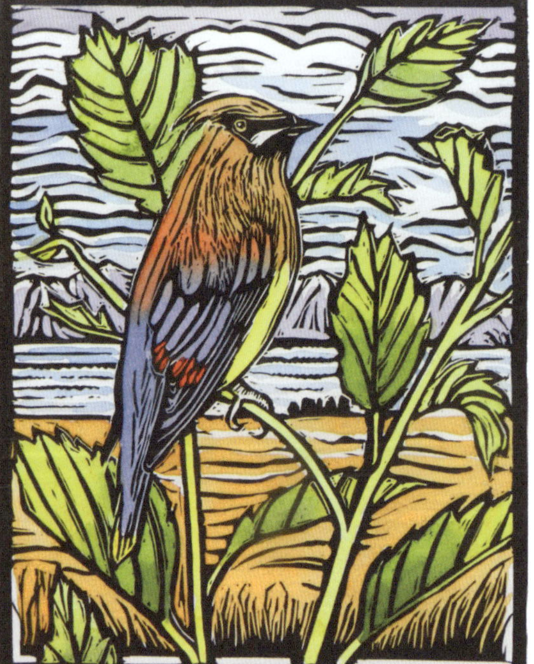

Pileated woodpecker *(Dryocopus pileatus)* • **WOODBLOCK PRINT**

The restoration of the Burke-Gilman Trail in Seattle has prompted some uncommon woodland birds to return. Volunteers have cleared blackberries, planted native species such as Oregon grape, currants, and bleeding hearts, and placed many nest boxes. All of this creates an inviting woodland habitat, and since the restoration, I've seen a pileated woodpecker three times in as many years.

For this print, I had access to a press and an encouraging teacher who helped me with the technical aspects of it—the process was entirely driven by curiosity on my part. When using heavy saturations of oil-based relief inks on a sturdy printmaking paper (as opposed to thinned-out inks on the delicate Japanese paper I used for the harlequin duck in "Shoreline & Beach"), a press is necessary. The print required four separate blocks with oil-based ink applied: one for the pale gray-blue of the tree and the bird's lighter feathers, one for the bird's red head, one for the gold background, and one for the darker lines of the trunk texture and the bird's feathers. It was very much a labor of love, taking many hours of carving and many hours of experimenting to achieve a print I was happy with.

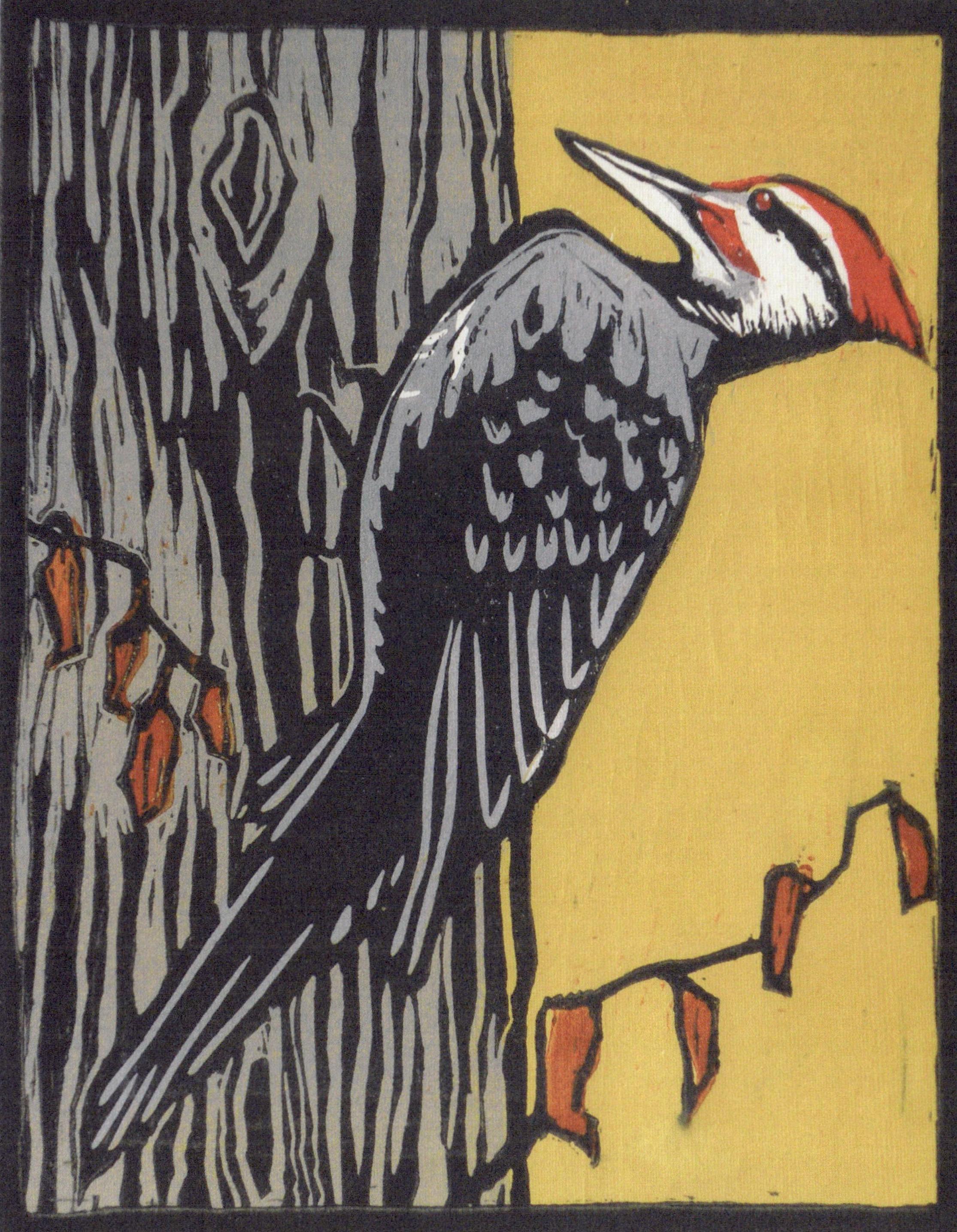

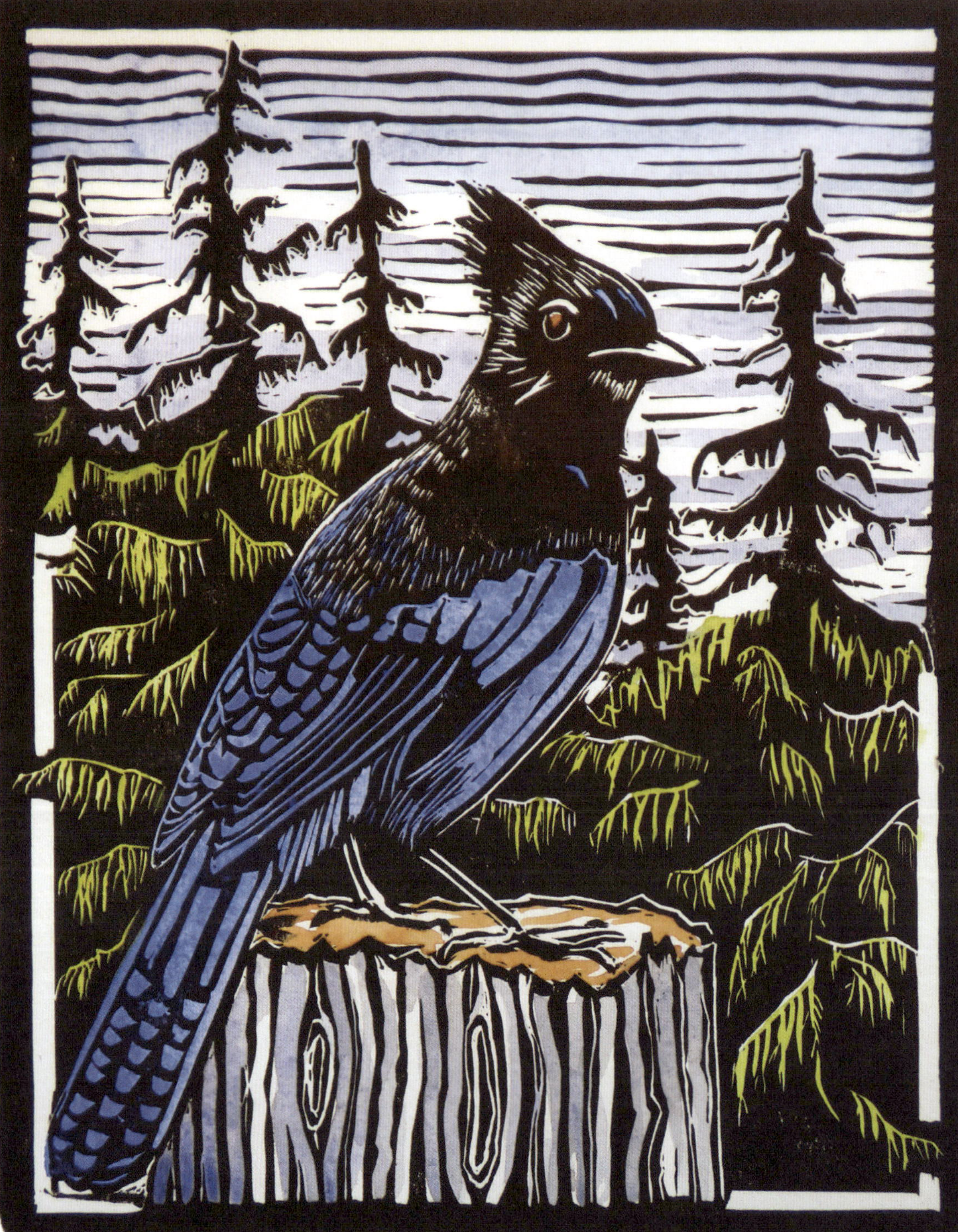

Steller's jay *(Cyanocitta stelleri)* • BLOCK PRINT

Steller's jays seem to appreciate conifer forests, but don't require wilderness, so they're seen in neighborhoods throughout the West between the Rockies and the Pacific. If you hear a repetitive call on high and see a bright flash of blue, you'll know a Steller's is nearby. In the block print, the black crest of the jay finds a counterpart in the dark cedar treetops. As you might witness on a windy day, they're both flexible enough to arch with the wind.

Ruby-crowned kinglet *(Regulus calendula)* • BLOCK PRINT

One day after heavy snow in Seattle, I walked in the park and saw this kinglet hopping in the snow beside a wild rosebush with hips festooned with snow. Kinglets are secretive birds and spend most of their time in large conifers, moving quickly, often in groups; it usually takes binoculars and patience to view them in the woods. It occurred to me then that a hungry bird, like a hungry wolf, will take a lot of risks, and that inclement weather can bring some rare sightings. I made the print to commemorate the snowy day and the bird's willingness to travel beyond its safe boundaries.

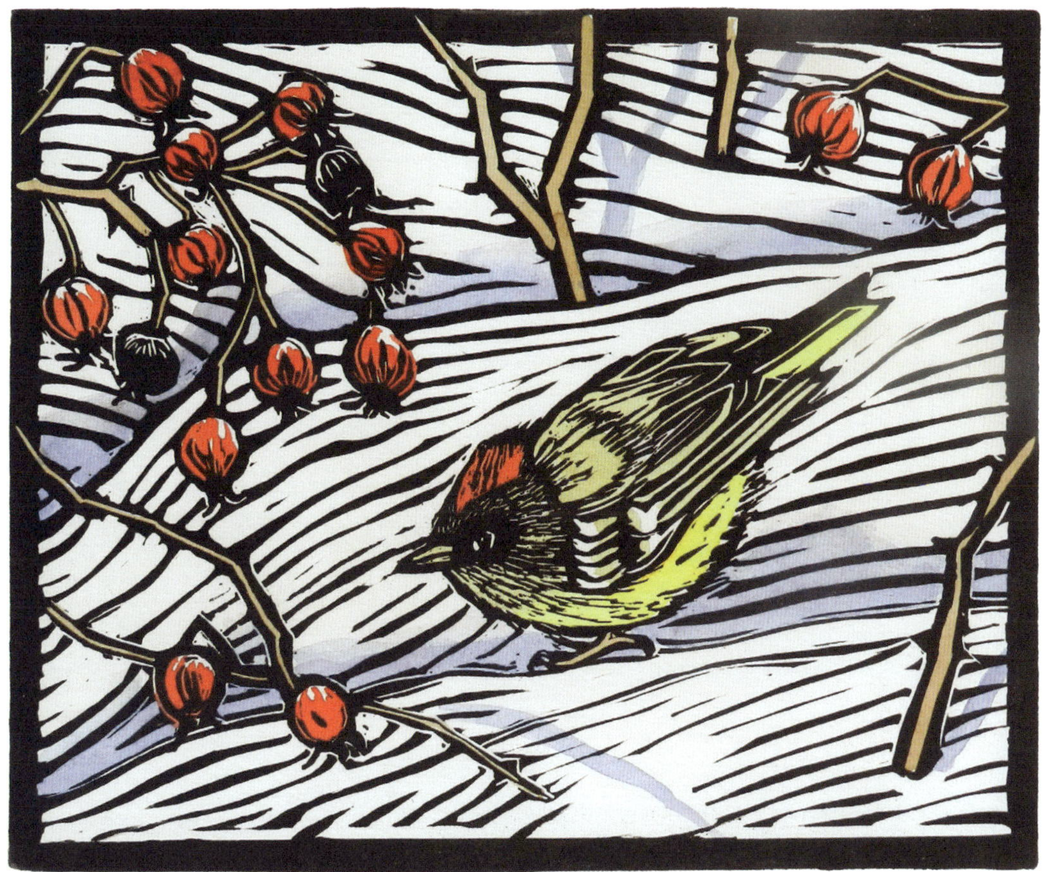

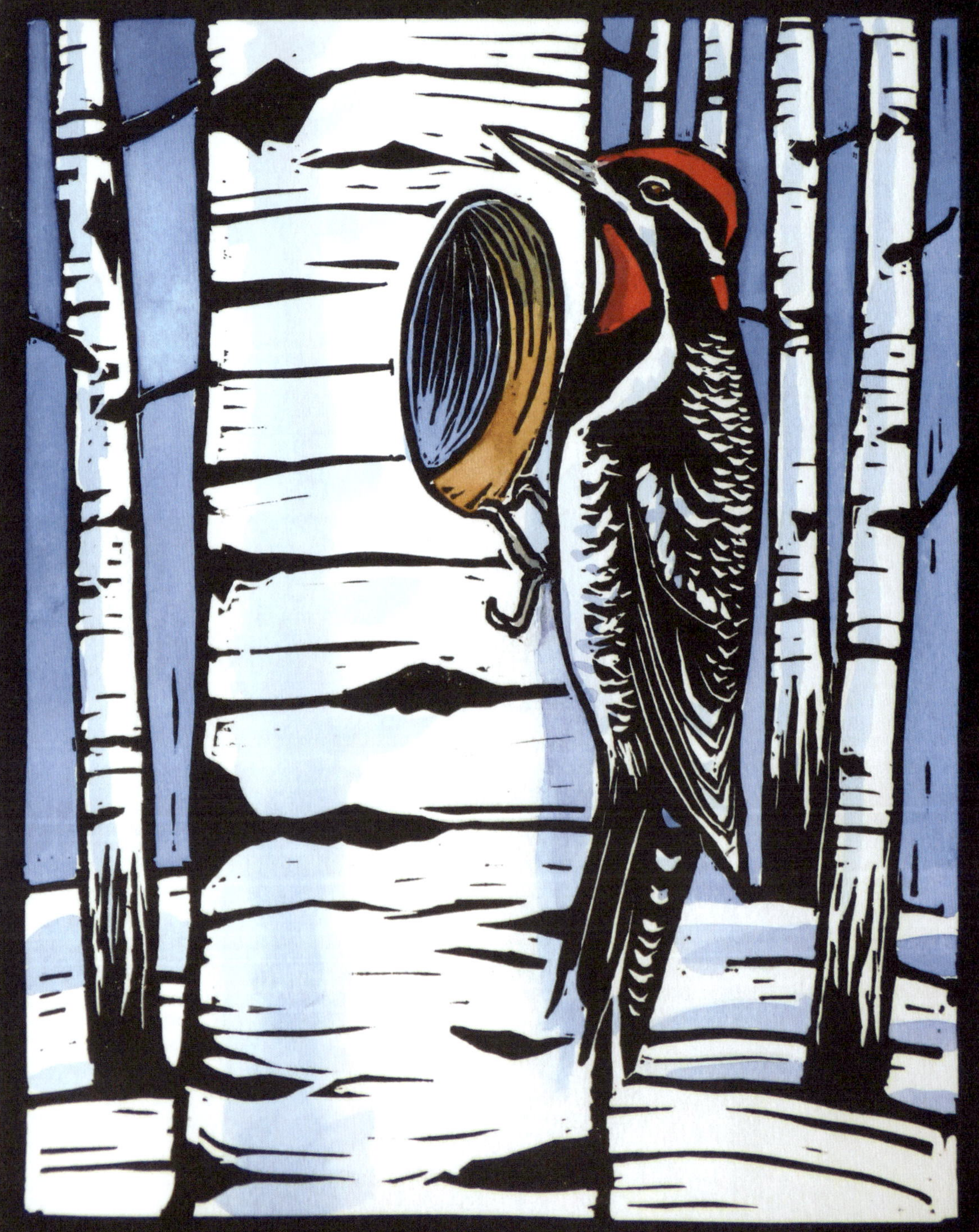

TECHNIQUE

Watercolor with White Gouache

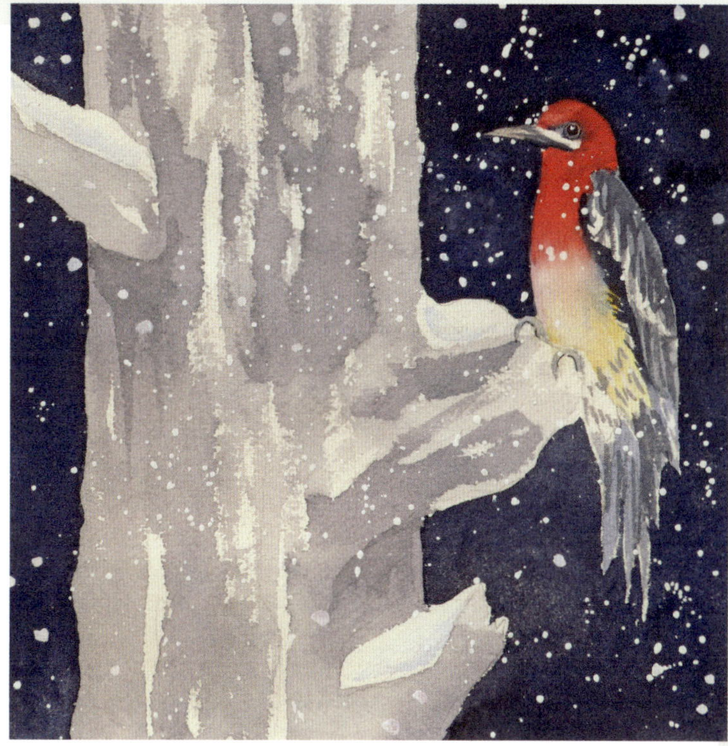

Although I didn't see this red-breasted sapsucker (*Sphyrapicus ruber*) in the snow, but rather in springtime in south central Oregon, I decided to explore the winter interpretation artistically, thinking its red head and breast would look dramatic against the white of snow. To depict the snow, once the watercolor was dry, I mixed up a fairly thick solution of white gouache (think of crème fraiche). It's important to achieve the right degree of saturation. If your mixture is too watery, the white paint will almost disappear once it's dry. If it's too thick, it won't spatter, so be sure to experiment first. I used a paintbrush to brush the gouache onto a toothbrush. After masking off the area outside the sketch with a few well-placed pieces of scrap paper, I dragged a chopstick across the toothbrush to spatter the paint, aiming it in the direction the flakes were meant to fall, usually not at an angle, but rather vertically. For larger snowflakes, tapping a loaded paintbrush with the handle of another paintbrush works well.

Red-naped sapsucker *(Sphyrapicus nuchalis)* • **BLOCK PRINT**

I used my imagination to situate the sapsucker on an aspen trunk, since I actually saw it in a birch tree near my home in Seattle. This bird is quite rare west of the Cascades and mostly prefers the drier woodland environment of areas east of the mountains, frequenting both conifers and aspens. Unlike other woodpeckers, sapsuckers drill symmetric holes both vertically and horizontally in tree trunks in order to reach the sap they rely on for food. This benefits many other species that also love to snack on the sap, including warblers. Bats, rodents, and butterflies also drink it, as do other insects. How convenient—the insects are another food source for the sapsuckers.

Nests WATERCOLOR SKETCHES

Bird nests are among the most ingenious artifacts of animal life on the planet, justifiably compared to the work of human architects. Nests evolved when birds became warm-blooded creatures as the climate cooled. At that point they couldn't leave their eggs in an open environment to hatch; they needed to incubate the eggs in a temperature-controlled space, with protection for themselves and their eggs. Early nests were probably like the more primitive ones still used today by many species—for example, the scraped depressions in the ground employed by killdeer. Other birds do little nest building—woodpeckers and some owls use existing cavities in trees. But many other birds have evolved beautiful structures. The passerine (songbird) species build cup-shaped nests with a foundation of mud and grasses, like the robin's nest shown here. Other species, including orioles, bushtits, vireos, and the occasional hummingbird, weave elegant hanging nests, like vertical hammocks! Some birds build nests each year, some for multiple broods in a single year, and others—especially birds of prey—reuse the same nests year after year, restoring them with each use.

Types of nest materials include seaweed, tules, rushes, reeds, grasses, sticks, mud, hair, wool, bark strips, feathers, paper, leaf mold, lichen, mosses, and pine needles. Some birds

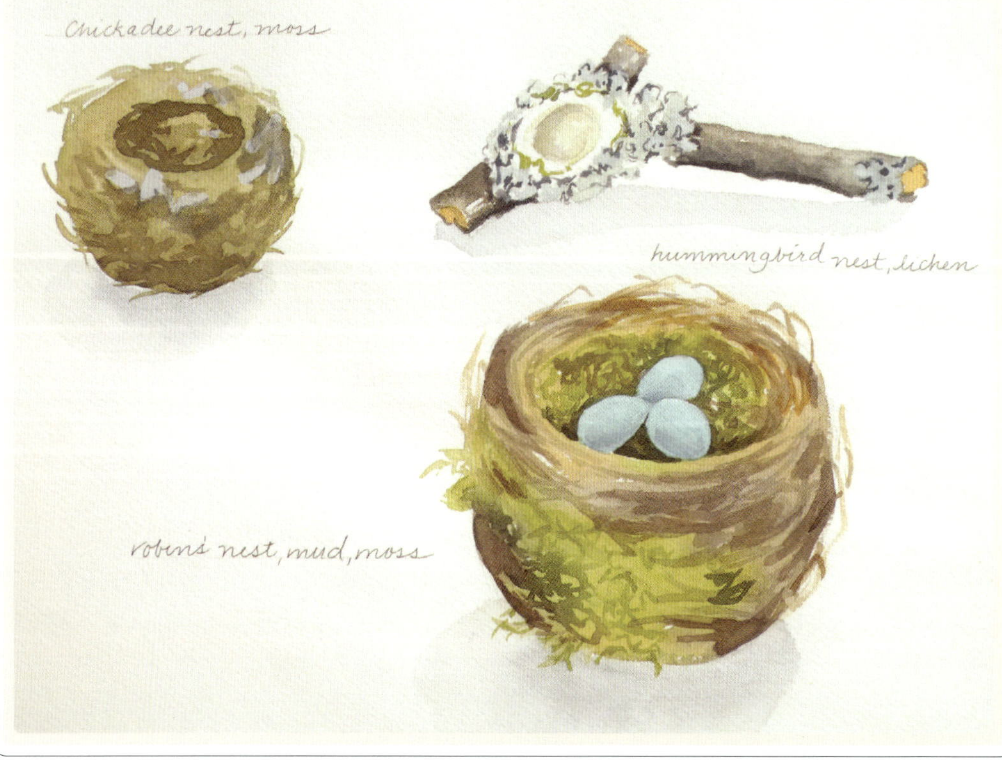

get creative with manmade objects—shorts, bath towels, brooms, old shoes, straw hats, and rag dolls have been found in osprey nests.

I borrowed three nests from Seattle Audubon to sketch and to share with my classes. The tiny Anna's hummingbird nest is so well camouflaged as to be invisible and is woven of spider silk and decorated with lichen. The third nest in the watercolor is a chickadee nest, made with moss, grasses, and a homely bit of dryer lint.

I discovered a nest in an oak sapling at Union Bay Natural Area in winter, when the young oak had only a few leaves clinging to its branches. In winter it's always a revelation to see how many trees and understory shrubs have sheltered nests that were safely hidden in the summer. On that gray, drizzly day, the nest was a poignant memory as well as a sweet anticipation of the life-bringing season of spring.

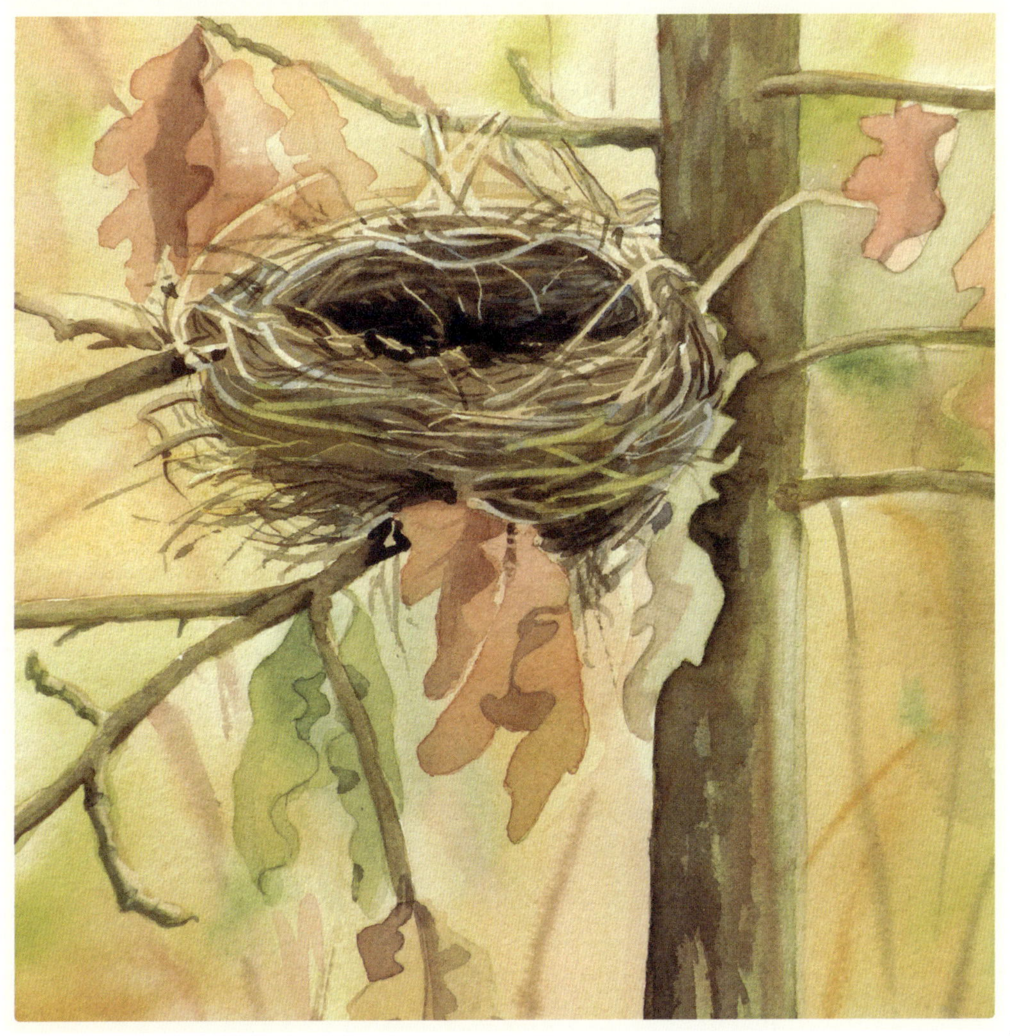

Wilson's and yellow warblers *(Cardellina pusilla, Setophaga petechia)* •

WATERCOLOR SKETCH

The Wilson's (top) was well concealed in bright alder and willow leaves during a visit my husband and I made to the Wood River Valley in the Upper Klamath Basin of southern Oregon. The sunny day turned the tree leaves almost as yellow as the bird, and I realized that the Wilson's bright plumage was actually very well camouflaged by a deciduous woods in full leaf. The fact that I hadn't ever seen one before is a testament!

On the same outing we also saw the yellow warbler (bottom two). Both warbler species like moist woods, bogs, and wetlands, which are abundant in mountain range drainages of the West.

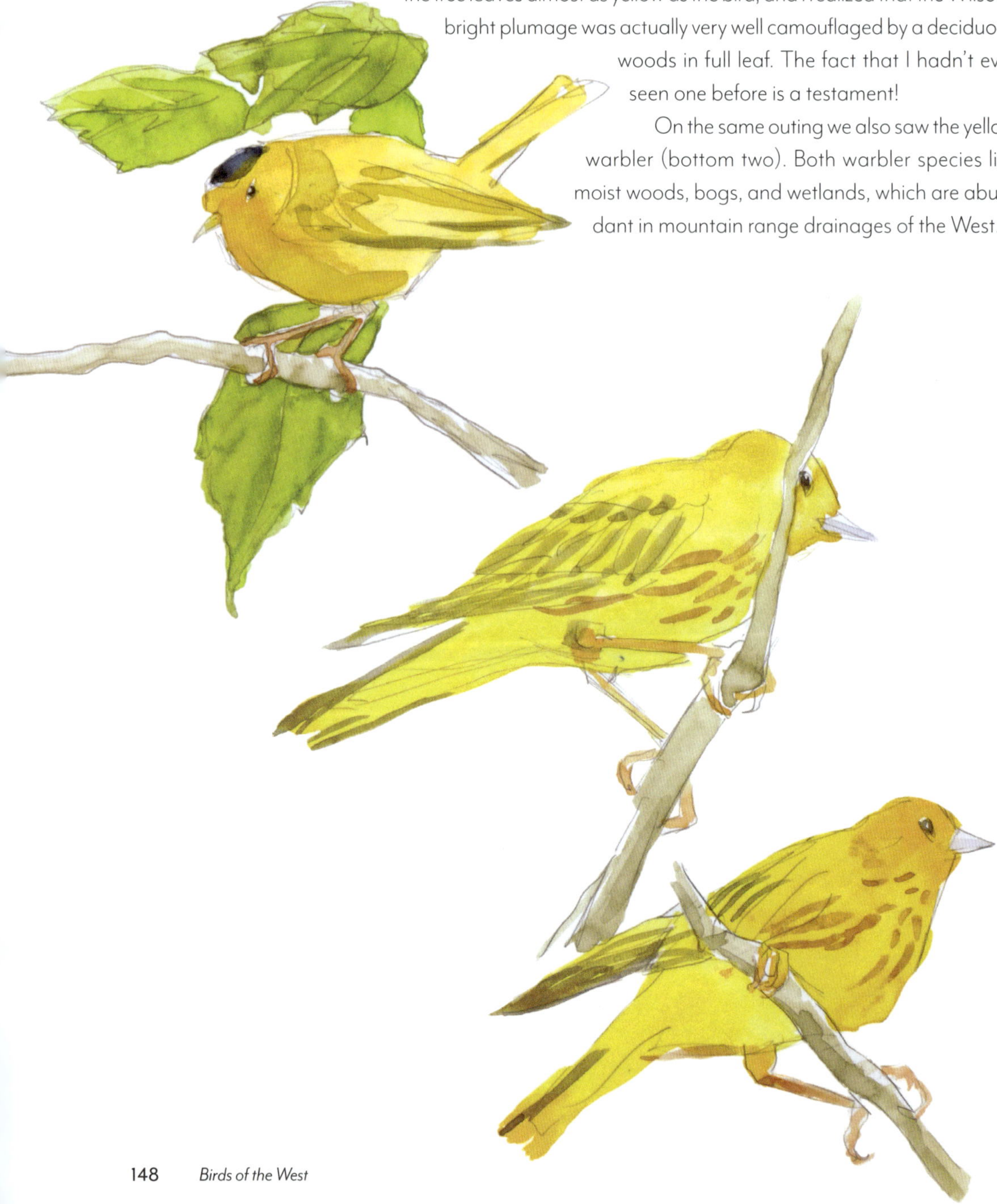

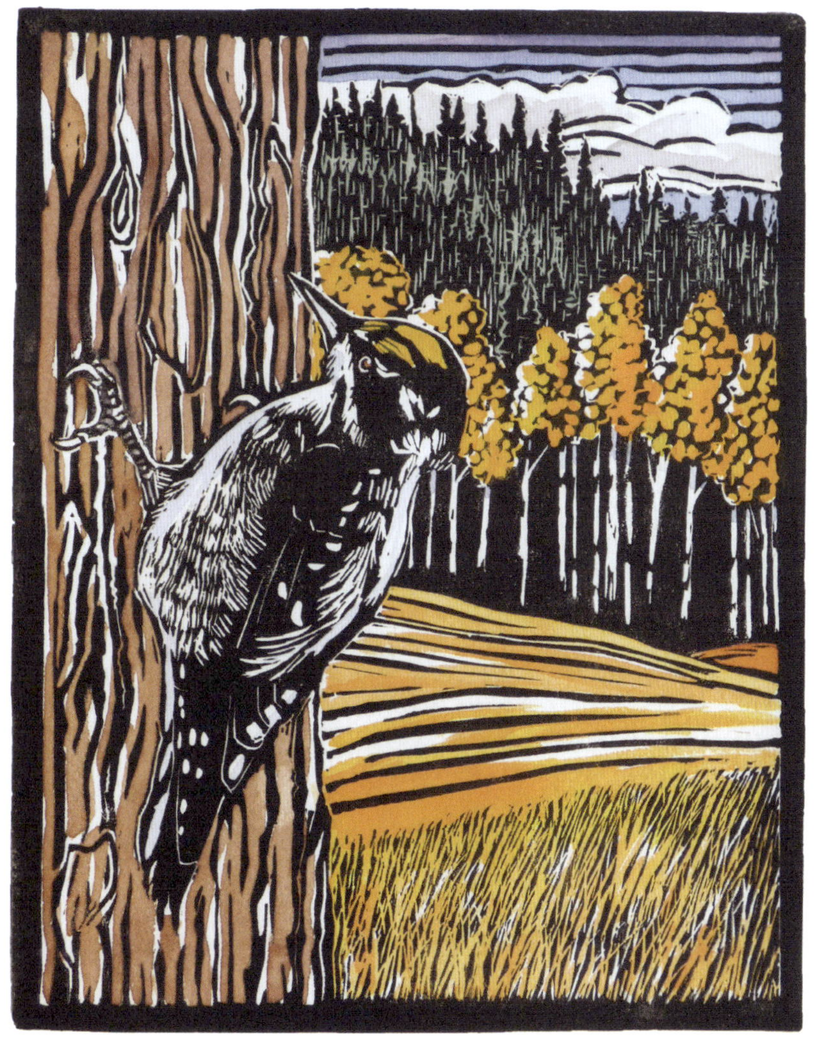

American three-toed woodpecker *(Picoides dorsalis)* • **BLOCK PRINT**

Both the three-toed and black-backed woodpeckers are missing a toe, unlike all other woodpeckers. My hiking companions and I saw this bird climbing a lodgepole pine along the Slough Creek Trail at Yellowstone. We spent about twenty minutes watching the bird, which was busy prying bark off the pine in search of insects and minded us not a bit. Like many of the creatures at Yellowstone, it was easy to view up close due to habituation and lack of human predation.

With artist's license, I changed the background trees to an aspen grove in the block print, thinking how dramatic the trunks would look against the golden background, and felt it was legitimate to do so since an aspen grove was within sight.

Brown creeper *(Certhia americana)* · **BLOCK PRINT**

You may never see a brown creeper unless you're attuned to movement. It's not that rare a bird, but it's so well camouflaged that it's almost invisible in the forest. I got into the habit of walking along the Burke-Gilman Trail in my neighborhood and decided to carry a small Panasonic Lumix camera with me so I wouldn't miss anything. I'd seen a pileated woodpecker there on several occasions, plus a barred owl, a peregrine falcon, and a sharp-shinned hawk. I took several photos of the creeper and combined the best of them for this block print. I was concerned that the bird would simply disappear in the block print unless I surrounded it with some bright color, and because it favors the trunks of maple trees along the trail, placing the creeper beside some chartreuse leaves was a logical choice.

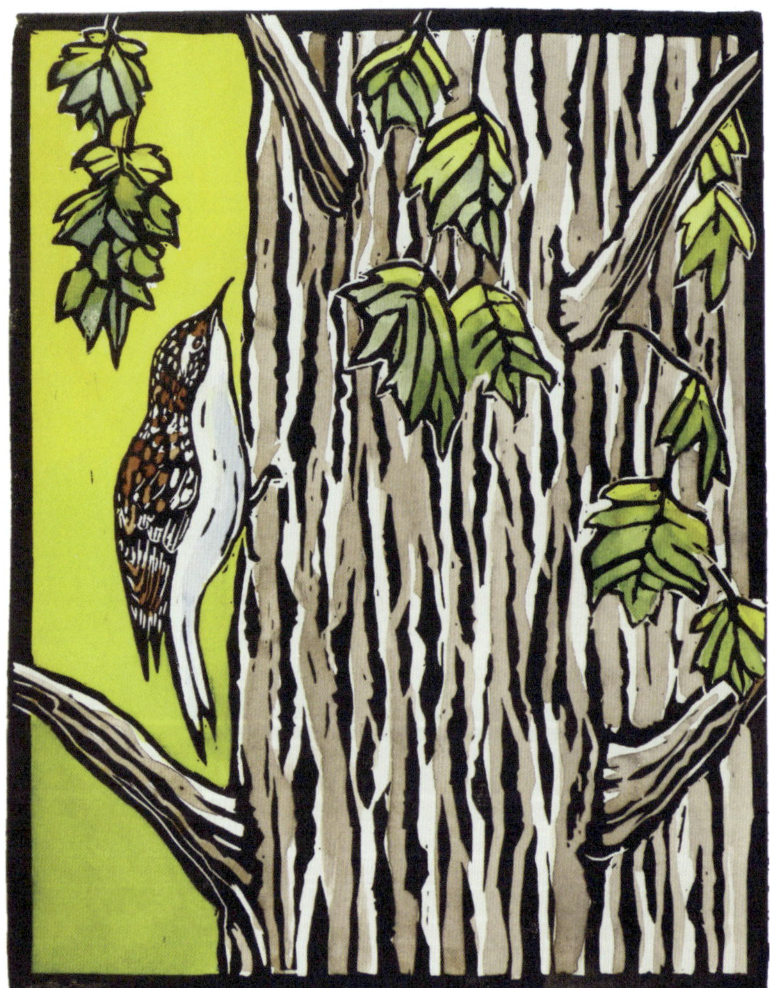

Northern saw-whet owl *(Aegolicus acadicus)* · **WATERCOLOR**

The saw-whet is a very small owl, eight inches tall, with dramatic rust-colored plumage on its breast and glowing golden eyes. A nocturnal species, it roosts in dense evergreens in winter, and you're likely to see it in a dark forest setting like the one pictured here. It's one of the most widespread owls in North America and winters all across the United States. In the Southwest, it's found in mountain forests. Its call is a high-pitched *toot-toot-toot* that, according to one guidebook, sounds a lot like a smoke detector going off. Earlier listeners likened the call to the sound of a saw being sharpened.

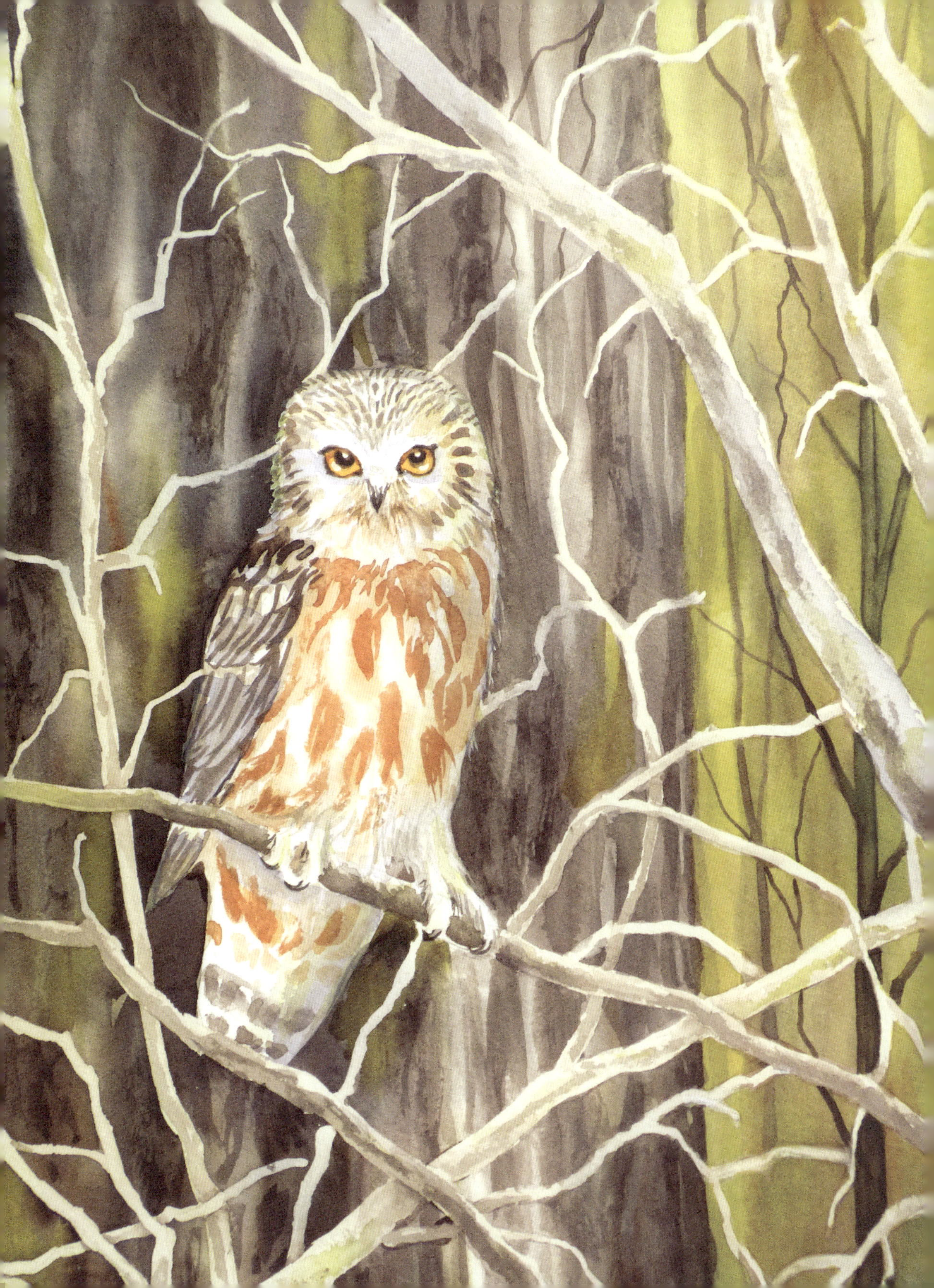

Eggs WATERCOLOR SKETCH

Early summer days are a jubilee time for birds. In the fields, around the house, in the barn, in the woods, in the swamp—everywhere love and songs and nests and eggs.

—**E. B. White,** *Charlotte's Web*

In his recent book *The Most Perfect Thing: Inside (and Outside) a Bird's Egg,* ornithologist Tim Birkhead compares the egg pigmentation process to an array of "paint guns." Each gun is genetically programmed to fire at a certain time so that the signature background color and spotting of a species' eggs is produced.

The coloration of bird eggs varies depending on the location of the nest. Birds that nest in holes don't need camouflage and often have white- or cream-colored eggs without markings. Birds that nest in the open need heavier pigmentation. Some zoologists think that birds that nest in trees have greener- and

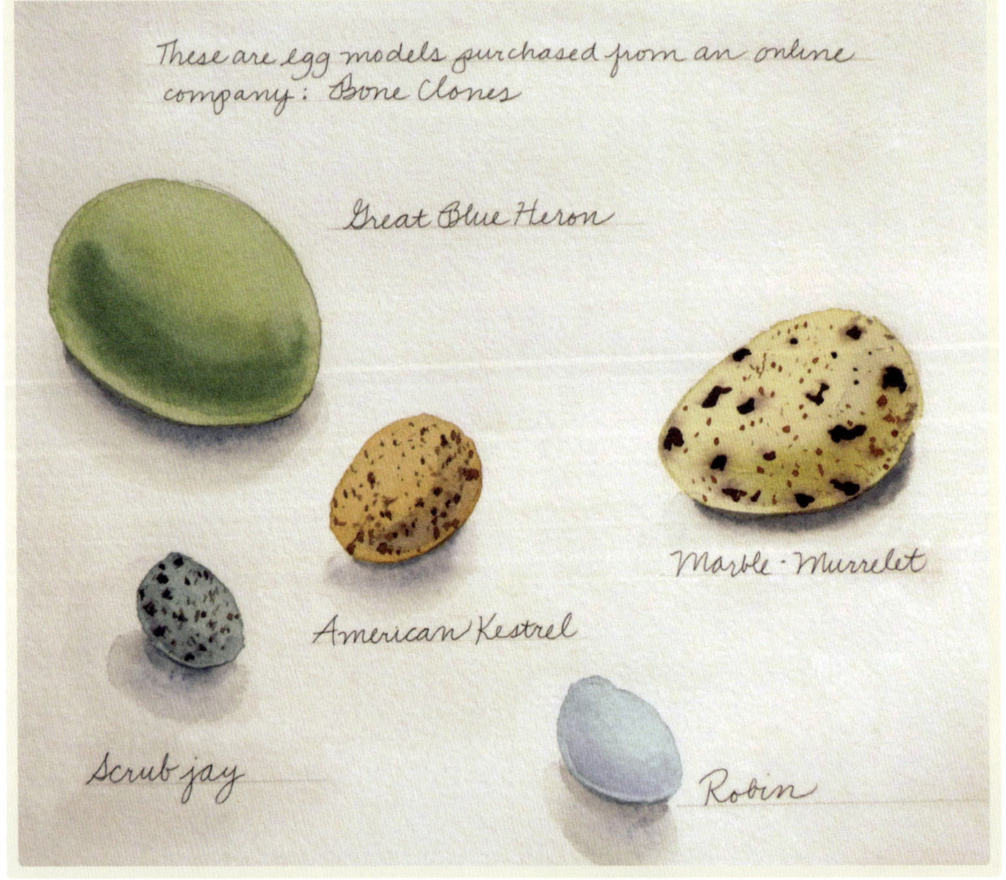

bluer-colored eggs. Markings are described as follows: blotched, spotted, dotted, splashed, scrawled, streaked, marbled, wreathed, capped, and overlaid.

Some birds have remarkably shaped eggs, and the question is: why are there so many different shapes? A recent theory is that the shape is based on how pointed and long a bird's wings are, which determines how strong a flier a bird is. Long and pointed wings are often found on birds that fly frequently or fly very long distances. For example, barn owls travel far and have very elongated, pointy eggs, whereas screech owls don't fly far or fast and have rounder, more symmetrical eggs.

As an artist, I find the colors of bird eggs irresistible, beginning, of course, with robin's egg blue, but the names of some of the more camouflaged and drab colors resonate with me just as strongly. In 1886, Robert Ridgway wrote a book called *A Nomenclature of Colors for Naturalists, and Compendium of Useful Knowledge for Ornithologists.* Egg collecting was an important part of bird study in the nineteenth century (though thankfully now illegal), and Ridgway created his guide to help in identification. In his book he names colors that are still used today by oologists, the scientists who study eggs. For the layperson, some of these names are antiquated but still worth knowing because they're so poetic: Brussels brown, sayal brown, Prout's brown, hazel, warm sepia, cartridge buff, bister, Saccardo's umber, court gray, greenish glaucous, aniline lilac, Rood's lavender, Quaker drab, Isabella, vinaceous drab, ecru drab, tawny olive, and many more.

I purchased the replica eggs painted here from a company called Bone Clones, which offers models of human, other mammal, and bird skeletons, as well as models of eggs and other fragile natural phenomena—an invaluable resource for teachers. I've brought the replicas to many classes and surprised participants by showing the incredibly tiny egg of a hummingbird, about ⅓-inch long. We've also compared the sizes of mallard and great blue heron eggs: the duck's egg is almost as large (1½-inch wide by 2¼-inch high) as the great blue heron's (1¾-inch wide by 2½-inch high). There's a very good reason for this: the duckling needs to be ready to swim and safely hide from predators at birth, whereas the heron chick has weeks to mature in its secure nest high above the ground.

Alpine & Tundra

mountain

peak

sierra

timberline

crag

butte

mesa

precipice

range

taiga

subalpine fir

Alaska yellow cedar

mountain hemlock

huckleberry

mountain ash

glacier lily

tiger lily

columbine

aster

shooting star

penstemon

gentian

monkshood

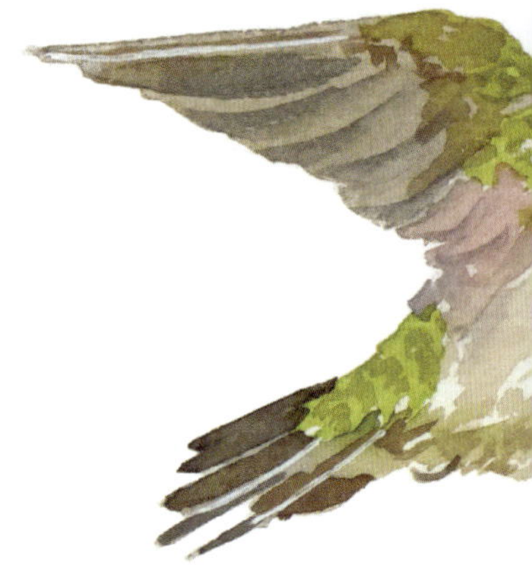

How hard to realize that every camp of men or beast has this glorious starry firmament for a roof! In such places standing alone on the mountain-top it is easy to realize that whatever special nests we make—leaves and moss like the marmots and birds, or tents or piled stone—we all dwell in a house of one room—the world with the firmament for its roof—and are sailing the celestial spaces without leaving any track.

—**John Muir,** *John of the Mountains: The Unpublished Journals of John Muir*

A ptarmigan in white winter plumage is nearly invisible in a snowfield—it's only the slight movement that signals its presence. In a high meadow on Mount Rainier in autumn, when perennial and annual flowers have shriveled back to their roots, a flock of mountain bluebirds alights on basalt boulders, the birds as blue as lapis lazuli in the slanting light of September. Ravens call to one another across miles of Douglas firs and lodgepole pines at Diablo Lake in the North Cascades. Calliope hummingbirds swarm a hiker wearing a fuchsia-colored T-shirt on the Green Mountain Trail near Glacier Peak. Having lunch beside a mountain stream, a hiker may be startled by a stout bird, the American dipper, that suddenly flies upstream from below and then continues vertically up a waterfall that hangs above. The dipper sings year-round, never migrates, and turns up like an old friend in many places—the Gardner River in Yellowstone, the Deschutes River in central Oregon, the Skykomish River on the west side of the Cascades, Sourdough Creek in the North Cascades.

Alpine habitat has much in common with arctic zones; stresses include low winter temperatures, a very short growing season, high winds, limited water in summer, and high ultraviolet light, as well as less carbon dioxide than in lower elevations. The plants that grow in this zone must be hardy: small conifers, shrubs, sedges, and wildflowers. All of these grow amid talus and boulders, cliffs, streams, tarns, and sometimes permanent snowfields. Constrained by such conditions, just a few species, including willow and rock ptarmigans, Savannah sparrows, brown-capped rosy finches, American pipits, and horned larks, complete their breeding and nesting cycles above tree line. Public lands are crucial for these birds and all alpine and arctic birds because those lands support 86 percent of the distribution of these species, a higher percentage than for birds dependent on any other terrestrial habitat.

I also include birds in this section that forage and nest in lower-elevation alpine zones, below tree line. Those areas have much larger populations of birds since they contain forest habitat, too.

American dipper *(Cinclus mexicanus)* •

SOLARPLATE INTAGLIO, WATERCOLOR

Late in October, the fall colors were spectacular in Tumwater Canyon, just off Highway 2 in the central Cascades. A month of sunny days and cold nights had created the perfect conditions for brilliant color. Earlier, my husband and I had walked along the Wenatchee River in Leavenworth, bathed in an almost extraterrestrial glow created by cottonwoods and bigleaf and vine maples, their leaves the same yellow-gold in every direction. Reluctantly we'd left and begun our drive home to Seattle. We stopped by the river in the canyon to eat a snack and saw an American dipper observing its world closely on a rock beside the river, dipping, diving, and swimming. I've watched these birds for years, and they're among my favorites. Not because of their color—they're a bit drab in camouflaged browns and grays. Nor because of their shape, which is anything but elegant; their bodies are stocky and almost comically stout, with short tails and wings. It's because they live year-round along watercourses, persevering in cold, rain, and wind, and never stop their singing. I've seen them in many national parks and forests: Yellowstone on the Gardner River, Mount Rainier National Park, and countless times at the North Cascades Institute in North Cascades National Park. I love watching them dive and swim. They fly low and also lift off like small helicopters, straight up a waterfall, disappearing into the mist and spray.

That October day it was utterly surprising when the dipper flew out way above the river, much higher than I had ever seen one fly, snatched a large moth out of the air, returned to its boulder perch with the moth securely in its beak, and proceeded to swallow it. Somehow this vision stayed with me and seemed a perfect metaphor for the day we had enjoyed. For the following weekend, snow was predicted for the east side and heavy rains for the wet west side of the Cascades as November began. The golden light, the warmth of the sixty-degree day, this remarkable bird catching one last airborne insect: *Carpe diem!* Seize the day!

The monochrome solarplate intaglio portrays the American dipper as I've seen it on other, misty days and gives the impression of the watery world of rushing water and vapors, perhaps the most common atmospheric environment for the dipper. The solarplate intaglio print is much like an etching. The manufacturer has already covered the plate with an emulsion. You place a watercolor sketch above the plate, then expose that to the sun or strong light, and a twenty-minute exposure transfers the sketch to the plate. After you rinse the emulsion off, you ink the plate, then wipe it, and the inks stays in the depressions formed from your marks being exposed to the light. Every place you haven't sketched, drawn lines, or painted light washes remains blank, and in the finished print you'll see only the paper in those areas. I used blue ink and light-blue-toned paper, and the result was something like a monochrome watercolor sketch.

One for the Dipper

(Cinclus mexicanus)

To be as sure
and light-footed among rapids
as the dipper:

slate-gray puff
of feather and song
twiglike dusky feet

dip, dip, on a sudsing rock
cheeps off upstream
no higher than spray . . .

one yesterday—
drinking delicate little
beakfuls

from a boulder
mid-Dungeness
wild with three weeks rain

—In Blue Mountain Dusk:
Poems by Tim McNulty

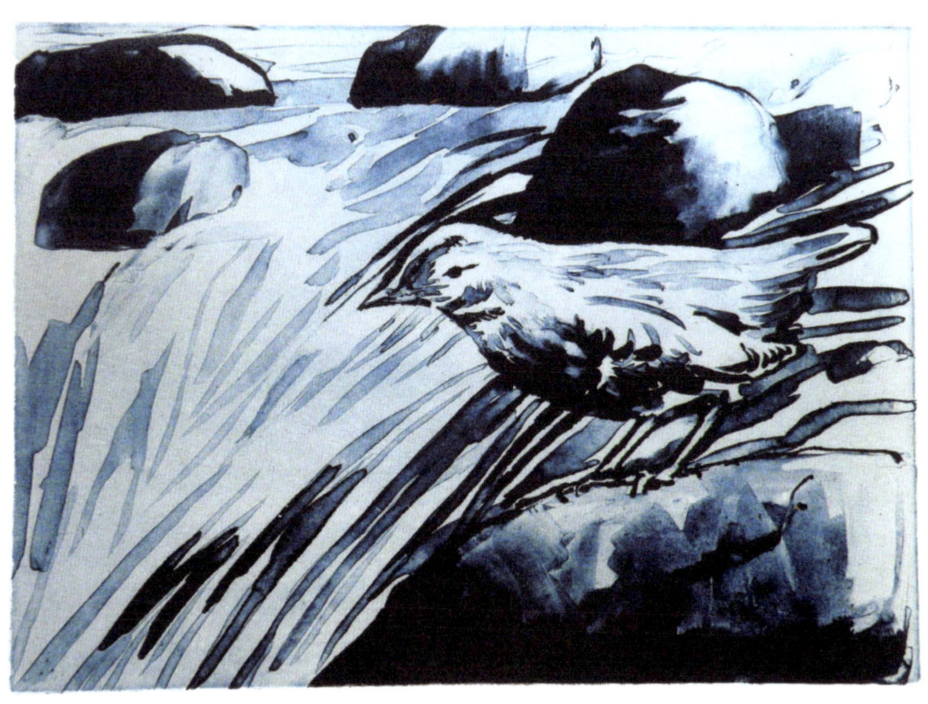

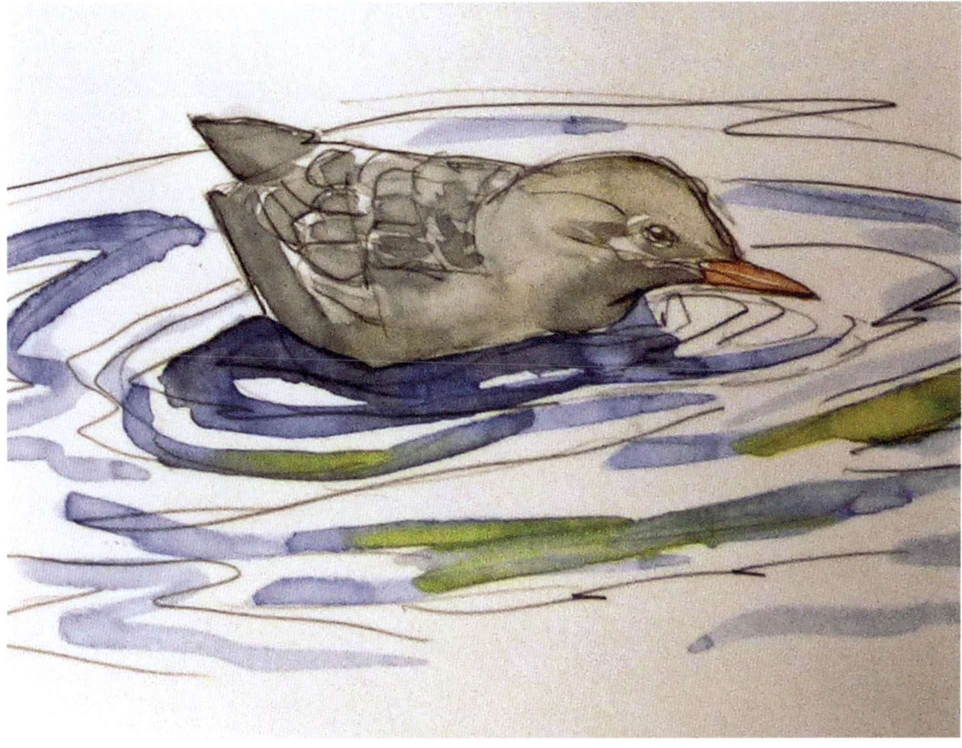

TECHNIQUE
Squaring Circles

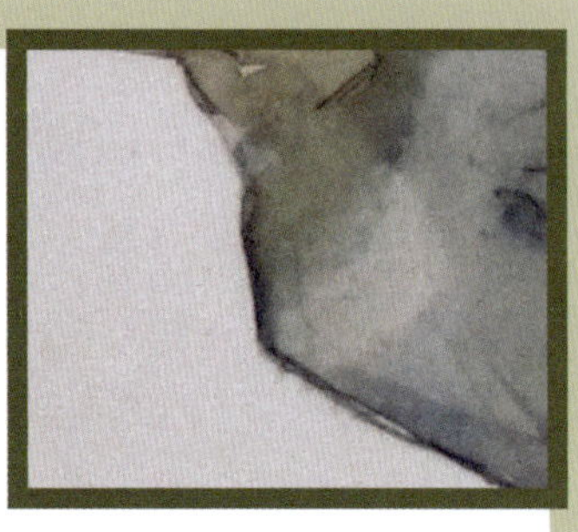

Art historians have always had a hard time distinguishing the drawings of Rembrandt from those of his students, who often worked side by side with him in his studio. One very clear sign that a work is Rembrandt's—and not his studio assistants'—is the quality of line. In an analysis of a drawing of a seated nude, previously thought to be the work of Rembrandt, curators noticed that a calf muscle was rendered with a very smooth curve. Rembrandt, by contrast, in a similar drawing of a nude, stroked in a bold straight line across the curve of the calf to strengthen and define the musculature. Notice the boxy shape of the American dipper (*Cinclus mexicanus*) in the watercolor sketches; the sharp angles help to convey the energy and strength of this strong swimmer. The dipper needs so much power to swim through rapids—blocking in angles on the bird's shape really conveys that necessary sturdiness.

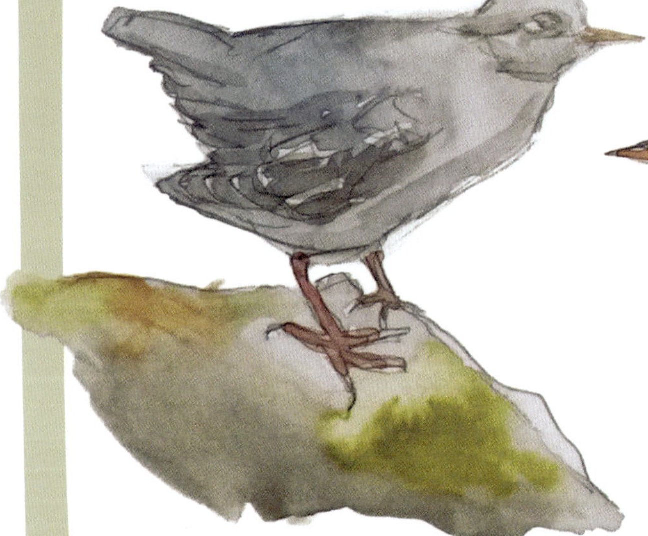

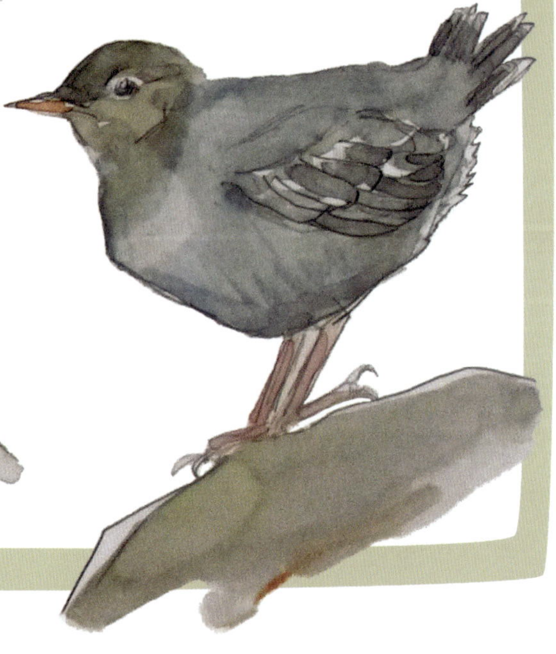

Common raven *(Corvus corax)* • WATERCOLOR SKETCH

Ravens are members of the highly intelligent corvid family. They, too, cache food and have remarkable visual memories. In addition, because ravens rely mostly on the fresh kill of other predators for food, it's important for them to understand the behavior of those predators and try to ascertain how dangerous they are since they spend so much time close to them—they have to test the waters to see just how far they can go. This requires logical thinking on the ravens' part.

"Elvis" definitely exemplifies corvid intelligence. A raven resident of Diablo Lake, site of the North Cascades Institute and the North Cascades Environmental Learning Center, Elvis was named by staff because of his fondness for the bacon-dripping-soaked newspapers composted in a shed by the dining hall. (Elvis Presley was partial to peanut butter and bacon sandwiches. Of course, the raven's mate is called Priscilla.) Elvis is very resourceful and capable of unzipping backpacks, since he's watched countless groups of schoolchildren who spend a week at a time at the Institute learning about the North Cascades. He's figured out that children are easy marks. Whenever my students and I paint there, we have to take care to watch our lunches and packs. My friend shared a photo of Elvis perched on a rock, and I decided to celebrate his bold posture and beautiful black coloration, using blue-gray as an underpainting first, to capture the highlights shining on his feathers. To paint this way, begin with the blue-gray and paint it everywhere. Paint the black second, after the blue-gray is dry, or try adding it while the blue-gray is still wet for softer edges and more subtle shading. This technique is suitable for any black subject with glossy blue-gray highlights.

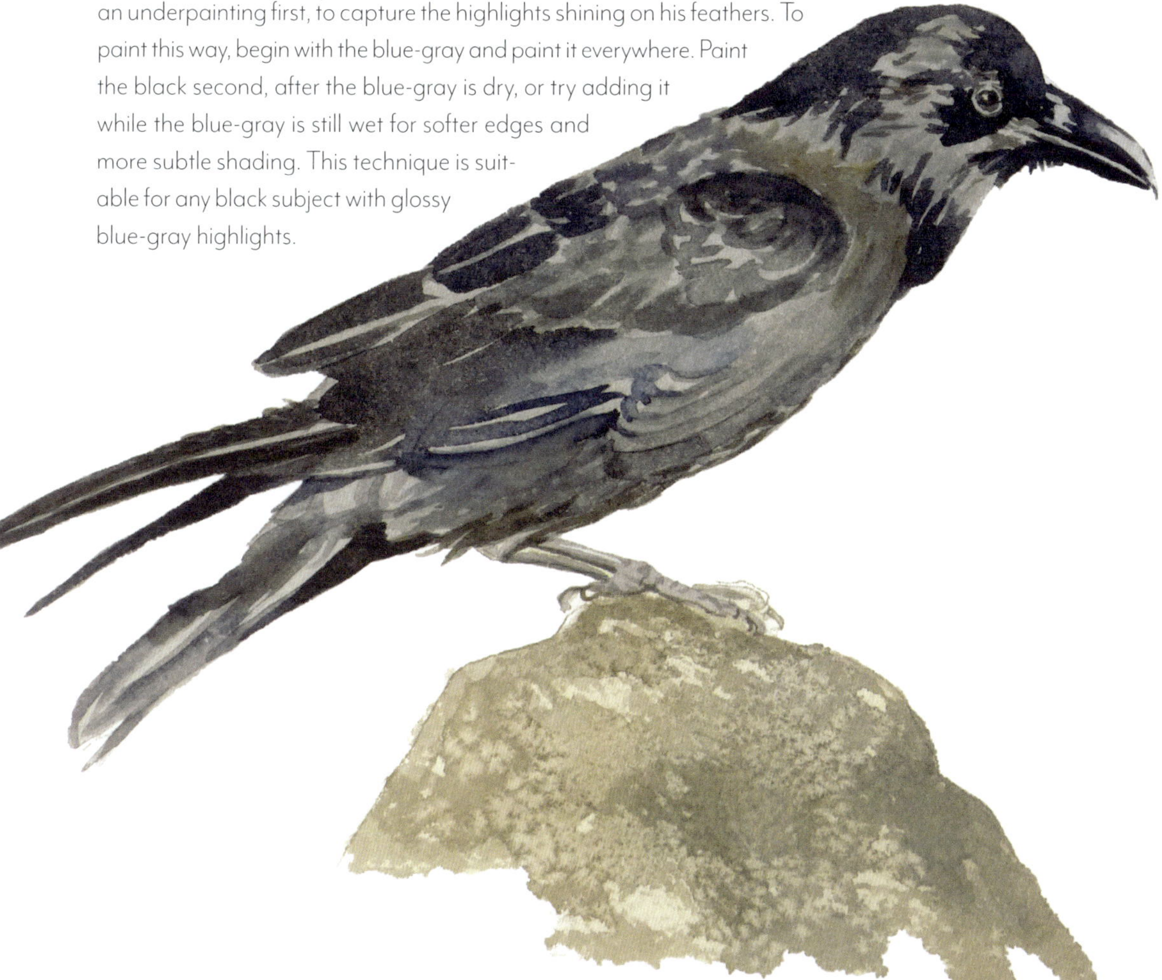

Mountain bluebird *(Sialia currucoides)* • **BLOCK PRINT, ETCHING**

One day we hiked the Wonderland Trail in Mount Rainier National Park past Sunrise, stopping just above Berkeley Park, where we saw a flock of bluebirds landing on twisted mountain hemlocks. Botanists use the German word *krummholz* ("crooked wood") to describe these gnarled trees deformed by high-altitude winds, and there are countless specimens at Mount Rainier. It was September, definitely late autumn in the high country, and the birds were probably migrating; seeing them was like a farewell to summer. They were moving quite frenetically from dwarf tree to dwarf tree, and I wasn't able to photograph or sketch them, so I only have my memory of them. But in late October in the high desert country of eastern Oregon, I saw another flock moving from juniper to juniper and managed to photograph a couple of them. I decided to try an etching. Quite unlike a watercolor or block print, the etching conveys the elegance and simplicity of the form of the bird, with the blue ink and light-blue-toned paper expressing the lovely hue of its plumage in a more subdued way.

The block print illustrates a bluebird sighting in Yellowstone in autumn, when colors had all turned russet and golden. The bluebird dazzled my hiking companions and me with its intense pure primary blue amid the neutral tints of the high, dry Yellowstone country of Rescue Creek.

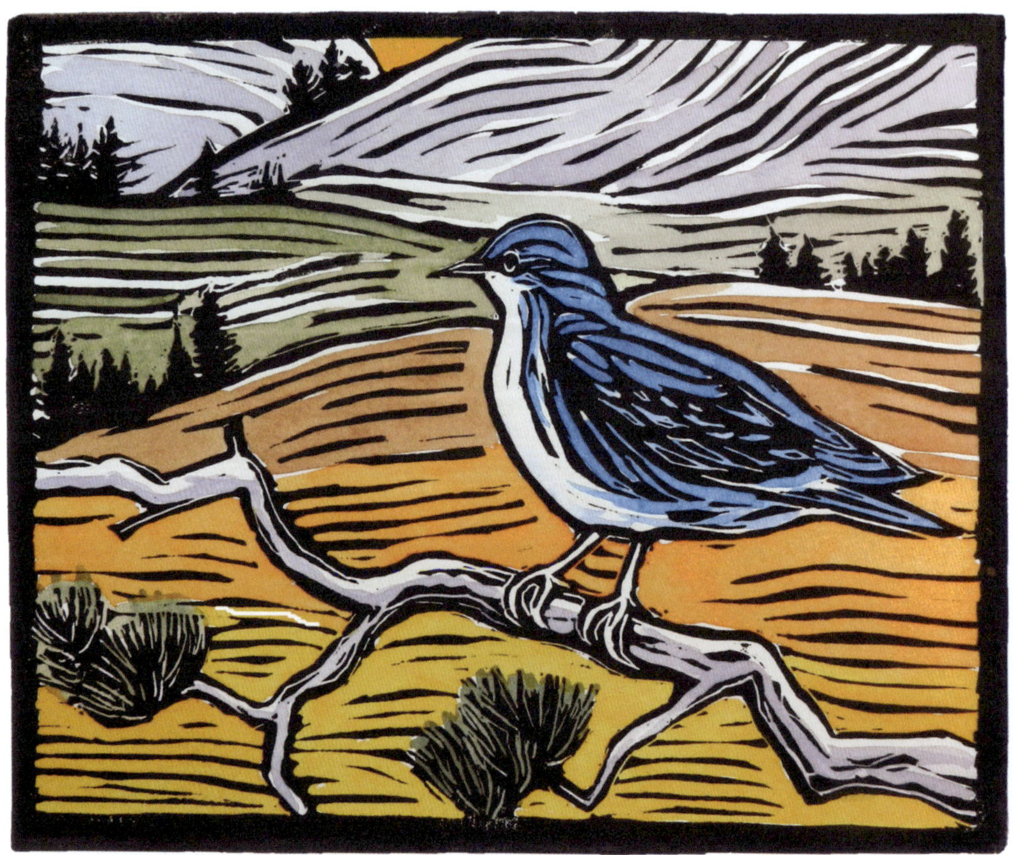

The bluebird carries the sky on his back.

—**Henry David Thoreau,** April 3, 1852, *Journals 1838–1859*

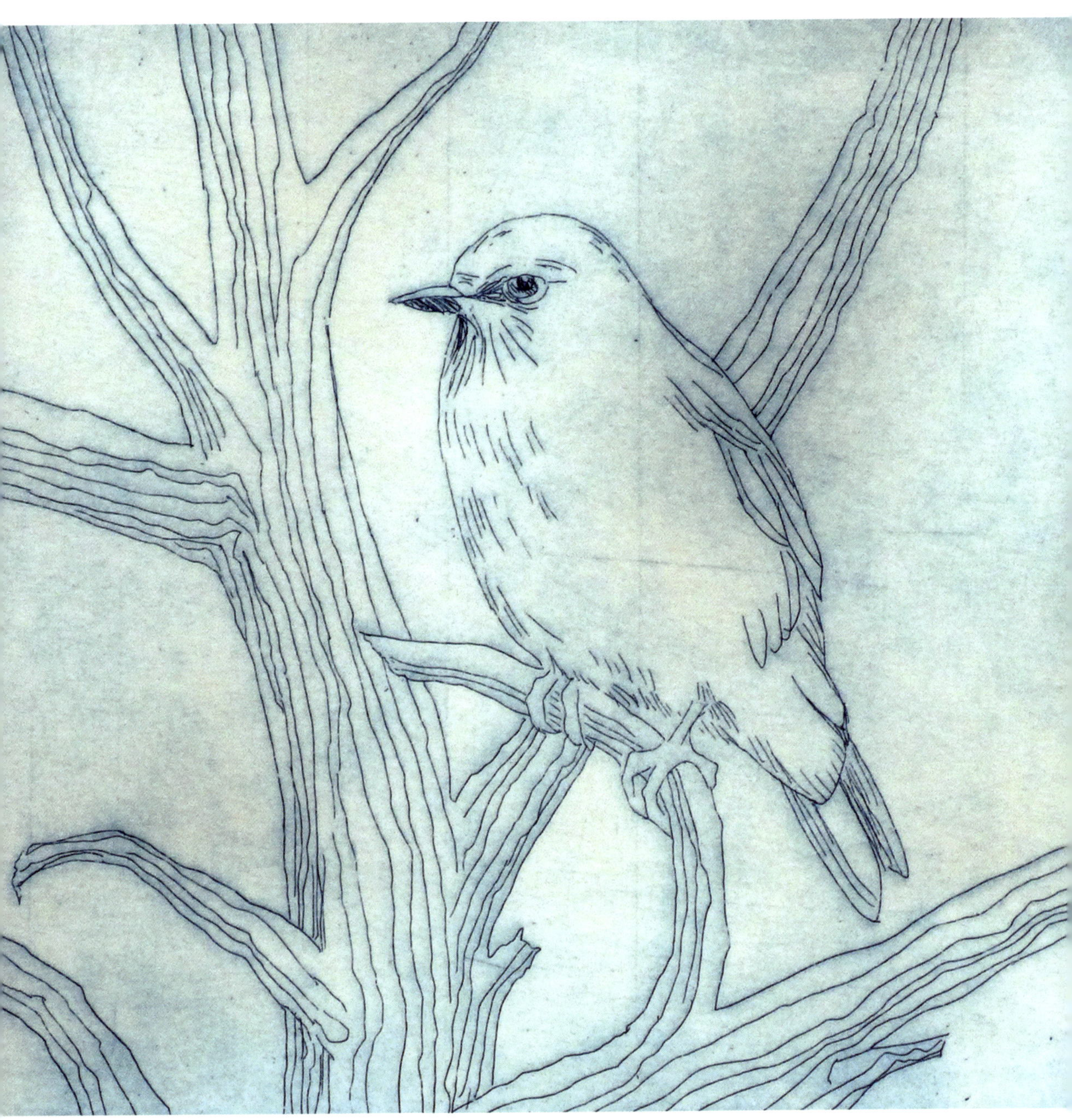

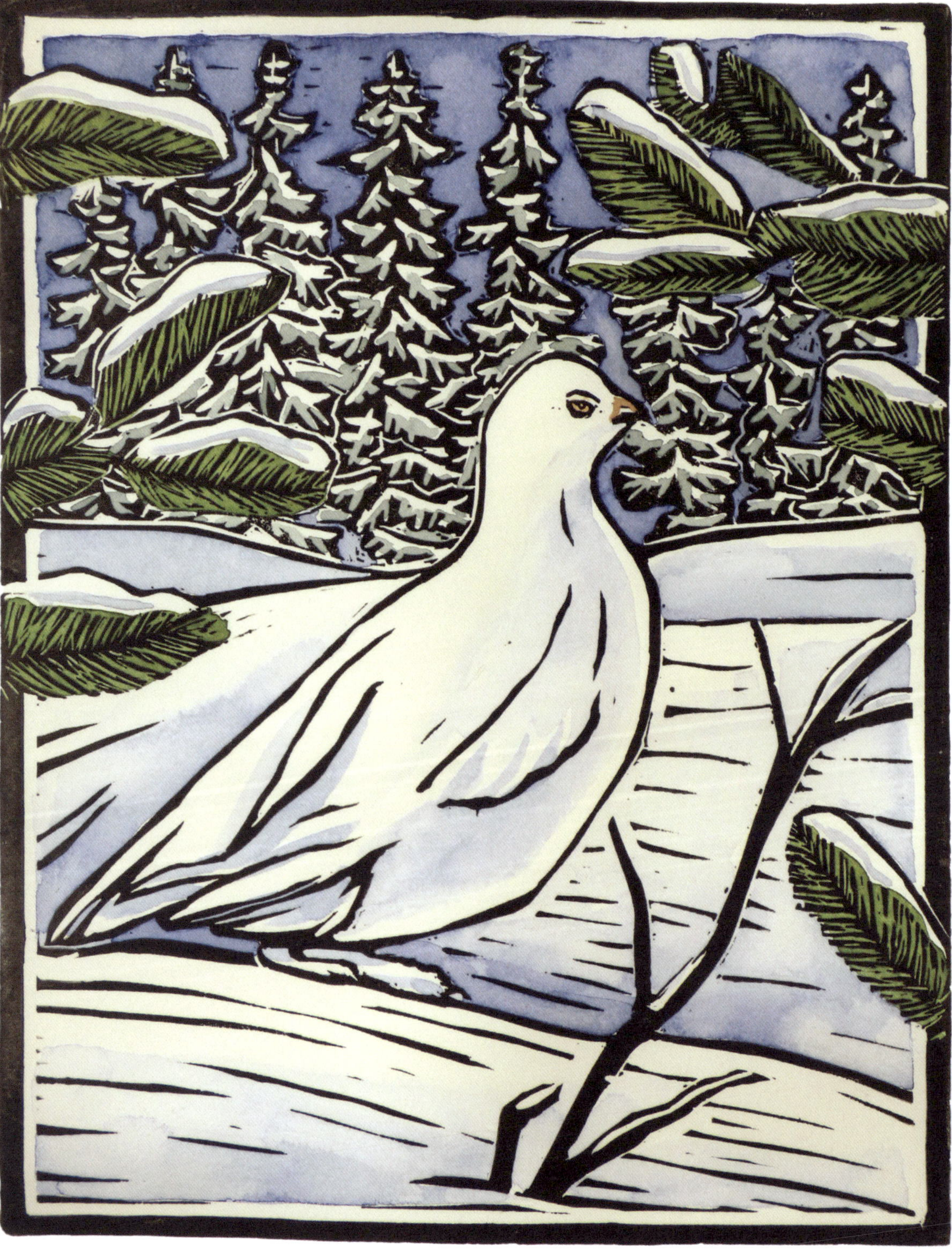

White-tailed ptarmigan *(Lagopus leucura)* · **BLOCK PRINT**

The ptarmigan has a remarkable ability to camouflage itself in winter with white feathers that look like snow. Ptarmigans molt three times a year. In summer the males have only a little bit of white on them—and the females none—but are instead mostly brown and black. They look much like the rocks in their high-altitude environment, which they choose for their nesting sites, specifically near willows, their main food source and also good cover for safety. The word "ptarmigan" originated in the Gaelic rendering of the bird's hoarse croak: *tarmachan*. The white-tailed ptarmigan is found only in high-altitude locations above tree line in Alaska and Canada and, in the contiguous United States, in the Cascades and Rockies of Washington, Idaho, Montana, Wyoming, and Colorado.

Great gray owl *(Strix nebulosa)* · **WATERCOLOR SKETCH ON TONED PAPER**

The great gray is the largest owl at twenty-seven inches long and is very much a boreal species, found in Canada and Alaska. It also lives in Washington, the southern part of its range, but only at high altitudes. The owl is able to turn its head 270 degrees, which compensates for its inability to move its eyes, so you see the back feathers of the owl in this watercolor sketch, even though its head is turned toward us. (In my sketch, the owl is turning its head only 180 degrees.) A similar pose is found on the owl in France's ancient Chauvet Cave; at 30,000 years old, Chauvet is one of the world's oldest cave art sites. The Chauvet long-eared owl has its very own cave, and its head is turned back, looking down toward the other animal art in a deeper cave. Art historians surmise that Stone Age people believed that owls had supernatural powers—their head turning must have amazed those early artists as much as it does us. I sketched the owl on toned paper (allowing the paper to show through), added watercolor, then used white gouache, and finally drew the delicate feathers with a white pen.

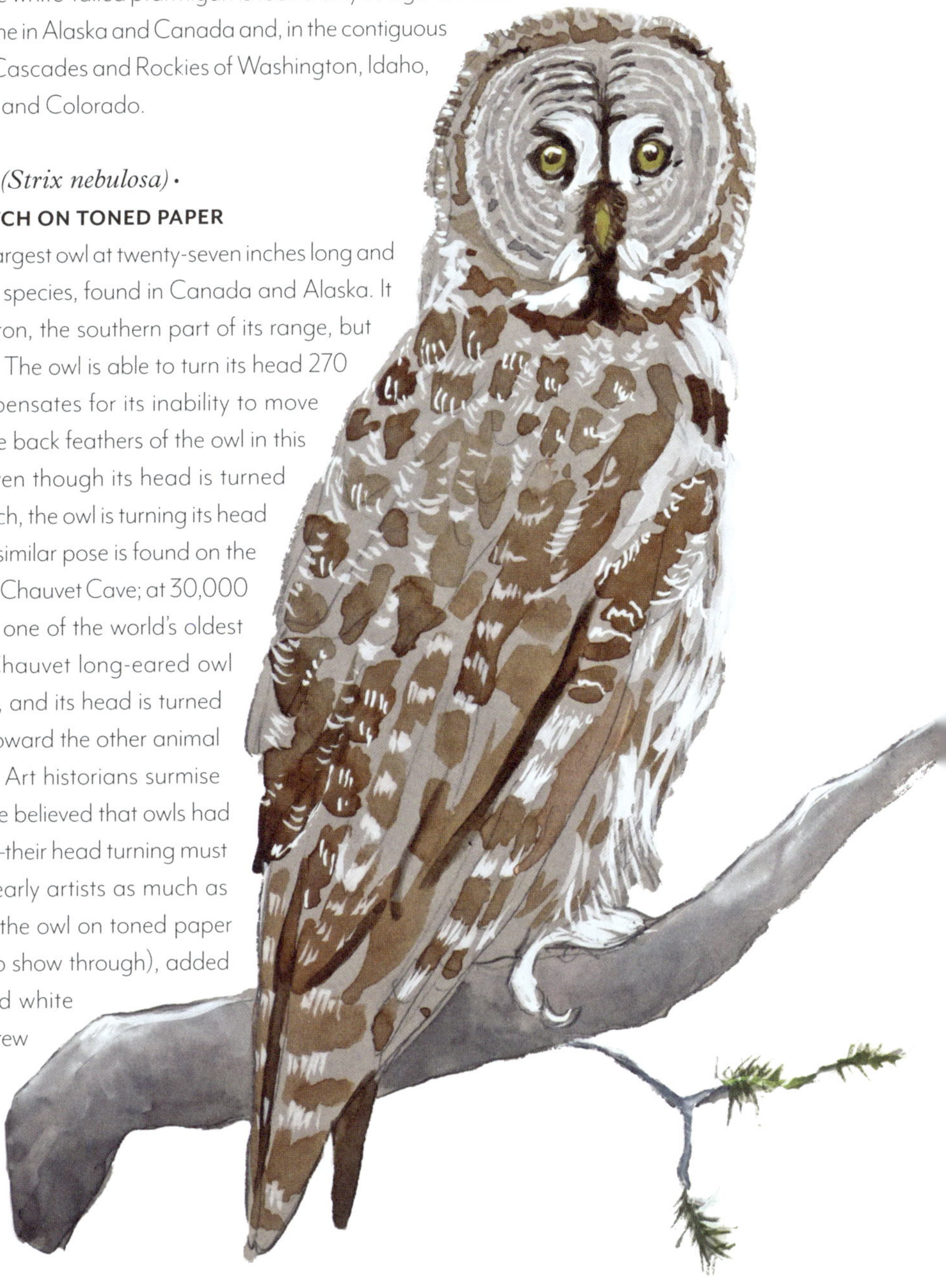

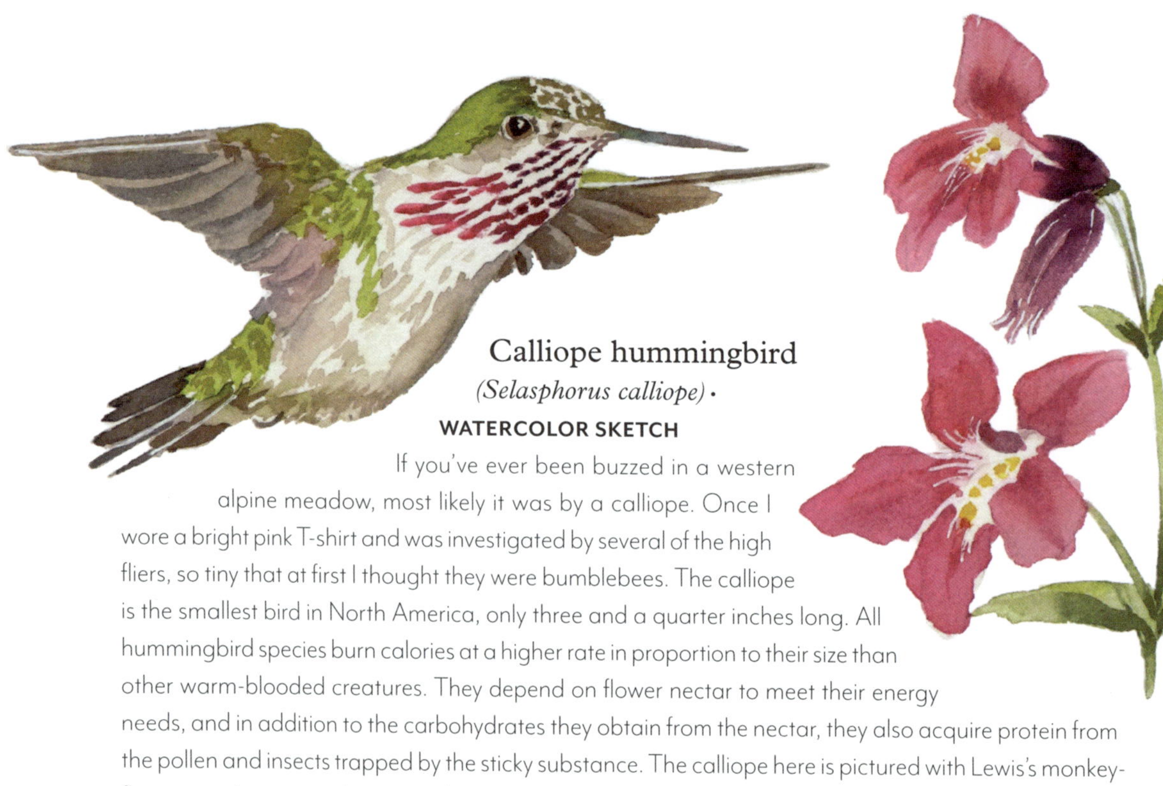

Calliope hummingbird *(Selasphorus calliope)* · WATERCOLOR SKETCH

If you've ever been buzzed in a western alpine meadow, most likely it was by a calliope. Once I wore a bright pink T-shirt and was investigated by several of the high fliers, so tiny that at first I thought they were bumblebees. The calliope is the smallest bird in North America, only three and a quarter inches long. All hummingbird species burn calories at a higher rate in proportion to their size than other warm-blooded creatures. They depend on flower nectar to meet their energy needs, and in addition to the carbohydrates they obtain from the nectar, they also acquire protein from the pollen and insects trapped by the sticky substance. The calliope here is pictured with Lewis's monkey-flower, an alpine gem that grows beside streams and in other moist areas at high elevations.

Western tanager *(Piranga ludoviciana)* · BLOCK PRINT

Tanagers are rare sightings, even though they're common and not endangered, because they spend much of their time foraging in the upper branches of conifers. I've seen them a couple of times in the Cascades, once on the Cascade River near Marblemount, high in some alders, with Eldorado Peak shimmering to the east. Another time they flew and landed briefly in lodgepole pines above Diablo Lake at the Overlook in North Cascades National Park. I find them so striking because we don't have very many brilliantly colored birds in the Pacific Northwest—their yellows and reds are hues you might see in the tropics. The word "tanager" comes from *tangara* and means "dancer" in the now-extinct Tupi language of southeast Brazil. Tanagers breed in mixed conifer and deciduous forests in western North America and winter in Mexico and Central America, where they also rely on forests. Traditionally, nature and Native American burning practices maintained these forests, but now it's up to forest managers to use controlled burning to keep these important habitats healthy.

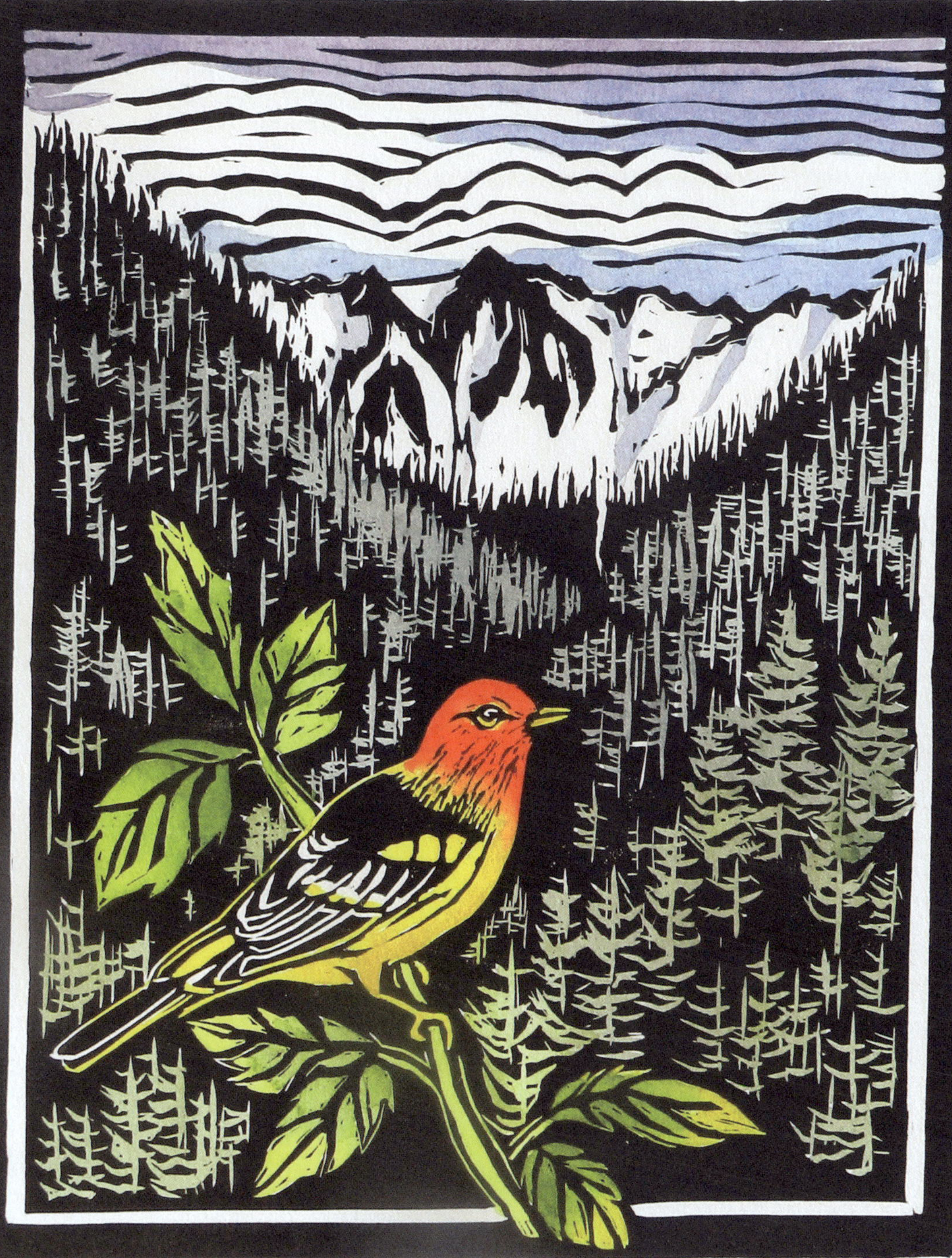

Clark's nutcracker *(Nucifraga columbiana)* · **BLOCK PRINT**

Clark's nutcrackers, a common sight in the North Cascades, cache whitebark pine seeds throughout the western mountains in all seasons. They dig trenches in the ground or in gravelly areas and place seeds in them; they also store seeds in cracks in trees, choosing whitebark pines, firs, and spruce trees at higher elevations in summer and then moving to lower forests of ponderosa pines and Douglas firs in fall and winter. Between September and December, a single bird can store up to 30,000 seeds. In winter and spring, the birds are able to retrieve the seeds by memory—up to six months after caching them! Whitebark pines grow near Blue Lake, just below Liberty Bell Mountain at Washington Pass, and I've seen the birds there on many occasions. This block print celebrates a Clark's that I saw at the Diablo Lake Overlook, farther west in the North Cascades.

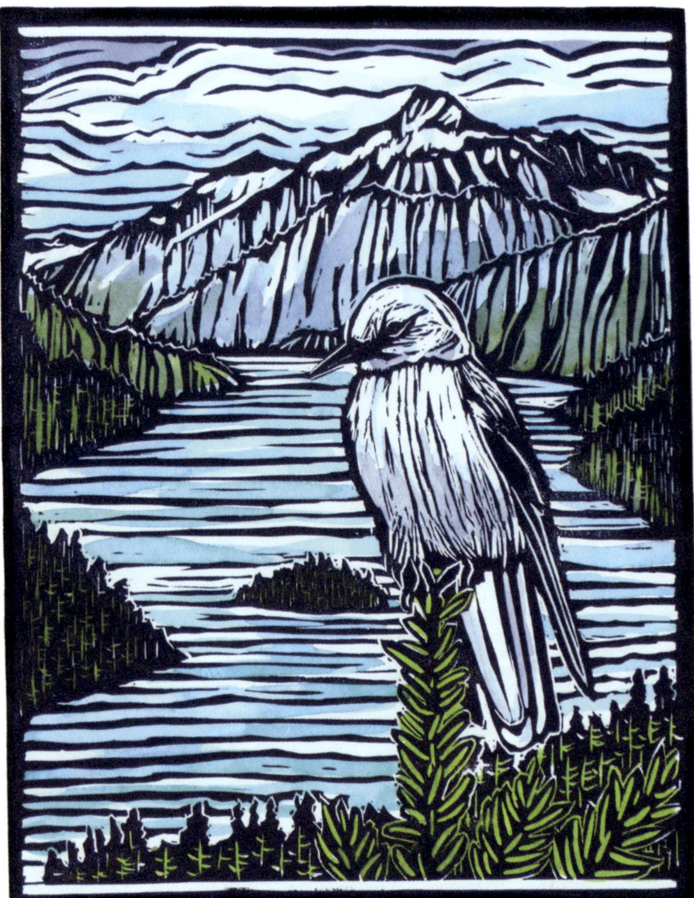

Canada jay *(Perisoreus canadensis)* · **WATERCOLOR**

Canada jays, members of the clever corvid family, are known as camp robbers, and they love to hang around human beings, waiting for handouts. They will gladly alight on your hand to snatch a bit of your sandwich and will amuse children with their antics and acrobatic flying. I decided to represent one in a more dignified pose, among the conifers where you often find them. I painted much of the background behind the bird with a wet-in-wet method, which takes very little time. I usually proceed with the subject bird once I've completed such a background because I don't want to spend hours on the background if the bird isn't turning out to my satisfaction. Canada jays are found throughout Canada and Alaska, Washington, Oregon, Idaho, western Montana, and the mountains of New Mexico.

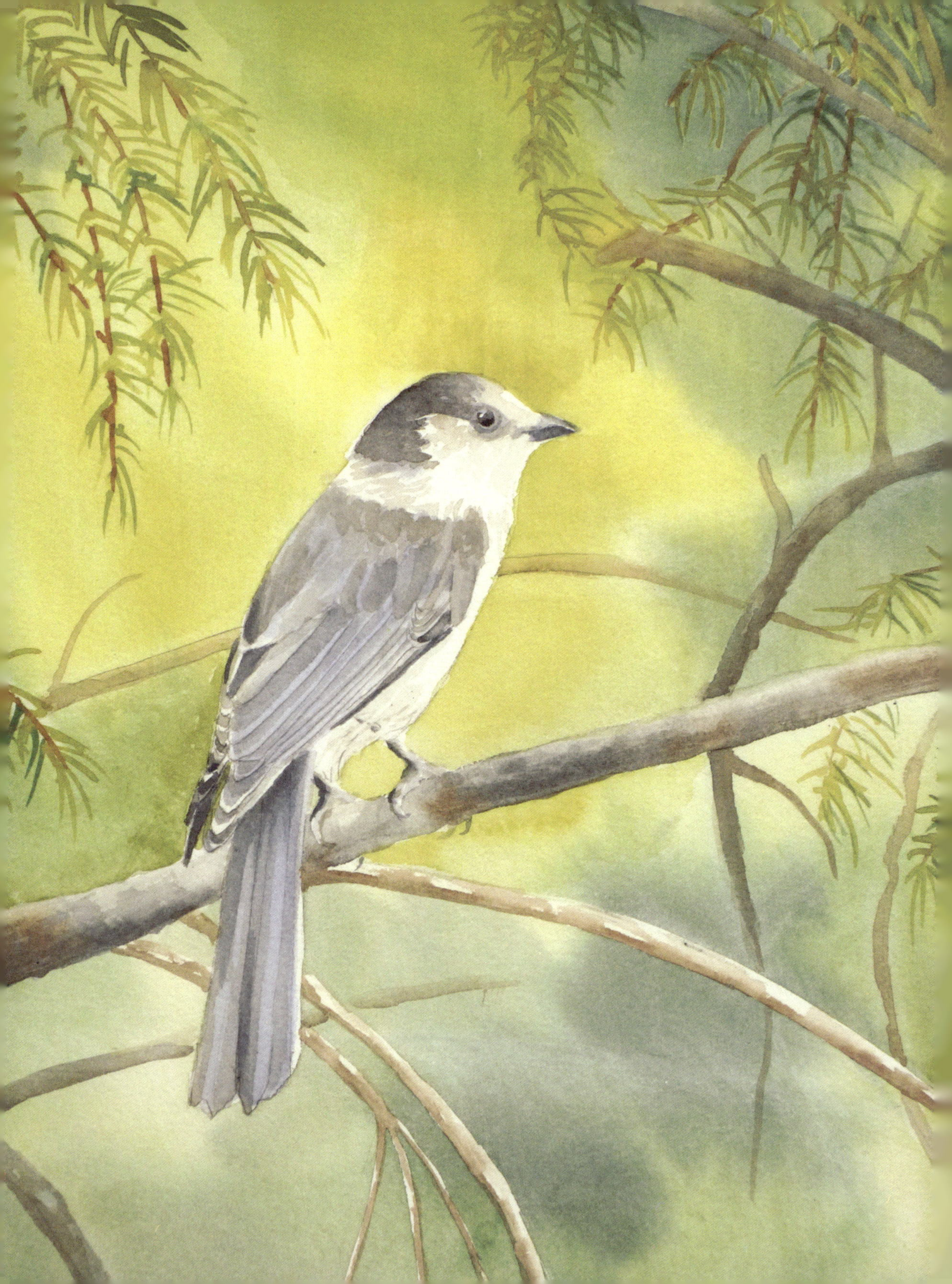

Acknowledgments

I offer thanks to my family and friends, who've accompanied me on so many of my outdoor excursions, as well as giving me invaluable advice and helpful criticism: David, Tom, Rose, Mich, Jane, Julie, Gerry, Dave, Kendall, Ilona, and Martin.

Everyone who has assisted me in publishing: including my agent, Anne Depue; book designer Kate Basart; Kate and Tom Burke and the rest of the staff at Pomegranate Publications; and Cary Cartmill of Digital Canvas Northwest. Special thanks on this second book to my brilliant editors at Skipstone (an imprint of Mountaineers Books), Kate Rogers and Mary Metz. In addition, editor Kirsten Colton was a great help with content and research; and Linda Gunnarson's keen editorial eye for detail and language refined my style immeasurably.

My friends at Seattle Audubon: Hanae Bettancourt, David Garcia, Leigh Hiura, Russ Steele, and Wendy Walker; and at Seward Park Audubon: Joey Manson and Marina Pita.

Photographers Glenn Dreger and Gerry Fuller.

Poets Jane Graham George of Wellington, New Zealand; John Daniel of Oregon; Ilona Popper of Montana; and Tim McNulty and Saul Weisberg of Washington State.

Graham Taylor of National Parks Conservation Association, Ranger Christy Pendley of Crater Lake National Park, and Fish and Wildlife officer Stephen Rooker of Tule Lake National Wildlife Refuge.

Colleagues at the outdoor institutes where I teach: Evan Holstrom, Christian Martin, Kiley Barbero, and Saul Weisberg of the North Cascades Institute; Mindy Chaffin, Carrie Hardison, and the staff of Sitka Center for Art and Ecology; Katy Fast and Katie Roloson of the Yellowstone Forever Institute; and Patrick Walker and Brook Steele of the Wenatchee River Institute.

Artists/staff at Daniel Smith Artists' Materials in Seattle, Washington, who keep me well supplied and wonderfully informed: Thom Wright, Joe Bosch, Janice Berkebile, Patrice Cox, James Love, Joan Wright, Justin Viau, and Deborah Burns.

McClain's Printmaking Supplies in Portland, Oregon: Alex Prentiss and her knowledgeable staff—Andrew, Kaitlyn, Jesse, Ally, Daniel, and Carolyn—who've answered countless questions by phone.

Librarians: Deborah Schneider, Jeff Kempe, Harriet Herschel, and the many branch librarians of the King County Library System; Brian Thompson, Tracy Mehlin, Rebecca Alexander, Jessica Anderson, and Laura Blumhagen at the Elisabeth C. Miller Library, University of Washington Botanic Gardens.

Printmaking teachers, artists, and friends: first teacher, Jocelyn Curry, who introduced me to the joy of printmaking; Roberta Long; Laurie Brown; Charles Spitzack, woodblock printmaker and teacher; and Virginia Hungate-Hawk, my ongoing mentor, who continues to share the mysteries of etching.

My many students, who inspire me.

Further Reading

FIELD GUIDES

Cuming, E. D. *British Birds: The Bodley Head Natural History*. Illustrated by J. A. Shepherd. London: John Lane Co., 1913.

Dunn, John L., and Jonathan Alderfer. *National Geographic Field Guide to the Birds of Western North America*. Washington, DC: National Geographic, 2008.

Harrison, Hal H. *Western Birds' Nests*. Peterson Field Guides. New York: Houghton Mifflin, 1979.

Peterson, Roger Tory. *Peterson Field Guide to Birds of North America*. New York: Houghton Mifflin Harcourt, 2008.

Sibley, David Allen. *The Sibley Guide to Birds*. 2nd ed. New York: Knopf, 2014.

Stokes, Donald, and Lillian Stokes. *The New Stokes Field Guide to Birds: Western Region*. New York: Little, Brown, 2013.

Swanson, Sarah, and Max Smith. *Must-See Birds of the Pacific Northwest*. Portland, OR: Timber Press, 2013.

NATURAL HISTORY

Churney, Marie, and Susan Williams. *Bogs, Meadows, Marshes, and Swamps*. Seattle: Mountaineers Books, 1996.

Kruckeberg, Arthur R. *The Natural History of Puget Sound Country*. Seattle: University of Washington Press, 1991.

Reedman, Ray. *Lapwings, Loons and Lousy Jacks: The How and Why of Bird Names*. Exeter, UK: Pelagic Press, 2016.

Scott, James C. *Against the Grain: A Deep History of the Earliest States*. New Haven: Yale University Press, 2017.

Taylor, Ronald J. *Sagebrush Country: A Wildflower Sanctuary*. Missoula, MT: Mountain Press, 1992.

ORNITHOLOGY

Birkhead, Tim. *The Most Perfect Thing: Inside (and Outside) a Bird's Egg*. London: Bloomsbury, 2016.

Hanson, Thor. *Feathers: The Evolution of a Natural Miracle*. New York: Basic Books, 2011.

Marzluff, John M. *Welcome to Subirdia: Sharing Our Neighborhoods with Wrens, Robins, Woodpeckers, and Other Wildlife*. New Haven: Yale University Press, 2014.

McFarland, Casey, and S. David Scott. *Bird Feathers: A Guide to North American Species*. Mechanicsburg, PA: Stackpole Books, 2010.

Price, A. Lindsay. *Swans of the World: In Nature, History, Myth and Art*. Tulsa, OK: Council Oak Books, 1995.

Prum, Richard O. *The Evolution of Beauty: How Darwin's Forgotten Theory of Mate Choice Shapes the Animal World—and Us*. New York: Doubleday, 2017.

BIRDS IN ART

Acton, David, Martin F. Krause, and Madeline Carol Yurtseven. *Gustave Baumann: Nearer to Art*. Santa Fe: Museum of New Mexico Press, 2015.

Chansigaud, Valerie. *All About Birds: A Short Illustrated History of Ornithology*. Princeton: Princeton University Press, 2010.

Daston, Lorraine J., and Katharine Park. *Wonders and the Order of Nature 1150–1750*. New York: Zone Books, 2001.

Kiser, Joy M. *America's Other Audubon*. Princeton: Princeton Architectural Press, 2012. (Biography and art of Genevieve Estelle Jones, painter of birds' nests and eggs)

Peterson, Roger Tory, and Virginia Marie Peterson. *Audubon's Birds of America: The Audubon Society Baby Elephant Folio*. Illustrated by John James Audubon. New York: Abbeville Press, 2003.

ART TECHNIQUE

Busby, John. *Drawing Birds*. Portland, OR: Timber Press, 2014.

Martin, Judy. *The Encyclopedia of Printmaking Techniques*. Tunbridge Wells, UK: Search Press, 2014.

Sparkes, W. E. *Lessons on Shading*. Mineola, NY: Dover Publications, 2007.

Treseder, Roberta Rice. *William S. Rice: California Block Prints*. Portland, OR: Pomegranate Communications, 2009.

Weller, Shane, ed. *German Expressionist Woodcuts*. New York: Dover Publications, 1994.

Wootton, Tim. *Drawing and Painting Birds*. Ramsbury, UK: The Crowood Press, 2010.

Resources

ART MATERIALS STORES

There are countless online resources and some fine, well-stocked retail outlets for art supplies. I recommend that you shop at retail art stores to get the best advice. The sales staffs are almost always artists and love helping you find just what you need.

- Artist and Craftsman Supply, www.artistcraftsman.com
- John Neal Bookseller, www.johnnealbooks.com
- McClain's Printmaking Supplies (online only), www.imcclains.com
- Paper and Ink Arts, www.paperinksarts.com
- University Bookstore, www.ubookstore.com

Supplies

The following list includes the materials that have performed best for me over the years.

DRAWING MATERIALS

- HB and 6B pencils; for field sketches and general sketching, mechanical pencils are ideal
- Staedtler white Mars Plastic eraser
- Pilot G-Tec pen, .38 and .5 nib widths
- Duke drawing pen; nib gives the option of thick and thin lines for sketching
- Stylist felt-tip pen; dissolves into a nice blue-black, excellent for quick sketches
- Staedtler brush pens, a variety of grays and browns
- Signo Uni-ball broad white pen, for small details on feathers and other highlights
- Stillman & Birn archival-quality sketchbooks; available in spiral-bound and softbound, in white, ivory, gray, and tan. The colored papers are ideal for making sketches on toned paper with white gouache.

WATERCOLOR MATERIALS

- Watercolor papers: Arches 140 lb. cold press; Fabriano Artistico 140 lb. cold press; Lanaquarelle 140 lb. cold press; Saunders Waterford 140 lb coldpress. You can have these papers cut and spiral-bound into a sketchbook at an office supply store or specialty binder.
- Bristol or other drawing paper: 90 lb. weight (minimum) so it can handle a light watercolor wash
- Brushes: Da Vinci Maestro sable rounds, numbers 4 and 6, plus a ½" wide flat sable brush
- Hahnemühle sketchbooks, 100% cotton
- Palettes: John Pike Palette; San Francisco Slant Palette with multiple large wells for mixing washes
- Portable watercolor sets: Sennelier, Winsor & Newton, Van Gogh

WATERCOLOR TUBE PAINTS IN PRIMARY COLORS (A WARM AND A COOL OF EACH)

I prefer Daniel Smith watercolors. Other high-quality manufacturers are Winsor & Newton, Old Holland, Schmincke, Sennelier, and M. Graham.

- Blue: phthalo blue red shade, phthalo blue green shade
- Yellow: hansa yellow deep, hansa yellow medium
- Red: permanent alizarin crimson, pyrrol scarlet
- Other colors: cobalt blue, hansa yellow light, quinacridone burnt orange, carbazole violet, yellow ochre, perylene green, permanent white gouache

PRINTMAKING MATERIALS

- Safety-Kut carving blocks; available in various sizes but cheapest if you buy the biggest and cut your own
- Speedball carving tools and handle: tools numbers 1–5: U-gouge, big and small; V-gouge, big and small; square gouge
- Charbonnel etching inks: soft black, carbon black, and many other colors available
- Papers: Arches 140 lb. hot press; Fabriano Artistico 140 lb. hot press; Lanaquarelle 140 lb. hot press; Rives BFK printmaking for etching

EGG TEMPERA MATERIALS

- Dry ground pigments: available at art supply stores and online at Sinopia, www.sinopia.com; Kremer Pigments, www.kremer-pigmente.com/en; and Natural Pigments, www.naturalpigments.com
- Gessoed panels: True Gesso Panels, www.truegesso.com
- Koo Schadler: www.kooschadler.com

PRINTMAKING COOPERATIVES AND STUDIOS (FOR CLASSES, WORKSHOPS, AND PRESS TIME)

Seattle, Washington:

- Pratt Fine Arts Center, www.pratt.org
- Print Zero Studios, www.printzerostudios.com

Bellingham, Washington:

- Runaway Press, www.runaway.press

Portland, Oregon:

- Flight 64 Studio, www.flight64.org
- Multnomah Arts Center, www.multnomahartscenter.org
- Print Arts Northwest, www.printartsnw.org

San Francisco, California:

- Graphic Arts Workshop, www.graphicartsworkshop.org
- 3Fish Studios, www.3fishstudios.com

Index

Page numbers in italic refer to illustrations

About the Author

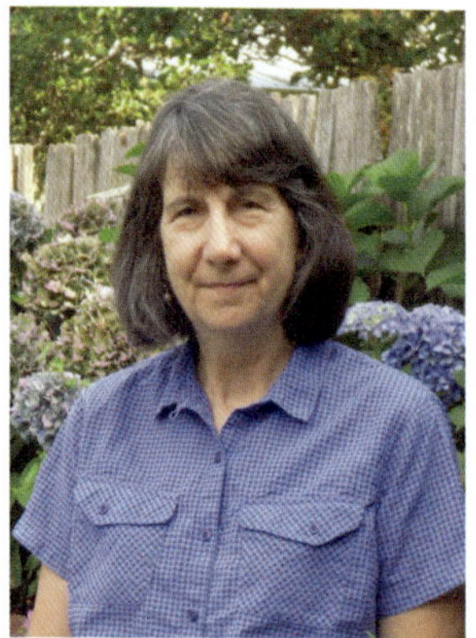

MOLLY HASHIMOTO explores parks and wildlife refuges all over the West, both in urban and wilderness settings, seeking inspiration for her sketches, paintings, and prints. For more than twenty-five years, her work has appeared in cards, books, and calendars published by Pomegranate Communications. Her subjects include mountain peaks, forests, trees, ferns and wildflowers, and coastal headlands and estuaries, but she is particularly known for her depictions of the marvelous birds of every ecosystem, and mammals and other creatures of all sizes and shapes.

Molly is dedicated to connecting people to nature through hands-on art experiences and for many months each year can be found teaching aspiring artists of all ages in Seattle. When she is not painting, making prints, and teaching in Seattle, she leads plein air watercolor painting and printmaking workshops at the North Cascades Institute, Yellowstone Forever Institute, Wenatchee River Institute, and Sitka Center for Art and Ecology.

SKIPSTONE is an imprint of independent nonprofit publisher MOUNTAINEERS BOOKS. It features thematically related titles that promote a deeper connection to our natural world through sustainable practice and backyard activism. Our readers live smart, play well, and typically engage with the community around them. Skipstone guides explore healthy lifestyles and how an outdoor life relates to the well-being of our planet, as well as of our own neighborhoods. Sustainable foods and gardens; healthful living; realistic and doable conservation at home; modern aspirations for community—Skipstone tries to address such topics in ways that emphasize active living, local and grassroots practices, and a small footprint.

Our hope is that Skipstone books will inspire you to effect change without losing your sense of humor, to celebrate the freedom and generosity of a life outdoors, and to move forward with gentle leaps or breathtaking bounds.

All of our publications, as part of our 501(c)(3) nonprofit program, are made possible through the generosity of donors and through sales of more than 800 titles on outdoor recreation, sustainable lifestyle, and conservation. To donate, purchase books, or learn more, visit us online:

www.skipstonebooks.org
www.mountaineersbooks.org

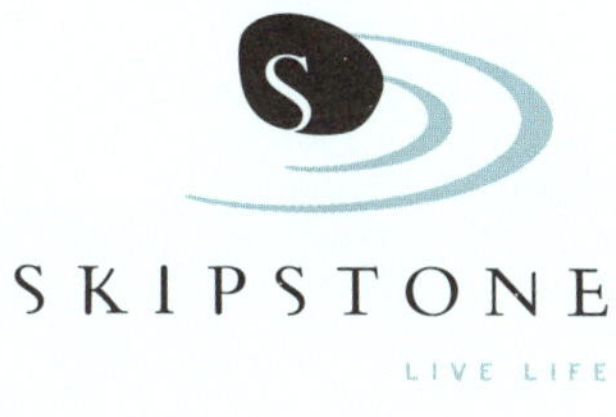

Also Available

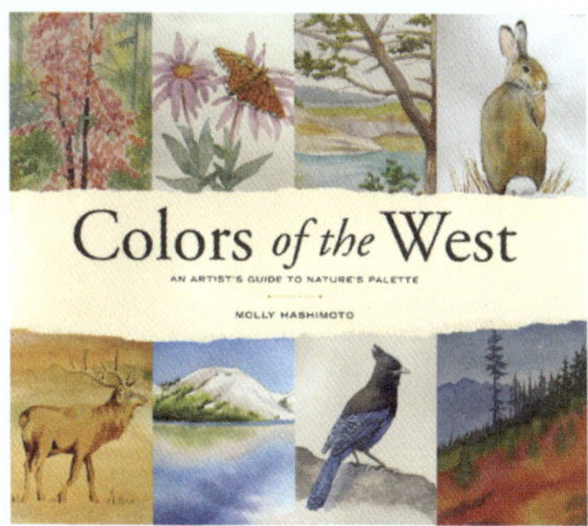

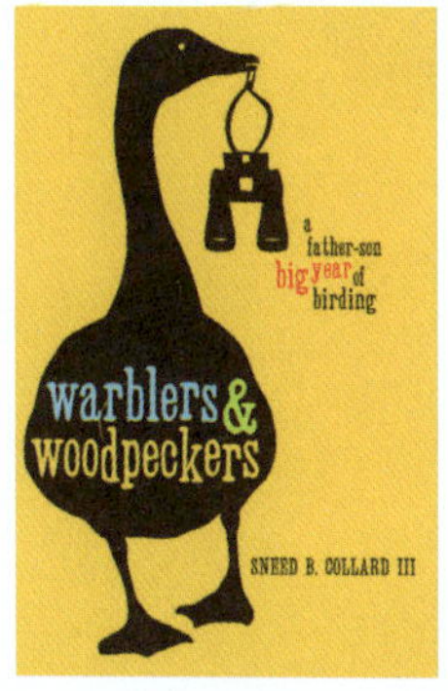

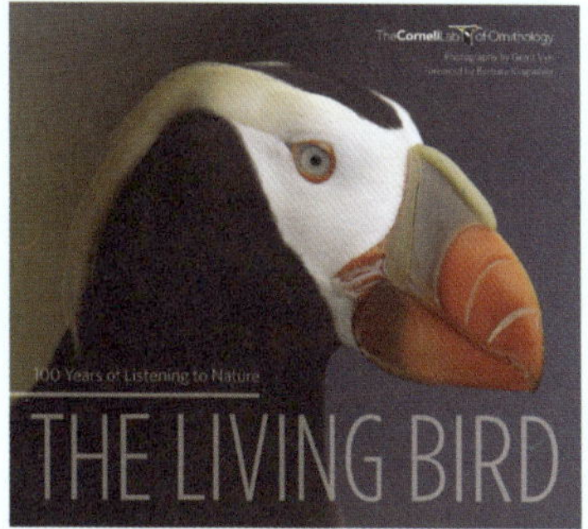

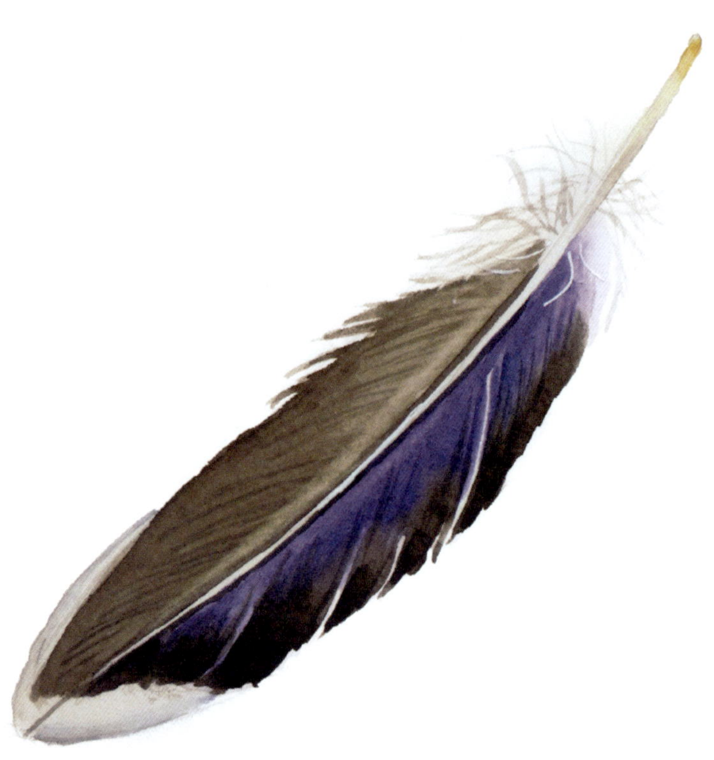